Pocket Rough Guide

# LONDON

written and researched by

## ROB HUMPHREYS

# Contents

# INTRODUCTION TO
# LONDON

London is a very big city. In fact, it's the largest capital in the European Union, stretching for more than thirty miles from east to west, and with a population of just under eight million. Ethnically and linguistically, it's also Europe's most diverse metropolis, offering cultural and culinary delights from right across the globe. The city dominates the national horizon, too: this is where most of the country's news and money are made, it's where central government resides and, as far as its inhabitants are concerned, provincial life begins beyond the circuit of the city's orbital motorway.

TOWER OF LONDON

## Best place for an alfresco drink

If you're lucky enough to be in London when the weather's fine, there's nothing like an alfresco drink, whether in a leafy outdoor beer garden, or by the banks of the Thames. For a great riverside view of the Dome, head to *The Gun* in Docklands (see p.113), or if you're wandering along the south bank of the Thames, *The Anchor* in Bankside (see p.127) is hard to beat. After an invigorating stroll on nearby Hampstead Heath, *The Flask* in Highgate (see p.155) is the perfect place to sink a pint.

For the visitor, it's a thrilling destination. The biggest problem for newcomers is that the city can seem bewilderingly amorphous, with no single predominant focus of interest. Londoners tend to cope with all this by compartmentalizing their city, identifying strongly with the neighbourhoods in which they work or live, just making occasional forays into the West End, London's shopping and entertainment heartland. As a visitor, the key to enjoying the London, then, is not to try and do everything in a single visit – concentrate on one or two areas and you'll get a lot more out of the place.

The capital's traditional sights – Big Ben, Westminster Abbey, Buckingham Palace, St Paul's Cathedral and the Tower of London – continue to draw in millions of tourists every year. Things change fast, though, and the regular emergence of new attractions ensures that there's plenty to do even for those who've visited before. In the last decade or so, all of London's world-class museums, galleries and institutions have been reinvented, from the Royal Opera House to the British Museum, and the tourist and transport infrastructure has had a major overhaul too, ready for the 2012 Olympics.

Monuments from the capital's glorious past are everywhere, from medieval banqueting halls and the great churches of Christopher Wren to the eclectic Victorian architecture of the triumphalist British Empire. There's also much enjoyment to be had from the city's quiet Georgian squares, the narrow alleyways of the City of London, the riverside walks, and the assorted quirks

## When to visit

Despite the temperateness of the English climate, it's impossible to say with any degree of certainty that the weather will be pleasant in any given month. With average daily temperatures of around 22°C, English summers rarely get unbearably hot, while the winters (average daily temperature 6–10°C) don't get very cold – though they're often wet. However, whenever you come, be prepared for all eventualities: it has been known to snow at Easter and rain all day on August Bank Holiday weekend. As far as crowds go, tourists stream into London pretty much all year round, with peak season from Easter to October, and the biggest crush in July and August, when you'll need to book your accommodation well in advance.

of what is still identifiably a collection of villages. And urban London is offset by surprisingly large expanses of greenery: Hyde Park, Green Park and St James's Park are all within a few minutes' walk of the West End, while, further afield, you can enjoy the more expansive parklands of Hampstead Heath and Richmond Park.

You could spend days just shopping in London, too, mixing with the upper classes in the "tiara triangle" around Harrods, or sampling the offbeat weekend markets of Portobello Road, Camden and Spitalfields. The music, clubbing and gay/lesbian scenes are second to none, and mainstream arts are no less exciting, with regular opportunities to catch first-rate theatre companies, dance troupes, exhibitions and opera. The city's pubs have always had heaps of atmosphere, but food is a major attraction too, with over fifty Michelin-starred restaurants and the widest choice of cuisines on the planet.

TRAFALGAR SQUARE

# LONDON AT A GLANCE

## >>EATING

With thousands of cafés, pubs and restaurants, you're never far from a good place to fill your stomach. For the widest choice, make for **Soho** or nearby **Covent Garden**, where you'll find everything from triple-starred restaurants to cheap Chinese and Indian. Head out of the centre, though, to sample the best of the city's diverse cuisines, whether Portuguese in **Ladbroke Grove** or Bangladeshi in **Tower Hamlets**. London's also a great place for snacking, whether from the take-away stalls at **Camden Market** during the week, or from **Borough Market** or around Spitalfields and **Brick Lane** over the weekend.

## >>DRINKING

Found on just about every street corner, the pub remains one of the nation's most enduring social institutions and its popularity in London sees no sign of waning. The City has probably the best choice of long-established drinking holes – though with the average pint costing over £3, it's worth knowing that you can pay half that at Sam Smith's pubs. **Soho** and **Hoxton** attract a clubbier crowd, so you'll find a wide choice of bars and clubs alongside good old fashioned pubs. For a riverside drink, head for the **South Bank** or **Docklands**, and for a lazy Sunday afternoon mosey on up to **Hampstead** or down to **Greenwich**.

## >>SHOPPING

From the folie de grandeur of Harrods to the street markets of Camden and Spitalfields, London is a shopper's playground. In the West End, **Oxford Street** is Europe's busiest shopping street, followed closely by Regent Street – here you'll find pretty much every mainstream shop you could wish for. **Charing Cross Road** remains the centre of the city's book trade, while **Covent Garden** has become a fashion and designer wear hotspot. **St James's** equips the English gentleman, **Bond Street** deals with the ladies, but for haute couture – and Harrods – head for **Knightsbridge** and Sloane Street. For something more offbeat, or vintage, head out to **Camden Market** or Spitalfields and Brick Lane.

## >>NIGHTLIFE

As well as two top-class **opera** houses, London has an enormous number of **theatres**, most of them centrally located in the West End districts of Soho and Covent Garden, and boasts more **comedy** venues than any other city in the world. Although you'll find **clubs** and **live music** venues all across the capital, Hoxton and Spitalfields remain the epicentre of the city's clubland. London is also the **gay** capital of Europe, with Old Compton Street in Soho still, so to speak, the city's main drag.

**OUR RECOMMENDATIONS FOR WHERE TO EAT, DRINK AND SHOP ARE LISTED AT THE END OF EACH PLACES CHAPTER.**

7

# **Day One** in London

**1 Parliament Square** > p.42.
Gaze at two of the capital's most remarkable buildings: the Houses of Parliament and Westminster Abbey.

**2 Whitehall** > p.39. This wide avenue is lined with grandiose governmental ministries and dotted with statues recalling the days of the British Empire.

**3 Churchill Museum** > p.41.
Explore the subterranean rooms used by Churchill and his War Cabinet during World War II.

**4 St James's Park** > p.46. One of London's smartest royal parks, with views across to Buckingham Palace, exotic ducks and even pelicans.

🍴 **Lunch** > p.51. Picnic in the park or tuck into some excellent British food on the lovely terrace at *Inn the Park*.

**5 Trafalgar Square** > p.36.
London's finest set-piece square, overlooked by the National Gallery and famous for its fountains and pigeons.

**6 Covent Garden Piazza** > p.68.
One of the city's few pedestrianized public spaces, Covent Garden's cobbled piazza is the place to see London's best buskers.

**7 British Museum** > p.78. One of the world's most amazing (and largest) museums, with everything from Egyptian mummies to Constructivist ceramics from the Russian Revolution.

🍴 **Dinner** > p.74. Experience the bustle of *Wong Kei* in the heart of Chinatown, before heading into the heart of Soho for a night of drinking and (maybe) dancing.

# Day Two in London

**1 Harrods** > p.139. The queen of department stores, Harrods is a sight in itself, especially the Art Nouveau food hall and the Di and Dodi shrine.

**2 Hyde Park** > p.128. Stroll along the Serpentine, go for a dip (if you're feeling brave) and check out the Diana Memorial Fountain.

**3 Serpentine Gallery** > p.132. Sample some contemporary art for free and then have tea at the architecturally cutting-edge summer pavilion.

**4 Albert Memorial** > p.132. Stop by this incredible, over-the-top neo-Gothic memorial to Queen Victoria's husband.

**Lunch** > p.140. Pause for lunch at *Daquise*, a Polish café that's changed very little since it was opened by Polish exiles shortly after the war.

**5 V&A** > p.135. South Kensington is home to a trio of fabulous museums, but the V&A's collection of applied arts is head and shoulders above the others.

**6 Kensington Palace** > p.132. Princess Diana's former residence houses a display of her glamorous frocks, as well as some finely frescoed rooms.

**7 Portobello Road Market** > p.136. Browse the antique shops or (if Saturday) the busy flea market.

**Dinner** > p.141 and p.142. Grab some of the best fish and chips in London at Greek-Cypriot *Costas Fish Restaurant* or go for a drink and meal at *The Cow*.

# Riverside London

London grew up around the Thames, and a stroll (or a boat ride) along its banks is one of the city's real treats.

**1 London Eye** > p.116. London's graceful millennial observation wheel has become one of the iconic symbols of the city despite its relative youth.

**2 South Bank** > p.114. The views along the river from the South Bank's car-free promenade are some of London's best.

**3 Tate Modern** > p.120. Feast your eyes on art from the last hundred years or so at the world's largest modern art gallery.

**4 Millennium Bridge** > p.120. London's only pedestrian-only river crossing offers great views of St Paul's Cathedral and the City.

**Lunch** > p.126. Sample some of the top-notch British produce on offer at Borough Market's stalls (Thurs–Sat only), or head upstairs for a feast at *Roast*.

**5 Boat to Greenwich** > p.157. Catch a Thames Clipper from London Bridge pier, and check out the Tower of London, Tower Bridge and Docklands development en route to SE10.

**6 Old Royal Naval College** > p.156. This is the one building in London which exploits its riverside position to best effect, and harbours two fantastic eighteenth-century interiors to boot.

**7 Somerset House** > p.70. Take the boat back to Festival Pier and cross Waterloo Bridge to the sole survivor of the grandiose palaces that once lined the Strand.

**Dinner** > p.74 and p.127. Enjoy the magnificent views over the river at *Tom's Terrace* or, for something a little cheaper, head for one of Fleet Street's pubs.

# The City

From the Romans to rogue traders, the City has more history than the rest of London combined.

**1 Sir John Soane's Museum** > p.88. The idiosyncratic home of the architect of the Bank of England is crammed with paintings and sculpture.

**2 Temple Church** > p.85. Fascinating medieval round church, famed for its effigy tombs and appearance in *The Da Vinci Code*.

**3 St Paul's Cathedral** > p.92. Climb up to the top of the dome of Wren's masterpiece for a fabulous view across the river.

🍴 **Lunch** > p.96 and p.97. Tuck into fresh, seasonal food at *The Café Below*, in the atmospheric crypt of St Mary-le-Bow, or pub grub at the wonderful Art Nouveau *Black Friar*.

**4 Museum of London** > p.91. From Roman mosaics to Wellington's boots, this museum encompasses the whole of London's history.

**5 Bank of England** > p.94. The Bank of England stands at the heart of the City, and forms part of a superb architectural set piece of Neoclassical edifices.

**6 City skyscrapers** > p.95. Stand outside Richard Rogers' Lloyds Building for a panoramic view of the City's latest generation of skyscrapers, including the iconic Gherkin.

**7 Old Spitalfields Market** > p.104. Though at its liveliest on Sundays, this old Victorian market hall has plenty of interest throughout the week.

🍴 **Dinner** > p.106. Have supper at *Café Naz*, a modern Bangladeshi restaurant on Brick Lane, and then head up the road for a night in trendy Shoreditch.

11

# Royal London

**1 Hampton Court Palace** This sprawling red-brick Tudor edifice is without a doubt the finest of London's royal palaces. **> p.168**

**2 Buckingham Palace** Unlike the rest of London's royal palaces, the Queen does actually live here (for some of the year, at least). > **p.48**

**3 Tower of London** England's most perfectly preserved medieval fortress and safe-deposit box for the Crown Jewels. > **p.108**

**4 Westminster Abbey** Venue for every coronation since William the Conqueror and resting place of countless kings and queens. > **p.42**

**5 Changing of the Guard** This daily royal ceremony is best viewed on Horse Guards Parade, where the Household Cavalry change shifts. > **p.40**

# Outdoor London

**1 St James's Park** Probably London's smartest royal park, with a fine array of exotic ducks and pelicans in the lake and a great café. **> p.46**

**2 Portobello Market** London's trendiest street market offers brilliant retro clothes, bric-à-brac, antiques, and fruit and veg. > **p.137**

**3 Thames boat ride** River services are now fast and frequent: hop on and off anywhere between Westminster and Greenwich. > **p.188**

**4 Hampstead Heath** North London's green lung and the city's most enjoyable public outdoor space. > **p.150**

**5 South Bank** Stroll along the riverbank's Thames Path from the London Eye to the Tate Modern and beyond. > **p.114**

# London for kids

**1 Double-decker bus** Head upstairs on an old double-decker for a scenic tour of some of London's most famous sights. **> p.189**

**2 Natural History Museum** With animatronic dinosaurs and an earthquake simulator, the Natural History Museum is sure to prove a winner. > **p.134**

**3 Diana Memorial Playground** The city's most sophisticated, imaginative and popular outdoor playground, just a short walk from Diana's former home. > **p.132**

**4 Pollock's Toy Museum** Doll's house-like museum of paper theatres, dolls and games above a toyshop. > **p.68**

**5 London Zoo** Opened in 1828 as the world's first scientific zoo, and still a guaranteed hit with children of all ages. > **p.146**

# Museums

**1 British Museum** The oldest and greatest public museum on the planet contains objects from every corner of the globe. **> p.78**

**2 National Maritime Museum** Imaginatively designed complex encompassing the old Royal Observatory as well as nautical exhibits. > **p.157**

**3 V&A** The world's greatest applied arts museum, with something for everyone, from Islamic art to Kylie Minogue's dressing room. > **p.135**

**4 Imperial War Museum** This military museum houses a huge art collection and gives a sober account of the horrors of war. > **p.117**

-every available piece of land must be cultivated

GROW YOUR OWN FOOD
supply your own cookhouse

**5 Sir John Soane's Museum** Part architectural set piece, part art gallery, the John Soane museum is small but perfectly formed. > **p.88**

# Food

**1 Afternoon tea** The classic English afternoon tea – sandwiches, scones and cream cakes – is as popular as ever. **> p.56**

**2 Dim Sum** This bargain spread of dumplings and other little morsels is a Chinatown lunchtime ritual. > **p.74**

**4 Pie and mash** London's most peculiar culinary speciality, topped by "liquor" (parsley sauce), is an acquired taste. > **p.96**

**3 Fish and chips** The national dish – fish in batter with deep-fried potato chips – remains as popular and tasty as ever. > **p.140**

**5 Curry** London is the best place in Europe for curry, with cuisine from all over the Indian subcontinent well represented. > **p.106**

# London art

**1 Kenwood House** Small but perfectly formed gallery of seventeenth- and eighteenth-century paintings, including works by Gainsborough, Rembrandt and Vermeer. > **p.150**

**2 Tate Modern** A wonderful hotchpotch of wild and wacky art, from video installations to gargantuan pieces that fill the vast turbine hall. > **p.120**

**3 Courtauld Institute** Quality, not quantity, is the hallmark of this gallery, best known for its superlative collection of Impressionist masterpieces. > **p.71**

**4 Tate Britain** The history of British painting from Holbein and Hogarth to Hockney and Hirst, plus pre-Raphaelites and Turners in abundance. > **p.44**

**5 National Gallery** A comprehensive overview of Western painting, from Renaissance classics in the airy Sainsbury Wing to fin-de-siècle Parisian works. > **p.38**

# Pubs

**1 Royal Oak** Beautiful Victorian pub with a great range of real ales from the Harvey's brewery in Sussex. **> p.127**

**2 Ye Olde Cheshire Cheese** A dark, snug seventeenth-century tavern hidden down an alleyway off Fleet Street – look out for the sign. > **p.99**

**3 Salisbury** Flamboyant late-Victorian pub a stone's throw from Trafalgar Square, replete with bronze nymphs and etched glasswork. > **p.76**

**5 The Lamb** Classic, beautifully preserved nineteenth-century pub in lovely Leadenhall Market. > **p.98**

**4 Dog & Duck** Soho pub with genuine character that retains its original decor of tiles and mosaics. > **p.75**

# Victorian London

**1 Albert Memorial** This bombastic monument to Queen Victoria's consort is a riot of semi-precious stones, marbles, bronze and gilding. **> p.132**

## 2 Westminster Cathedral

Still unfinished inside, London's neo-Byzantine Roman Catholic Cathedral represents the last gasp of the Victorian period. **> p.44**

**3 St Pancras Station** Revitalized Victorian railway station fronted by a gloriously over-the-top red-brick neo-Gothic hotel. **> p.81**

## 4 Houses of Parliament

A gargantuan, confident expression of nationhood, best known for its "Big Ben" clock-tower. **> p.43**

**5 Leadenhall Market** Cobblestones and graceful Victorian ironwork combine to create the City's most attractive market for luxury comestibles. **> p.94**

29

# Nightlife

**1 Live music** Originally a train engine shed, the *Roundhouse* is one of London's most atmospheric music venues. > **p.149**

**2 Theatre** The country's top actors and directors ensure that high standards are maintained at the South Bank's National Theatre. **> p.119**

**3 Jazz** London's most famous jazz club, *Ronnie Scott's* is an intimate venue that nevertheless attracts big names. **> p.77**

**4 Cabaret** *Madame JoJo's* is a louche Soho institution that puts on variety, drag acts and comedy, but also disco, rock and funk. **> p.77**

**5 Clubs** *Fabric* in Clerkenwell is one of the city's finest clubs, with a devastating soundsystem and both DJs and live bands. **> p.99**

# Modern London

**1 Lloyds Building** Lloyds' high-tech City offices, designed by Richard Rogers in the mid-1980s, are still strikingly contemporary. > **p.95**

**3 Canary Wharf** Cesar Pelli's stainless steel skyscraper is the centrepiece of the Canary Wharf Docklands development. > **p.112**

**2 The Gherkin** This unusual cone-shaped affair is – for now, at least – the most distinctive lofty addition to the City skyline. > **p.95**

**4 Millennium Bridge** This flashy millennial footbridge connects St Paul's Cathedral with the Tate Modern. > **p.120**

**5 City Hall** Norman Foster's eco-friendly headquarters for the Greater London Authority bears a close resemblance to a giant car headlight. > **p.125**

# Whitehall and Westminster

Whitehall is synonymous with the faceless, pinstriped bureaucracy who run the various governmental ministries located here, while Westminster remains home to the Houses of Parliament. Both are popular with visitors thanks to the Changing of the Guard, and familiar landmarks such as Nelson's Column, Big Ben, and Westminster Abbey, London's most historic church.

Political, religious and regal power has emanated from Whitehall and Westminster for almost a millennium. It was King Edward the Confessor who first established this spot as London's royal and ecclesiastical power base in the eleventh century. He built his palace and abbey some three miles upstream from the City of London, and it was in the abbey that the embryonic English parliament used to meet in the Middle Ages.

## TRAFALGAR SQUARE

⊖ Charing Cross. MAP P.37, POCKET MAP G16

As one of the few large public squares in London, Trafalgar Square has been a focus for political demonstrations since it was laid out in the 1820s. Most days, however, it's scruffy urban pigeons that you're more likely to encounter, as they wheel around the square hoping some unsuspecting visitor will feed them (though, it is, in fact, illegal to do so). Along with its fountains, the square's central focal point is the deeply patriotic **Nelson's Column**, which stands 170ft high and is topped by a 17-foot statue of the one-eyed, one-armed admiral who defeated the French (and died) at the 1805 Battle of Trafalgar. Nelson himself is actually quite hard to see – not so the giant bronze lions at the base of the column, which provide a popular photo opportunity. Stranded on a nearby traffic island is an equestrian statue of Charles I, while in the square's northeastern corner is one of George IV, which he himself originally commissioned for the top of Marble Arch. The **fourth plinth**, in the northwest corner, was built for an equestrian statue of William IV, but remained empty until 1999, since when it's been used to

VIEW OF NELSON'S COLUMN, TRAFALGAR SQUARE

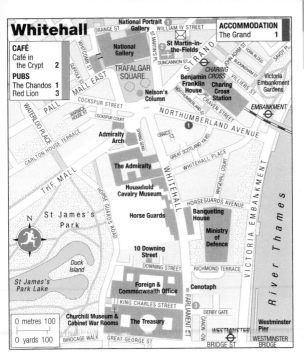

| ACCOMMODATION | |
| --- | --- |
| The Grand | 1 |

| CAFÉ | |
| --- | --- |
| Café in the Crypt | 2 |
| **PUBS** | |
| The Chandos | 1 |
| Red Lion | 3 |

display alternating works of modern sculpture (Ⓦwww.london.gov.uk/fourthplinth).

## ST MARTIN-IN-THE-FIELDS

Duncannon St ⊖ Charing Cross ☎ 020/7766 1100, Ⓦ www.stmartin-in-the-fields.org. Mon–Wed 10am–7pm Thurs–Sat 10am–10pm, Sun noon–7pm. Free. MAP P.37, POCKET MAP G16

Something of a blueprint for eighteenth-century churches across the empire, St Martin-in-the-Fields is fronted by a magnificent Corinthian portico and topped by an elaborate tower and steeple. Designed by James Gibbs and completed in 1726, the barrel-vaulted interior features ornate, sparkling white Italian plasterwork and is best appreciated while listening to one of the church's free **lunchtime concerts** (Mon, Tues and Fri) or ticketed, candle-lit evening performances. Down in the newly expanded **crypt** – accessible via an entrance north of the church – there's a licensed **café** (see p.45), shop, gallery and **brass-rubbing centre** (Mon–Sat 10am–6pm, Sun noon–6pm).

## NATIONAL GALLERY

Trafalgar Square ⊖ Charing Cross
☎ 020/7747 2885, Ⓦ www.nationalgallery
.org.uk. Daily 10am–6pm, Wed till 9pm. Free.
MAP P.37, POCKET MAP G16

Despite housing more than 2300 paintings, the main virtue of the National Gallery is not so much the collection's size, but its range, depth and sheer quality. A quick tally of the **Italian** masterpieces, for example, includes works by Uccello, Botticelli, Mantegna, Piero della Francesca, Veronese, Titian, Raphael, Michelangelo and Caravaggio. From **Spain** there are dazzling pieces by El Greco, Velázquez and Goya; from the **Low Countries**, van Eyck, Memling and Rubens, and an array of Rembrandt paintings that features some of his most searching portraits. Poussin, Claude, Watteau and the only Jacques-Louis David paintings in the country are the early highlights of a **French** contingent, which also has a particularly strong showing of Cézanne and the Impression-ists. **British** art is also well represented, with important works by Hogarth, Gainsbor-ough, Stubbs and Turner, though for twentieth-century British art – and many more Turners – you'll need to move on to Tate Britain on Millbank (see p.44).

To view the collection chronologically, begin with the **Sainsbury Wing**, the softly-softly, postmodern 1980s adjunct which is linked to – and playfully imitates – the original Neoclassical building. However, with more than a thousand paintings on permanent display, you'll need stamina to see everything in one day, so if time is tight your best bet is to home in on your areas of special interest, having picked up a gallery plan at one of the information desks. Audioguides are available for a "voluntary contribution" – much better, though, are the gallery's **free guided tours** (daily 11.30am and 2.30pm), which set off from the Sainsbury Wing foyer, and focus on a representative sample of works.

## NATIONAL PORTRAIT GALLERY

St Martin's Place ⊖ Charing Cross ☎ 020/7306 0055, Ⓦ www.npg.org.uk. Daily 10am–6pm, Thurs & Fri till 9pm. Free.
MAP P.37, POCKET MAP G16

Founded in 1856 to house uplifting depictions of the good and the great, the National Portrait Gallery has some fine individual works. However, many of the studies are of less interest than their subjects, and the overall impression is of an overstuffed shrine to famous Brits rather than a museum offering any insight into the history of portraiture. Nevertheless, it is fascinating to trace who has been deemed worthy of admiration at any moment: aristocrats and artists in previous centuries, warmongers and imperialists in the early decades of the twentieth century, writers and poets in the 1930s and 1940s, and latterly, sportsmen and women, politicians and film and pop stars. The NPG's audioguide (£2) gives useful biographical background information and the gallery's **special exhibitions** (for which there's often an entrance charge) are well worth seeing – the photography shows, in particular, are usually excellent.

## WHITEHALL

Westminster or Charing Cross. MAP P.37, POCKET MAP G17–G18

Whitehall, the unusually broad avenue connecting Trafalgar Square to Parliament Square, is synonymous with the faceless, pinstriped bureaucracy charged with the day-to-day running of the country. Yet during the sixteenth and seventeenth centuries it served as the chief residence of England's kings and queens. Having started out as the London seat of the Archbishop of York, **Whitehall Palace** was confiscated and embellished by Henry VIII after a fire at Westminster made him homeless; it was here that he celebrated his marriage to Anne Boleyn in 1533, and where he died fourteen years later. Described by one contemporary chronicler as nothing but "a heap of houses erected at diverse times and of different models, made continuous", it boasted some two thousand rooms and stretched for half a mile along the Thames. Not much survived the fire of 1698, and subsequently, the royal residences shifted to St James's and Kensington. Since then, the key governmental ministries and offices have migrated here, rehousing themselves on an ever-increasing scale.

The statues dotted along Whitehall today recall the days when this street stood at the centre of an empire on which the sun never set, while just beyond the Downing Street gates, in the middle of the road, stands Edwin Lutyens' **Cenotaph**, commemorating the dead of both world wars. Eschewing any kind of Christian imagery, the plain monument is inscribed simply with the words "The Glorious Dead" and remains the focus of the country's Remembrance Sunday ceremony, held here in early November.

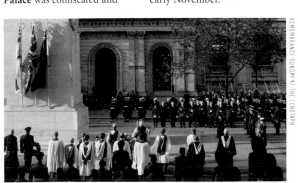

REMEMBRANCE SUNDAY AT THE CENOTAPH

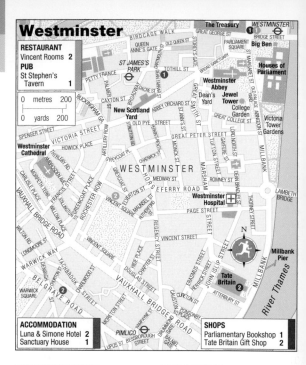

# Westminster

**RESTAURANT**
Vincent Rooms 2

**PUB**
St Stephen's
Tavern 1

0 metres 200

0 yards 200

**ACCOMMODATION**
Luna & Simone Hotel 2
Sanctuary House 1

**SHOPS**
Parliamentary Bookshop 1
Tate Britain Gift Shop 2

## BANQUETING HOUSE

Whitehall ⊖ Westminster ⓦ www.hrp
.org.uk. Mon–Sat 10am–5pm. £4.50. MAP P.37,
POCKET MAP G18

One of the few sections of
Whitehall Palace to escape
the 1698 fire, the Banqueting
House was one of the first
Palladian buildings to be built
in England. The one room
open to the public has no
original furnishings, but is well
worth seeing for the superlative **Rubens ceiling paintings**
commissioned by Charles I
in the 1630s, depicting the
union of England and Scotland,
the peaceful reign of his
father, James I, and finally his
apotheosis (ask for an audioguide). Charles himself walked
through the room for the last
time in 1649, when he stepped
onto the executioner's scaffold
from one of its windows.

## HORSE GUARDS

Whitehall ⊖ Charing Cross or Westminster.
MAP P.37, POCKET MAP G18

Outside this modest building,
built in 1745 and once the
old palace guard house, two
mounted sentries of the
**Queen's Household Cavalry**
and two horseless colleagues,
all in ceremonial uniform,
are posted daily from 10am
to 4pm. With nothing in
particular to guard nowadays,
the sentries are basically here
for the tourists, though they are
under orders not to smile. Try
to coincide your visit with the
**Changing of the Guard**, when
a squad of mounted Household
Cavalry in full livery arrives to
relieve the guards (Mon–Sat
11am, Sun 10am) – if you
miss it, turn up at 4pm for the
elaborate **daily inspection** by
the Officer of the Guard.

## HOUSEHOLD CAVALRY MUSEUM

Whitehall ⊖ Westminster ☎ 020/7930 3070.
ⓦ www.householdcavalrymuseum.org.uk.
Daily: March–Sept 10am–6pm; Oct–Feb
10am–5pm. £6. MAP P.37, POCKET MAP G17

Round the back of Horse
Guards, you'll find the Household Cavalry Museum, where
you can try on a trooper's
elaborate uniform, complete a
horse quiz and learn about the
regiments' history. With the
stables immediately adjacent,
it's a sweet-smelling place, and
– horse-lovers will be pleased
to know – you can see the
beasts in their stalls through
a glass screen. Don't miss the
pocket Riot Act on display,
which ends with the wise
warning: "must read correctly:
variance fatal".

## 10 DOWNING STREET

⊖ Westminster ⓦ www.number10.gov.uk.
MAP P.37, POCKET MAP G18

Since the days of Margaret
Thatcher, London's most
famous address has been
hidden behind wrought-iron
security gates. A pretty plain,
seventeenth-century terraced
house, no. 10 has been home to
every British **prime minister**
since it was presented to Robert
Walpole, Britain's first PM, by
George II in 1732.

## CHURCHILL MUSEUM AND
## CABINET WAR ROOMS

King Charles St ⊖ Westminster ☎ 020/7930
6961. ⓦ cwr.iwm.org.uk. Daily 9.30am–6pm.
£12. MAP P.37, POCKET MAP G18

In 1938, in anticipation of Nazi
air raids, the basement of the
civil service buildings on the
south side of King Charles
Street was converted into the
**Cabinet War Rooms**. It was
here that Winston Churchill
directed operations and held
Cabinet meetings for the
duration of World War II. The
rooms have been left pretty
much as they were when they
were finally abandoned on
VJ Day 1945, making for an
atmospheric underground
trot through wartime London.
Also in the basement is the
excellent **Churchill Museum**,
where you can hear snippets
of Churchill's most famous
speeches and check out his
trademark bowler, spotted bow
tie and half-chewed Havana,
not to mention his wonderful
burgundy zip-up "romper suit".

# WESTMINSTER ABBEY

Parliament Square ⊖ Westminster
☎ 020/7654 4900, ⓦ www.westminster-abbey
.org. Mon–Fri 9.30am–4.30pm, Wed until 6pm,
Sat 9.30am–2.30pm, though hours can vary.
£12. MAP P.40, POCKET MAP G19

Venue for every coronation since William the Conqueror, and burial place of kings and queens, Westminster Abbey embodies much of England's history.

Entry is via the north transept, cluttered with monuments to politicians. Adjacent is the central sanctuary, site of the coronations, and the wonderful **Cosmati floor mosaic**, constructed in the thirteenth century by Italian craftsmen. At the east end lies the abbey's most dazzling architectural set piece, the **Lady Chapel**, added by Henry VII in 1503 as his future resting place. With its intricately carved vaulting and fan-shaped gilded pendants, the chapel represents the final spectacular gasp of the English Perpendicular style. The public is no longer admitted to the **Shrine of Edward the Confessor**, the sacred heart of the building, except on a guided verger tour (£3), though you do get to inspect Edward I's **Coronation Chair**, a decrepit oak throne dating from around 1300 and still used for coronations. Nowadays, the abbey's royal tombs are upstaged by **Poets' Corner**, in the south transept. The first occupant, Geoffrey Chaucer, was buried here in 1400, not because he was a poet but because he lived nearby. By the eighteenth century, however, this zone had become an artistic pantheon, and since then has been filled with tributes to all shades of talent from William Blake to John Betjeman.

Doors in the south choir aisle lead to the **Great Cloisters** (daily 8am–6pm; free with Abbey ticket), rebuilt after a fire in 1298. At the eastern end of the cloisters lies the octagonal **Chapter House** (daily 10.30am–4pm; free), where the House of Commons met from 1257. The thirteenth-century decorative paving tiles and apocalyptic wall-paintings have survived intact. Close by is the **Abbey Museum** (daily 10.30am–4pm; free), filled with generations of bald royal death masks and wax effigies. From the cloisters you can make your way to the little-known **College Garden** (Tues–Thurs: April–Sept 10am–6pm; Oct–March 10am–4pm; free), a 900-year-old stretch of green which now provides a quiet retreat; brass band concerts take place in July and August between 12.30 and 2pm.

It's only after exploring the cloisters that you get to see the **nave** itself: narrow, light and, at over a hundred feet in height, by far the tallest in the country. You exit via the west door.

WESTMINSTER ABBEY

# HOUSES OF PARLIAMENT

Parliament Square ⊖ Westminster ☎ 020/7219 3000, ⓦ www.parliament.uk.
MAP P.40, POCKET MAP H19

Also known as the **Palace of Westminster**, the Houses of Parliament are one of London's best-known monuments and the ultimate symbol of a nation once confident of its place at the centre of the world. The city's finest example of Victorian Gothic Revival, the complex is distinguished above all by the ornate, gilded clock-tower popularly known as **Big Ben**, after the thirteen-ton main bell that strikes the hour (and is broadcast across the airwaves by the BBC).

The original medieval palace burnt to the ground in 1834, but **Westminster Hall** survived, and its huge oak hammerbeam roof –and sheer scale – make it one of the most magnificent secular medieval halls in Europe; you get a glimpse of it en route to the public galleries. For centuries, the hall housed England's highest court of law and witnessed the trials of, among others, William Wallace, Guy Fawkes and Charles I.

To watch the proceedings in either the House of Commons or the Lords, simply join the queue for the **public galleries** (known as Strangers' Galleries) outside St Stephen's Gate. The public is let in slowly (from 4pm Mon, 1pm Tues–Thurs, 10am Fri); security checks are tight, and the whole procedure can take an hour or more. To avoid the queues, turn up an hour or more later, when the crowds have usually thinned; call ☎ 020/7219 4272 to check that the place is open.

To see **Question Time** (Mon 2.30pm, Tues–Thurs 11.30am),

BIG BEN

when the House is at its most raucous and entertaining, UK citizens must book a ticket several weeks in advance from their local MP. If you're here in late summer, you can also see Parliament by way of a **guided tour** (Mon–Sat only; £7; booking line ☎ 0870/906 3773), in which visitors get to walk through the two chambers, see some of the state rooms reserved for the Queen, and admire Westminster Hall. It's a good idea to book in advance, or you can simply head for the ticket office on Abingdon Green, opposite Victoria Tower and its adjacent gardens.

## JEWEL TOWER

Abingdon St ⊖ Westminster. Daily: April–Oct 10am–5pm; Nov–March 10am–4pm. £3.
MAP P.40, POCKET MAP J9

The Jewel Tower is another remnant of the medieval palace. It once formed the corner of the original fortifications, and was constructed in around 1365 by Edward III as a giant strongbox for the crown jewels. These days, it houses an excellent exhibition on the history of parliament – worth checking out before you visit the Houses of Parliament.

## WESTMINSTER CATHEDRAL

Victoria St ⊖ Victoria ☎ 020/7798 9055, ⓦ www.westminstercathedral.org.uk. Mon–Fri 7am–7pm, Sat 8am–7pm, Sun 8am–8pm. Free. MAP P.40, POCKET MAP G9

Begun in 1895, the stripy neo-Byzantine, Roman Catholic Westminster Cathedral is one of London's most surprising churches, as well as one of the last – and the wildest – monuments to the

Victorian era. Brick-built, and decorated with hoops of Portland stone, it culminates in a magnificent 274-foot tapered **campanile**, served by a lift (daily 9.30am–12.30pm and 1–5pm; £3). The interior is only half finished, so to get an idea of what the place should eventually look like, explore the side chapels whose rich, multicoloured decor uses over one hundred types of marble from around the world. Be sure, too, to check out the low-relief Stations of the Cross, sculpted by Eric Gill during World War I.

## TATE BRITAIN

Millbank ⊖ Pimlico ☎ 020/7887 8888, ⓦ www.tate.org.uk. Daily 10am–5.50pm. Free.
MAP P.40, POCKET MAP J10

A purpose-built gallery founded in 1897 with money from Henry Tate, inventor of the sugar cube, Tate Britain is devoted almost exclusively to British art from 1500 to the present day. In addition, the gallery showcases contemporary British artists and sponsors the Turner Prize, the country's most prestigious modern-art award.

The pictures are rehung more or less annually, but always include a fair selection of works by British artists such as Hogarth, Constable, Gainsborough, Reynolds and Blake, plus foreign artists like van Dyck who spent much of their career over here. The ever-popular **Pre-Raphaelites** are well represented, as are established twentieth-century greats including Stanley Spencer and Francis Bacon and living artists such as David Hockney and Lucian Freud. Lastly, don't miss the Tate's outstanding **Turner collection**, displayed in the Clore Gallery.

# Shops

### PARLIAMENTARY BOOKSHOP

12 Bridge St ⊖ Westminster. Mon–Thurs
9.30am–5.30pm, Fri 9am–4pm. MAP P.40,
POCKET MAP G19

Pick up copies of *Hansard*
(the word-for-word account of
parliament), the government's
white and green papers and
plenty of political literature.

### TATE BRITAIN GIFT SHOP

Millbank ⊖ Pimlico. Daily 10am–5.50pm.
MAP P.40, POCKET MAP J10

Lots of art posters, from
Constable to Turner Prize
nonsense, plus loads of funky,
arty accessories.

# Cafés and restaurants

### CAFÉ IN THE CRYPT

St Martin-in-the-Fields, Duncannon St
⊖ Charing Cross. Mon–Wed 8am–8pm, Thurs–
Sat 8am–10.30pm, Sun 11am–6pm.
MAP P.37, POCKET MAP G16

The self-service buffet food
is standard fare, but there are
regular veggie dishes, and
the handy (and atmospheric)
location – below the church in
the crypt – makes this an ideal
spot to fill up before hitting
the West End. Fortnightly jazz
nights (Wed 8pm).

### VINCENT ROOMS

76 Vincent Square ⊖ Victoria or St James's
Park ☎ 0207/802 8391, ⊛ www.westking
.ac.uk. Mon–Fri noon–2pm, plus some eves
6–9pm; closed Easter, July, Aug and Xmas.
MAP P.40, POCKET MAP H9

Elegant brasserie serving up
dishes cooked by the student
chefs of Westminster Kingsway
College, where Jamie Oliver
learnt his trade.

PARLIAMENTARY BOOKSHOP

# Pubs

### THE CHANDOS

29 St Martin's Lane ⊖ Charing Cross.
Mon–Sat 11am–11pm, Sun noon–10.30pm.
MAP P.37, POCKET MAP G16

If you can get one of the booths
downstairs, or the leather sofas
upstairs in the more relaxed
Opera Room Bar, then you'll
find it difficult to leave this Sam
Smith's pub.

### RED LION

48 Parliament St ⊖ Westminster. Mon–Fri
11am–11pm, Sat 11am–9.30pm, Sun
noon–10.30pm. MAP P.37, POCKET MAP G18

Classic old pub with good
grub, convenient for Westminster Abbey and Parliament.
Popular with MPs, who are
called to vote by a division bell
in the bar.

### ST STEPHEN'S TAVERN

10 Bridge St ⊖ Westminster. Mon–Fri
11am–11pm, Sat 11am–8pm, Sun noon–6pm.
MAP P.40, POCKET MAP H19

A beautifully restored and
opulent Victorian pub, built
in 1867, wall to wall with civil
servants and MPs (there's a
division bell), and serving good
real ales.

# St James's

An exclusive little enclave sandwiched between St James's
Park and Piccadilly, St James's was laid out in the 1670s close
to the royal seat of St James's Palace. Regal and aristocratic
residences overlook nearby Green Park and the stately avenue
of The Mall, while gentlemen's clubs cluster along Pall Mall
and St James's Street, and jacket-and-tie restaurants and
expense-account gentlemen's outfitters line Jermyn Street.
Hardly surprising, then, that most Londoners rarely stray into
this area. Plenty of folk, however, frequent St James's Park,
with large numbers heading for the Queen's chief residence,
Buckingham Palace, and the adjacent Queen's Gallery and
Royal Mews.

## THE MALL

Charing Cross. MAP P.47, POCKET MAP G17-E18

The tree-lined sweep of The
Mall was laid out in the
early twentieth century as a
memorial to Queen Victoria.
The bombastic **Admiralty
Arch** was erected to mark the
eastern entrance to The Mall,
from Trafalgar Square, while
at the other end, in front of
Buckingham Palace, stands the
ludicrously overblown **Victoria
Memorial**, Edward VII's tribute
to his mother. The Mall is best
visited on a Sunday, when it's
closed to traffic.

## ST JAMES'S PARK

St James's Park www.royalparks
.gov.uk. MAP P.47, POCKET MAP F18

St James's Park is the oldest of
London's royal parks, having
been enclosed for hunting
purposes by Henry VIII and
later opened to the public by
Charles II. It was landscaped by
Nash in the 1820s, and today
its tree-lined lake is a favourite
picnic spot for Whitehall's civil
servants. Pelicans chill out at
the eastern end, and there are
exotic ducks, swans and geese
aplenty. From the bridge across
the lake there's also a fine view

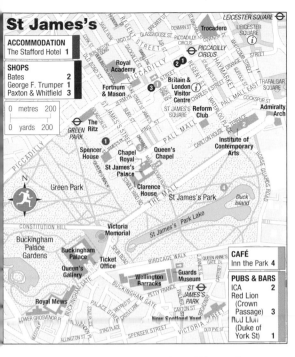

## St James's

**ACCOMMODATION**
The Stafford Hotel 1

**SHOPS**
Bates 2
George F. Trumper 1
Paxton & Whitfield 3

| 0 | metres | 200 |
| 0 | yards | 200 |

**CAFÉ**
Inn the Park 4

**PUBS & BARS**
ICA 2
Red Lion (Crown Passage) 3
Red Lion (Duke of York St) 1

over to Westminster and the jumble of domes and pinnacles along Whitehall, with the London Eye peeking over it all – even dull Buckingham Palace looks majestic from here.

## GUARDS MUSEUM

Birdcage Walk ⊖ St James's Park
☎ 020/7414 3271, ⊕ www.theguardsmuseum
.com. Daily 10am–4pm. £3. MAP P.47, POCKET
MAP E19

The Neoclassical facade of the **Wellington Barracks**, built in 1833 and fronted by a parade ground, runs along the south side of St James's Park. In a bunker opposite the barracks' modern chapel, the Guards Museum endeavours to explain the complicated evolution of the Queen's Household Regiments, and provides a potted military history since the Civil War. Among the exhibits are the guards' glorious

scarlet and blue uniforms, a lock of Wellington's hair and a whole load of war booty, from Dervish prayer mats plundered from Sudan in 1898 to items taken from an Iraqi POW during the 1990 Gulf War.

ADMIRALTY ARCH

## BUCKINGHAM PALACE

Buckingham Gate ⊖ Green Park ⓦ www
.royal.gov.uk. Aug & Sept daily 9.45am–6pm.
Advance booking on ☎ 020/7766 7300.
£16.50. MAP P.47, POCKET MAP D19

The graceless colossus of
Buckingham Palace, popularly
known as "Buck House", has
served as the monarch's permanent London residence only
since Queen Victoria's reign.
Bought by George III in 1762,
the building was overhauled
in the late 1820s, and again in
time for George V's coronation
in 1913, producing a Neoclassical monolith that's about as
bland as it's possible to be.

For two months of the year,
the hallowed portals are grudg-
ingly nudged open to the public;
timed tickets are sold from the
marquee-like box office in Green
Park at the western end of The
Mall. The interior, however,
is a bit of an anticlimax: of
the palace's 775 rooms, you're
permitted to see around twenty,
and there's little sign of life as
the Queen decamps to Scotland
every summer. If the decor is
disappointing, at least the art on
display is top-notch, with several
van Dycks, two Rembrandts,
two Canalettos, a Poussin, a
de Hooch and a wonderful
Vermeer hanging in the Picture
Gallery.

For the other ten months of
the year, the palace is closed to
visitors – not that this deters
the crowds who mill around
the railings and gather in some
force to watch the Foot Guards'
**Changing of the Guard**
ceremony (April–July daily
11.30am; Sept–March alternate
days; no ceremony if it rains).
If the Queen is at home, the
Royal Standard flies from the
roof of the palace and four
guards patrol; if not, the Union
flag flutters aloft and just two
guards stand out front.

## QUEEN'S GALLERY

Buckingham Gate ⊖ Victoria ⓦ www.royal
.gov.uk. Daily 10am–5.30pm. £8.50. MAP P.47,
POCKET MAP D19

The changing exhibitions here
are drawn from the **Royal
Collection**, the vast array of
artworks snapped up by the
royal family over the centuries,
which is three times larger than
that at the National Gallery.
Among the thousands of works
the curators have to choose
from are some incredible
masterpieces by Michelangelo,
Reynolds, Gainsborough,
Vermeer, van Dyck, Rubens,
Rembrandt and Canaletto, as
well as numerous Fabergé eggs
and heaps of Sèvres porcelain.

BUCKINGHAM PALACE

## ROYAL MEWS

Buckingham Gate ⊖ Victoria Ⓦ www
.royal.gov.uk. Aug & Sept daily 10am–5pm;
Oct–July daily except Fri 11am–4pm. £7.50.
MAP P.47, POCKET MAP D19

ST JAMES'S PALACE

At the Nash-built Royal Mews,
you can view the **Queen's
horses** – or at least their
backsides – in their luxury
stables, along with an exhibition
of equine accoutrements, but
it's the royal carriages, lined
up under a glass canopy in the
courtyard, that are the main
attraction. The most ornate is
the **Gold State Coach**, made for
George III in 1762, smothered
in 22-carat gilding, panel paintings by Cipriani, and weighing
four tons, its axles supporting
four life-size Tritons blowing
conches. Eight horses are
needed to pull it and the whole
experience apparently made
Queen Victoria feel quite sick;
since then it has only been used
for coronations and jubilees.
The mews also house the Royal
Family's fleet of five Rolls-Royce
Phantoms and three Daimlers,
none of which is obliged to
carry numberplates.

## ST JAMES'S PALACE

Marlborough Rd ⊖ Green Park Ⓦ www.royal
.gov.uk. MAP P.47, POCKET MAP E18

Originally built by Henry VIII
for Anne Boleyn, St James's
Palace became the principal
royal residence after Whitehall
Palace burnt to the ground in
1698, until the court moved
down the road to Buckingham
Palace under Queen Victoria.
The imposing red-brick gate-
tower that forms the main
entrance, and the **Chapel
Royal**, are all that remain of
the original Tudor palace. The
rambling complex is off-limits
to the public, though you can
attend services at the Chapel
Royal (Oct to Easter Sun
8.30am and 11.15am), venue
for numerous royal weddings,
and at the Neoclassical **Queen's
Chapel** (Easter Sun to July Sun
8.30am and 11.15am).

## The gentlemen's clubs

The **gentlemen's clubs** of St James's remain the final bastions of
the male chauvinism and public-school snobbery for which England
is famous. Their origins lie in the coffee- and chocolate-houses of
the eighteenth century, though the majority were founded in the post-
Napoleonic peace of the early nineteenth century by those who yearned
for the officers' mess; drinking, whoring and gambling were the major
features of early club life. The oldest clubs – like White's, Brooks's and
Boodle's – still boast a list of members that includes royals, politicians and
the military top brass. The **Reform Club**, on Pall Mall, from which Phileas
Fogg set off in Jules Verne's *Around the World in Eighty Days*, is one of the
more "progressive" – it's one of the few to admit women as members.

## CLARENCE HOUSE

Stable Yard Rd ⊖ Green Park ☎ 020/7766 7303, ⓦ www.royal.gov.uk. Aug & Sept daily 10am–4pm. £8. MAP P.47, POCKET MAP E18

Built in the 1820s by John Nash for the future William IV, and used as his principal residence, Clarence House was home to the **Queen Mother**, widow of George VI, until 2002, and is now the official London home of Charles and Camilla. A handful of rooms can be visited over the summer when the royals are in Scotland. Visits must be booked in advance and are by guided tour only, and the rooms are pretty unremarkable, so apart from a peek behind the scenes in a working royal palace, and a few mementos of the Queen Mum, the main draw is the twentieth-century British paintings on display by the likes of Walter Sickert and Augustus John.

## SPENCER HOUSE

St James's Place ⊖ Green Park ⓦ www .spencerhouse.co.uk. Feb–July & Sept–Dec Sun 10.30am–5.45pm. No under 10s. £9. MAP P.47, POCKET MAP E18

Most of St James's palatial residences are closed to the public, with the exception of this superb Palladian mansion, built between 1756 and 1766. Ancestral home of the late Diana, Princess of Wales, it was last lived in by the family in 1926. Inside, guides take you on an hour-long tour through eight of the state rooms. **The Great Room** features a stunning coved and coffered ceiling in green, white and gold, while the **Painted Room** is a feast of Neoclassicism, decorated with murals in the "Pompeian manner". The most outrageous decor, though, is in **Lord Spencer's Room**, with its astonishing gilded palm-tree columns.

## GREEN PARK

⊖ Green Park ⓦ www.royalparks.gov.uk. MAP P.47, POCKET MAP D18

Laid out on the burial ground of the old lepers' hospital by Henry VIII, Green Park was left more or less flowerless – hence its name (officially "The Green Park") – and, apart from the springtime swaths of daffodils and crocuses, it remains mostly meadow, shaded by graceful London plane trees. In its time, however, it was a popular place for duels (banned from neighbouring St James's Park), ballooning and fireworks displays. One such display was immortalized by Handel's *Music for the Royal Fireworks*, performed here on April 27, 1749 to celebrate the Peace of Aix-la-Chapelle, which ended the eight-year War of the Austrian Succession – over ten thousand fireworks were let off, setting fire to the custom-built Temple of Peace and causing three fatalities. The music was a great success, however. Along the east side of the park runs the wide path of **Queen's Walk**, laid out for Queen Caroline, wife of George II, who had a little pavilion built nearby.

LORD SPENCER'S ROOM, SPENCER HOUSE

# Shops

### BATES

21a Jermyn St ⊖ Piccadilly Circus. Mon–Fri
9am–5pm, Sat 9.30am–1pm and 2–4pm.
MAP P.47, POCKET MAP F16

A proper "gentlemen's hatter"
selling everything from
boaters and panamas to tweed
caps and felt hats – look out
for Binks, the stray cat, who
entered the shop in 1921 and
is now displayed in a glass
cabinet, sporting a cigar and
top hat.

### GEORGE F. TRUMPER

20 Jermyn St ⊖ Piccadilly Circus.
Mon–Fri 9am–5.30pm, Sat 9am–5pm.
MAP P.47, POCKET MAP F16

Founded in 1875, this impeccably discreet "Gentlemen's
Perfumer" is *the* barber of
choice, with a shaving school
that will teach you how to
execute the perfect wet shave.

### PAXTON & WHITFIELD

93 Jermyn St ⊖ Piccadilly Circus. Mon–Sat
9.30am–6pm. MAP P.47, POCKET MAP E16

Quintessentially English, this
200-year-old cheese shop
offers a very traditional range
of British and European
varieties, plus a good range of
wine and port.

# Cafés

### INN THE PARK

St James's Park ⊖ Westminster or
St James's Park. Mon–Fri 8am to dusk, Sat &
Sun 9am to dusk. MAP P.47, POCKET MAP F18

The panoramic windows of this
curving wooden building look
onto the park's lake. The restaurant serves delicious but pricey
British food, while the classy
takeaway section provides
sandwiches, salads and cakes
for a top-notch picnic.

INN THE PARK

# Pubs and bars

### ICA

94 The Mall ⊖ Charing Cross. Mon
noon–11pm, Tues–Sat noon–1am, Sun
noon–10.30pm. MAP P.47, POCKET MAP F17

Cool, late-opening drinking
venue, with a noir dress code
observed by the arty crowd and
staff, and sweaty DJ nights at
the weekends.

### RED LION

23 Crown Passage ⊖ Green Park. Mon–Sat
11am–11.30pm. MAP P.47, POCKET MAP E17

Hidden away in a passageway
off Pall Mall, this is a genuinely
warm and cosy local, with
super friendly bar staff, well-
kept Adnams beer and excellent
sandwiches.

### RED LION

2 Duke of York St ⊖ Piccadilly Circus. Mon–
Sat 11.30am–11pm. MAP P.47, POCKET MAP E16

Glorious old Victorian gin
palace with elegant etched
mirrors and lots of polished
wood. Offers a commendable
selection of ales, including a
weekly guest choice, voted for
by its customers.

# Mayfair and Marylebone

A whiff of exclusivity still pervades the streets of Mayfair, particularly Bond Street and its tributaries, where designer clothes emporia jostle for space with jewellers, bespoke tailors and fine art dealers. Most Londoners, however, stick to the more prosaic pleasures of Regent and Oxford streets, home to the flagship branches of the country's most popular chain stores. It's here that Londoners are referring to when they talk of the West End. Marylebone, to the north of Oxford Street, may not have quite the pedigree and snob value of Mayfair, but it's still a wealthy and aspirational area, and its mesh of smart Georgian streets and squares are a pleasure to wander, especially the chi-chi, village-like quarter around the High Street.

## PICCADILLY CIRCUS

Piccadilly Circus. MAP P.53, POCKET MAP F16
Characterless and congested it may be, but for many Londoners, Piccadilly Circus is the nearest their city comes to having a centre. Originally laid out in 1812 and now a major traffic bottleneck, it's by no means a picturesque place, and is probably best seen at night when the spread of vast illuminated signs (a feature since the Edwardian era) provide a touch of Las Vegas dazzle, and when the human traffic is at its most frenetic. Somewhat inexplicably, Piccadilly Circus attracts a steady flow of tourists, who come here to sit on the steps of the central fountain, topped by an aluminium statue popularly known as **Eros**. Despite the bow and arrow, it depicts not the god of love but the Angel of Christian Charity, and was erected to commemorate the Earl of Shaftesbury, a Bible-thumping social reformer who campaigned against child labour.

EROS, PICCADILLY CIRCUS

## TROCADERO

13 Coventry St Piccadilly Circus.
Mon–Thurs & Sun 10am–midnight, Fri & Sat 10am–1am. MAP P.53, POCKET MAP F16
Originally an opulent restaurant from 1896 until its

## Mayfair

**ACCOMMODATION**
Claridge's    1

**VENUES**
Dover Street    1

| SHOPS | |
|---|---|
| Browns | 1, 3 |
| Charbonnel et Walker | 5 |
| Fortnum & Mason | 7 |
| Hamleys | 4 |
| Liberty | 2 |
| Waterstone's | 6 |

| CAFÉS | |
|---|---|
| Mô | 8 |
| Sotheby's | 5 |
| Tibits | 6 |
| The Wolseley | 11 |

| RESTAURANTS | |
|---|---|
| Kiku | 13 |
| Patterson's | 2 |
| Wild Honey | 3 |

| PUBS & BARS | |
|---|---|
| Audley | 9 |
| Guinea | 7 |
| The Windmill | 4 |

| TEAROOMS | |
|---|---|
| Claridge's | 1 |
| Fortnum & Mason | 10 |
| The Lanesborough | 14 |
| The Ritz | 12 |

closure in 1965, this tacky glorified amusement arcade, casino and multiplex cinema has had millions poured into it in an unsuccessful attempt to find a winning formula. Among the more unusual incumbents are **Amora** (Mon–Thurs 1pm–midnight, Fri–Sun 11am–midnight; £15; ☏0871/230 9876, ⓦwww.amoralondon.com), an erotic (and allegedly educational) exhibition dedicated to the joys of sex, and a branch of **Ripley's Believe It or Not!** (daily 10am–midnight; £17.95; ☏020/3238 0022, ⓦwww.ripleyslondon.com), the world's largest odditorium, a sort-of waxwork version of a Victorian freak show.

TAXI IN PICCADILLY CIRCUS

## REGENT STREET

⊖ Piccadilly Circus or Oxford Circus.
MAP P.53, POCKET MAP D14–E16

Drawn up by John Nash in 1812 as both a luxury shopping street and a new, wide triumphal approach to Regent's Park, Regent Street was the city's first real attempt at dealing with traffic congestion. At the same time, it helped clear away a large area of slums, and create a tangible borderline to shore up fashionable Mayfair against the chaotic maze of Soho. Even today, it's still possible to admire the stately intentions of Nash's plan, particularly evident in the **Quadrant**, the street's partially arcaded section which curves westwards from Piccadilly Circus. During the course of the nineteenth century, however, the increased purchasing power of the city's middle classes brought the tone of the street "down", and heavyweight stores catering for the masses now predominate.

## PICCADILLY

⊖ Piccadilly Circus or Green Park. MAP P.53,
POCKET MAP F16–C18

Piccadilly apparently got its name from the ruffs or "pickadills" worn by the dandies who promenaded along this wide boulevard in the late seventeenth century. Despite its fashionable pedigree, and the presence of **The Ritz** halfway along, it's no place for promenading in its current state, with traffic careering down it nose to tail day and night. Infinitely more pleasant places to window-shop are the various **nineteenth-century arcades** leading off the street, originally built to protect shoppers from the mud and horse-dung on the streets, but now equally useful for escaping exhaust fumes.

## BURLINGTON ARCADE

Piccadilly ⊖ Green Park. Mon–Sat 8am–7pm,
Sun 11am–5pm. MAP P.53, POCKET MAP D16–E16

Awash with mahogany-fronted jewellers and gentlemen's outfitters, the Burlington Arcade is Piccadilly's longest and most expensive nineteenth-century arcade. It was built in 1819 for Lord Cavendish, then owner of neighbouring Burlington House, to prevent commoners throwing rubbish into his garden. Upholding Regency decorum, it is still illegal to whistle, sing, hum, hurry, carry large packages or open

umbrellas on this small stretch – the arcade's beadles (known as Burlington Berties), in their Edwardian frock-coats and gold-braided top hats, take the prevention of such criminality very seriously.

## ROYAL ACADEMY

Burlington House, Piccadilly ⊖ Green Park
☎ 020/7300 8000, ⓦ www.royalacademy
.org.uk. Daily 10am–6pm, Fri till 10pm.
Tickets £6–12. MAP P.53, POCKET MAP E16

The Royal Academy of Arts (RA) occupies the enormous Burlington House, one of the few survivors of the aristo-cratic mansions that once lined Piccadilly. The country's first-ever formal art school, the Academy was founded in 1768 by a group of English painters including Thomas Gainsbor-ough and Joshua Reynolds, the first president, whose statue now stands in the main courtyard, palette in hand. The Academy usually has two or three art exhibitions on at any one time, but is best known for its **Summer Exhibition**, which opens in June and runs until mid-August. Anyone can enter paintings in any style, and the lucky winners' works get exhibited and sold. In addition, RA "Academicians" are allowed to display six of their own works – no matter how awful. The result is a bewildering display, which gets annually panned by the critics. As well as hosting exhibitions, the RA has a small selection of works from its own collection on **permanent display** in the newly restored white and gold John Madejski Fine Rooms (Tues–Fri 1–4.30pm, Sat and Sun 10am–6pm; free; free guided tours Tues, Thurs and Fri 1pm, Wed 1 and 3pm, Sat 11.30am). Highlights include a Rembrandtesque self-portrait by Reynolds, as well as works

BURLINGTON ARCADE

by the likes of John Constable, Stanley Spencer and David Hockney.

## ROYAL INSTITUTION

21 Albemarle St ⊖ Green Park ☎ 020/7409 2992, ⓦ www.rigb.org. Mon–Fri 9am–9pm; free. MAP P.53, POCKET MAP Q16

Founded in 1799 "for teaching by courses of philosophical lectures and experiments the application of science to the common purposes of life", the Royal Institution is a scientific institution best known for its six Christmas Lectures, begun by **Michael Faraday** and designed to popularize science among schoolchildren. In the basement, there's an enjoyable interactive **museum** aimed at both kids and adults, where you can learn about the ten elements that have been discovered at the RI, and the famous experiments that have taken place here: Tyndall's blue sky tube, Humphry Davy's early lamps and Faraday's explorations into electricity and electromagneticism – there's even a reconstruction of Faraday's lab from the 1850s.

## BOND STREET AND AROUND

⊖ Bond Street or Green Park. MAP P.53,
POCKET MAP C15–D16

While Oxford Street, Regent
Street and Piccadilly have all
gone downmarket, Bond Street
has carefully maintained its
exclusivity. It is, in fact, two
streets rolled into one: the
southern half, laid out in the
1680s, is known as Old Bond
Street; its northern extension,
which followed less than fifty
years later, is New Bond Street.
Both are pretty unassuming
architecturally, but the shops
that line them – and those of
neighbouring Conduit Street
and South Molton Street – are
among the flashiest in London,
dominated by **perfumeries**,
**jewellers** and **designer clothing**
emporia such as Versace, Gucci
and Yves Saint-Laurent.

In addition to fashion, Bond
Street is also renowned for
its auction houses, the oldest
of which is **Sotheby's**, at

no. 34–35. The viewing galleries
(free) are open to the public, as
are the auctions themselves.
Bond Street's **art galleries** are
another favourite place for the
wealthy to offload their
heirlooms; for contemporary
art, head for neighbouring Cork
Street. Both locations' galleries
have somewhat intimidating
staff, but if you're interested,
walk in and look around.
They're only shops, after all.

## SAVILE ROW

⊖ Green Park. MAP P.53, POCKET MAP D15–E16
A classic address in sartorial
matters, Savile Row has been *the*
place to go for bespoke tailoring
since the early nineteenth
century. **Gieves & Hawkes**,
at no. 1, were the first tailors
to establish themselves here,
back in 1785, with Nelson and
Wellington among their first
customers, while modernist
**Kilgour**, at no. 8, famously
made Fred Astaire's morning

## Afternoon tea

The classic English **afternoon tea** – assorted sandwiches, scones and
cream, cakes and tarts, and, of course, lashings of tea – is available
all over London. The best venues are the capital's top hotels and most
fashionable department stores; a selection of the best is given below
(see also p.61). Expect to spend £20–40 a head, and leave your jeans and
trainers at home – most hotels will expect "smart casual attire", though
only *The Ritz* insists on jacket and tie. It's essential to book ahead.

**Claridge's** Foyer Restaurant, 49 Brook St ⊖ Bond Street ☏ 020/7409 6307.
Daily 3–5.30pm. MAP P.53, POCKET MAP C15

**Fortnum & Mason** St James's Restaurant, 181 Piccadilly ⊖ Green Park or
Piccadilly Circus ☏ 0845/602 5694. Mon–Sat 2–7pm, Sun 2–5pm. MAP P.53,
POCKET MAP E16

**Lanesborough** Apsley's Restaurant
Hyde Park Corner ⊖ Hyde Park Corner
☏ 020/7259 5599. Daily 3.30–6pm.
MAP P.53, POCKET MAP B18

**The Ritz** Palm Court, 150 Piccadilly
⊖ Green Park ☏ 020/7493 8181. Daily
11.30am, 1.30, 3.30, 5.30 and 7.30pm.
MAP P.53, POCKET MAP D17

coat for *Top Hat*, helping to popularize Savile Row tailoring in the US. **Henry Poole & Co**, who moved to no. 15 in 1846, has cut suits for the likes of Napoleon III, Dickens, Churchill and de Gaulle, and invented the short smoking jacket (originally designed for the future Edward VII), later popularized as the tuxedo.

## HANDEL HOUSE MUSEUM

25 Brook St ⊖ Bond Street ☎ 020/7495 1685, Ⓦ www.handelhouse.org. Tues–Sat 10am–6pm, Thurs till 8pm, Sun noon–6pm. £5. MAP P.53, POCKET MAP C15

The German-born composer **George Frideric Handel** (1685–1759) spent the best part of his life in London, producing all his best-known works at what's now the Handel House Museum. The composer used the ground floor of the building as a sort of shop where subscribers could buy scores, while the first floor was employed as a rehearsal room. Although containing few original artefacts, the house has been painstakingly restored, and its atmosphere is enhanced by music students who come to practise on the harpsichords. For information on more formal recitals that regularly take place, see the website. Access to the house is via the chic cobbled yard at the back.

## ST GEORGE'S CHURCH

St George's St ⊖ Oxford Circus ☎ 020/7629 0874, Ⓦ www.stgeorgeshanoversquare.org. Mon–Fri 8am–4pm, Sun 8am–noon. MAP P.53, POCKET MAP D15

The much-copied Corinthian portico of St George's Church was the first of its kind in London when built in the 1720s. The church has long been Mayfair's most fashionable wedding venue, and those who tied the knot here have included the Shelleys,

SELFRIDGE'S, OXFORD STREET

Benjamin Disraeli, George Eliot and Teddy Roosevelt. Handel, a confirmed bachelor, was a church warden for many years and even had his own pew.

## OXFORD STREET

⊖ Marble Arch, Bond Street, Oxford Circus or Tottenham Court Road. MAP PP.53 & 59, POCKET MAP F14–15, E6–H6

The old Roman road to Oxford has been London's main **shopping** mecca for the last century. Today, despite successive recessions and sky-high rents, this aesthetically unremarkable two-mile hotchpotch of shops is still one of the world's busiest streets. East of Oxford Circus, it forms the northern border of Soho; to the west, the one great landmark is **Selfridges**, a huge Edwardian pile fronted by giant Ionic columns, with the Queen of Time riding the ship of commerce and supporting an Art Deco clock above the main entrance. The store was opened in 1909 by Chicago millionaire Gordon Selfridge, who flaunted its 130 departments under the slogan, "Why not spend a day at Selfridges?"; he was later pensioned off after an altercation with the Inland Revenue.

## WALLACE COLLECTION

Hertford House, Manchester Square
Bond Street ☎ 020/7563 9500, ⓦ www
.wallacecollection.org. Daily 10am–5pm. Free.
MAP P.59, POCKET MAP B14

Housed in a miniature eighteenth-century French-style chateau, the Wallace Collection is an old-fashioned place, with exhibits piled high in glass cabinets, paintings covering every inch of wall space and a bloody great armoury. The collection is best known for its eighteenth-century French paintings (especially Watteau); look out, too, for Franz Hals' *Laughing Cavalier*, Titian's *Perseus and Andromeda*, Velázquez's *Lady with a Fan* and Rembrandt's affectionate portrait of his teenage son, Titus. Labelling can be pretty terse and paintings occasionally move about, so you might consider renting an audioguide.

## RIBA

66 Portland Place ⊖ Regent's Park
☎ 020/7580 5533, ⓦ www.architecture
.com. Mon–Fri 8am–6pm, Tues until 9pm; Sat
8am–5pm. Free. MAP P.59, POCKET MAP C12

With its sleek 1930s Portland-stone facade, the headquarters of the **Royal Institute of British Architects** is easily the finest building on Portland Place. Inside, the main staircase remains a wonderful period piece, with etched glass balustrades, walnut veneer and two large columns of black marble rising up on either side. You can view the interior en route to the institute's often thought-provoking first-floor architectural exhibitions (free) and to its café. The excellent ground-floor bookshop is also worth a browse.

## MADAME TUSSAUDS

Marylebone Rd ⊖ Baker Street ☎ 0870/999
0046, ⓦ www.madametussauds.com. Mon–Fri
9.30am–5.30pm, Sat & Sun 9am–6pm. From
£22. MAP P.59, POCKET MAP A12

Madame Tussaud's waxworks have been pulling in the crowds ever since the good lady arrived in London from France in 1802 bearing the sculpted heads of guillotined aristocrats. The entrance fee is extortionate, the likenesses occasionally dubious and the automated dummies inept, but you can still rely on finding London's biggest queues here – to avoid joining them, book

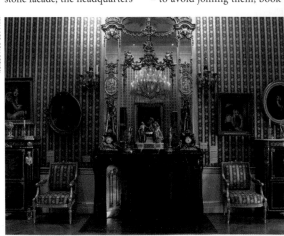

## Marylebone

Sherlock
Holmes
Museum

Madame Tussauds

RIBA

Broadcasting
House

John
Lewis

**SHOPS**
Daunt Books 1
Selfridges 2

**VENUES**
The Quebec 2
Wigmore Hall 1

**ACCOMMODATION**
Central YHA 1
Edward Lear Hotel 4
Lincoln House Hotel 2
Wigmore Court Hotel 3

**CAFÉS**
Abu Ali 9
Golden Hind 6
Patisserie Valerie
at Sagne 3
Paul Rothe & Son 8

**RESTAURANTS**
Fairuz 1
Phoenix Palace 1
The Providores
& Tapa Room 4
Truc Vert 10

**PUBS & BARS**
Dover Castle 2
Golden Eagle 7

your ticket online. There are photo opportunities galore throughout the first few sections, which are peppered with contemporary **celebrities** from the BBC to Bollywood. Keep your eyes out for the elderly and diminutive Madame Tussaud herself, and the oldest wax model, Madame du Barry, Louis XV's mistress, who gently respires as Sleeping Beauty – in reality she was beheaded in the French Revolution, as was Madame Tussaud's uncle. The **Chamber of Horrors**, the most popular section of all, is irredeemably tasteless, and now features live, costumed actors who jump out at you in the dark (you can opt out of this). The Tussauds finale is a manic five-minute "ride" through the history of London in a miniaturized taxi cab, followed by a thirty-minute high-tech presentation, usually on a celebrity/Hollywood-inspired theme, projected onto the dome of the adjoining Auditorium (formerly the Planetarium).

## SHERLOCK HOLMES MUSEUM

239 Baker St ⊖ Baker Street ☏ 020/7935 8866. ⓦ www.sherlock-holmes.co.uk. Daily 9.30am–6pm. £6. MAP P.59, POCKET MAP A12

Sherlock Holmes's fictional address was 221b Baker Street, hence the number on the door of the museum. Unashamedly touristy, the place is stuffed full of Victoriana and life-size models of characters from the books. It's an atmospheric and very competent exercise in period reconstruction – you can even don a deerstalker to have your picture taken by the fireside, looking like the great detective himself.

# Shops

## BROWNS

24–27 & 50 South Molton St ⊖ Bond Street.
Mon–Sat 10am–6.30pm, Thurs till 7pm.
MAP P.53, POCKET MAP C15

London's largest range of
designer wear, with big international names under the same
roof as the more cutting-edge,
up-and-coming designers,
and catering equally well for
women as for men.

## CHARBONNEL ET WALKER

1 Royal Arcade, 28 Old Bond St ⊖ Green Park.
Mon–Sat 10am–6pm. MAP P.53, POCKET MAP D16

Established in 1875, this is
where Her Majesty stocks up
on chocolate, which comes
presented in the most exquisite
wrapping.

## DAUNT BOOKS

83 Marylebone High St ⊖ Baker Street. Mon–
Sat 9am–7.30pm, Sun 11am–6pm.
MAP P.59, POCKET MAP B13

Wide and inspirational range of
travel literature, as well as the
usual guidebooks, presented
by expert staff in the beautiful,
galleried interior of this famous
shop.

LIBERTY

## FORTNUM & MASON

181 Piccadilly ⊖ Green Park or Piccadilly
Circus. Mon–Sat 10am–8pm, Sun noon–6pm.
MAP P.53, POCKET MAP E16

Beautiful and eccentric
300-year-old store with
heavenly murals, cherubs,
chandeliers and fountains as
a backdrop to its perfectly
English offerings. Justly famous
for its fabulous, pricey food,
it also specializes in upmarket
designer clothes, furniture,
luggage and stationery.

## HAMLEYS

188–196 Regent St ⊖ Oxford Circus. Mon–Fri
10am–8pm, Sat 9am–8pm, Sun noon–6pm.
MAP P.53, POCKET MAP D15

Possibly the world's largest toy
shop, and certainly a feast for
the eyes of most small children,
with lots of gadget demonstrations going on throughout its
six floors of mayhem.

## LIBERTY

210–220 Regent St ⊖ Oxford Circus. Mon–Sat
10am–7pm, Thurs till 8pm, Sun noon–6pm.
MAP P.53, POCKET MAP D15

A fabulous, partly mock-Tudor
emporium of luxury. Best
known for its fabrics, though it
is, in fact, a full-blown department store.

## SELFRIDGES

400 Oxford St ⊖ Bond Street. Mon–Sat
9.30am–8pm, Thurs till 9pm, Sun noon–6pm.
MAP P.59, POCKET MAP B14

London's first great department
store, and still one of its best:
a huge, airy mecca of clothes,
food and furnishings.

## WATERSTONE'S

203–206 Piccadilly ⊖ Piccadilly Circus.
Mon–Sat 9am–10pm, Sun noon–6pm. MAP P.53,
POCKET MAP E16

This flagship bookstore –
Europe's largest – boasts a café,
bar, gallery and events rooms
as well as five floors of books.

# Cafés

### ABU ALI

136–138 George St ⊖ Marble Arch. Daily
9am–11pm. MAP P.59, POCKET MAP E6
Lebanese equivalent of a
working men's club, serving
honest fare from tabbouleh to
kebabs, all terrific value. Wash
it all down with fresh mint tea.

### GOLDEN HIND

73 Marylebone Lane ⊖ Bond Street. Mon–Fri
noon–3pm & 6–10pm, Sat 6–10pm.
MAP P.59, POCKET MAP B2
Marylebone's heritage fish-
and-chip restaurant, founded
in 1914, serves classic cod and
chips from around a fiver, as
well as slightly fancier fare.

PATISSERIE VALERIE AT SAGNE

### MÔ

25 Heddon St ⊖ Piccadilly Circus. Mon–Sat
noon–11pm. MAP P.53, POCKET MAP E16
Serving reasonably priced
and delicious snacks, this
is London's ultimate Arabic
pastiche tearoom, with tables
and hookahs spilling out onto
the pavement of a quiet little
Mayfair alleyway.

### PATISSERIE VALERIE AT SAGNE

105 Marylebone High St ⊖ Bond Street.
Mon–Fri 7.30am–7pm, Sat 8am–7pm, Sun
9am–6pm. MAP P.59, POCKET MAP B14
Founded as Swiss-run *Maison
Sagne* in the 1920s, and
preserving its wonderful decor
from those days, the café is
now a branch of the *Valerie*
chain, but remains Marylebone's finest.

### PAUL ROTHE & SON

35 Marylebone Lane ⊖ Bond Street. Mon–Fri
8am–6pm, Sat 11.30am–5.30pm. MAP P.59,
POCKET MAP B3
Old-fashioned deli established
in 1900, selling "English &
Foreign Provisions", offering a
choice of two soups (one meat,
one vegetarian), plus toasties

and sandwiches made to order.
Take away or sit at one of the
formica tables inside the shop.

### SOTHEBY'S

34–35 New Bond St ⊖ Oxford Circus. Mon–Fri
9.30am–4.45pm. MAP P.53, POCKET MAP O15
Sotheby's café-restaurant
is by no means cheap, but
the lunches are exquisitely
prepared, and the excellent
afternoon teas are a fraction of
the price of the nearby hotels.

### TIBITS

12–14 Heddon St ⊖ Piccadilly Circus. Mon–
Wed 9am–10.30pm, Thurs–Sat 9am–midnight,
Sun 10am–10.30pm. MAP P.53, POCKET MAP E16
Spacious, modernist Swiss
German veggie café serving
up vast range of salads and hot
dishes from across the globe.

### THE WOLSELEY

160 Piccadilly ⊖ Green Park ☏ 020/7409 6996.
Mon–Fri 7am–midnight, Sat 8am–midnight,
Sun 8am–11pm. MAP P.53, POCKET MAP O17
The Viennese-inspired food is
good if rather pricey, but the
big draw is the lofty and stylish
1920s interior (built as the
showroom for Wolseley cars).
It's a great place for breakfast or
a cream tea and very popular
so book ahead.

# Restaurants

### FAIRUZ

3 Blandford St ⊖ Baker Street ☎ 020/7486 8108. Mon–Sat noon–11pm, Sun noon–10.30pm. MAP P.59, POCKET MAP B13

Busy, informal Lebanese restaurant, named after the famous diva, with an epic list of mezze, delicate and fragrant charcoal grills and one or two oven-baked dishes. Mains £12–20.

### KIKU

17 Half Moon St ⊖ Green Park ☎ 020/7499 4208. Mon–Sat noon–2.30pm & 6–10.15pm, Sun 5.30–9.45pm. MAP P.53, POCKET MAP C17

"Kiku" translates as pricey, but at least this place serves up top-quality sushi and sashimi (£3–5). Take a seat at the traditional sushi bar and wonder at the dexterity of the knife man. Set lunch £20.

### PATTERSON'S

4 Mill St ⊖ Oxford Circus ☎ 020/7499 1308. Mon–Fri noon–3pm & 6–11pm, Sat 5–11pm. MAP P.53, POCKET MAP D15

A very smart family-run restaurant serving mostly local and organic produce – the

TRUC VERT

seafood is sourced from the chef's hometown of Eyemouth in Scotland. The Modern European cooking looks and tastes superb. Mains (lunch) £10; (evening) £20.

### PHOENIX PALACE

3–5 Glentworth St ⊖ Baker Street ☎ 020/7486 3515. Mon–Sat noon–11.30pm, Sun 11am–10.30pm. MAP P.59, POCKET MAP A12

There's plenty to choose from here with dishes from all over China. Better still, the cooking is good and the portions large. Mains £8–11.

### THE PROVIDORES & TAPA ROOM

109 Marylebone High St ⊖ Baker Street or Bond Street ☎ 020/7935 6175. Mon–Fri 9am–11pm, Sat 10am–11pm, Sun 10am–10pm. MAP P.59, POCKET MAP B13

Outstanding fusion restaurant split into two: snacky *Tapa Room* downstairs and an elegant restaurant upstairs. In both the food, which may sound like an untidy assemblage on paper, is original and wholly satisfying. Mains £18–26.

### TRUC VERT

42 North Audley St ⊖ Bond Street ☎ 020/7491 9988. Mon–Sat 7.30am–midnight, Sun 9am–3pm. MAP P.59, POCKET MAP B15

An upmarket but friendly restaurant, offering quiches, salads, pâtés, cakes and pastries. The menu changes daily and begins early with breakfast; also has a small deli section. Mains £15–18.

### WILD HONEY

12 St George St ⊖ Oxford Circus or Bond Street ☎ 020/7758 9160. Mon–Sat noon–2.30pm & 6–11pm, Sun noon–3pm & 6–10.30pm. MAP P.53, POCKET MAP D15

Very popular wood-panelled restaurant with friendly service, serving up slow-cooked, UK-sourced haute cuisine. Mains £14–20.

# Pubs and bars

## AUDLEY

41 Mount St ⊖ Bond Street or Green Park.
Mon–Sat 11am–11pm, Sun noon–10.30pm.
MAP P.53, POCKET MAP B16

A grand Mayfair pub, with its
original Victorian burgundy
lincrusta ceiling, chandeliers
and clocks.

## DOVER CASTLE

43 Weymouth Mews ⊖ Regent's Park or Great
Portland Street. Mon–Sat 11.30am–11pm, Sun
noon–10.30pm. MAP P.59, POCKET MAP C13

A quiet, traditional boozer
hidden away down a pictur-
esque mews. Green upholstery,
dark wood and a strapwork
ceiling add to the atmosphere.
Cheap Sam Smith's bitter too.

## GOLDEN EAGLE

59 Marylebone Lane ⊖ Bond Street. Mon–
Sat 11am–11pm, Sun noon–7pm. MAP P.59,
POCKET MAP B13

Proper old neighbourhood
pub, made up of one single
room – they even have regular
singalongs on the old "Joanna"
(Tues, Thurs and Fri).

## GUINEA

30 Bruton Place ⊖ Bond Street or Oxford
Circus. Mon–Fri 11.30am–11.30pm, Sat
6–11pm. MAP P.53, POCKET MAP C16

Pretty, old-fashioned, flower-
strewn mews pub, serving good
Young's bitter and excellent
steak and kidney pies. Invari-
ably packed to its tiny rafters.

## THE WINDMILL

6–8 Mill St ⊖ Oxford Circus. Mon–Fri 11am–
midnight, Sat noon–4pm. MAP P.53,
POCKET MAP D15

Convivial, well-regarded pub
just off Regent Street, and a
perfect retreat for exhausted
shoppers. The Young's beers are
top-notch, as are the steak and
kidney pies, for which the pub
has won numerous awards.

DOVER CASTLE

# Venues

## DOVER STREET

8–10 Dover St ⊖ Green Park ☎ 020/7629 9813,
🌐 www.doverst.co.uk. MAP P.53, POCKET MAP D17

London's largest jazz restaurant
has music and dancing every
night until 3am, plus Modern
British food. Attracts an older
crowd. Dress smart.

## THE QUEBEC

12 Old Quebec St ⊖ Marble Arch
☎ 0871/971 4055. Mon–Thurs noon–2am,
Fri & Sat noon–3am, Sun noon–1am.
MAP P.59, POCKET MAP A15

Long-established and busy gay
venue with a downstairs disco
and late licence. Especially
popular with the older crowd,
and believed to be the oldest
gay pub in London.

## WIGMORE HALL

36 Wigmore St ⊖ Bond Street ☎ 020/7935
2141, 🌐 www.wigmore-hall.org.uk
MAP P.59, POCKET MAP C14

With its near-perfect acoustics,
this intimate classical and
chamber music/song recital
venue – originally built as a
piano showroom – is a favourite with artists and audiences
alike. Book well in advance.

# Soho and Covent Garden

Soho is very much the heart of the West End, home to more theatres and cinemas than any other single area in London. As the city's premier red-light district for centuries, it retains an unorthodox and slightly raffish air that's unique in central London. Conventional sights are few and far between, yet it's a great area to wander through – whatever the hour there's always something going on. Soho is also a very upfront gay quartier, focused around Old Compton Street. More sanitized and brazenly commercial, Covent Garden is one of London's chief tourist attractions, thanks to its buskers, pedestrianized piazza and old Victorian market hall. Some three centuries ago the piazza was the great playground of eighteenth-century London. Nowadays, while the market is pretty, but touristy, the streets to the north boast some very fashionable boutiques.

## LEICESTER SQUARE

⊖ Leicester Square. MAP PP.66–67.
POCKET MAP G16

By night, when the big cinemas and nightclubs are doing brisk business and the buskers are entertaining passers-by, Leicester

ODEON, LEICESTER SQUARE

Square is one of the most crowded places in London; on a Friday or Saturday night, it can seem as if half the youth of the city's suburbs have congregated here to get drunk, supplemented by a vast number of tourists. It wasn't until the mid-nineteenth century that the square began to emerge as an entertainment zone, with accommodation houses (for prostitutes and their clients) and music halls such as the grandiose Empire and the **Hippodrome** (just off the square), both of which still stand today. Cinema moved in during the 1930s – a golden age evoked by the sleek black lines of the **Odeon** on the east side – and maintains its grip on the area. The **Empire** is the favourite for big red-carpet premieres and, in a rather half-hearted imitation of the Hollywood tradition, there are even handprints-of-the-stars indented into the pavement of the square's southwestern corner.

## CHINATOWN

⊖ Leicester Square. MAP PP.66–67.
POCKET MAP F15–G15

A self-contained jumble of shops, cafés and restaurants, Chinatown is one of London's most distinct and popular ethnic enclaves. Centred around **Gerrard Street**, it's a tiny area of no more than three or four blocks, thick with the aromas of Chinese cooking and peppered with ersatz touches. Few of London's 60,000 Chinese actually live in Chinatown, but it nonetheless remains a focus for the community: a place to do business or the weekly shopping, celebrate a wedding, or just meet up for meals – particularly on Sundays, when the restaurants overflow with Chinese families tucking into dim sum. Most Londoners come to Chinatown simply to eat – easy and inexpensive enough to do. Cantonese cuisine predominates, and you're unlikely to be disappointed wherever you go.

CHINATOWN

## CHARING CROSS ROAD

⊖ Leicester Square. MAP PP.66–67.
POCKET MAP F14–G16

Charing Cross Road, which marks Soho's eastern border, boasts the highest concentration of bookshops anywhere in London. One of the first to open here, in 1906, was **Foyles** at no. 119 – Éamon de Valera, George Bernard Shaw, Walt Disney and Arthur Conan Doyle were all once regular customers. You'll find more of Charing Cross Road's original character at the string of specialist and secondhand bookshops south of Cambridge Circus. One of the nicest places for specialist and antiquarian book-browsing is **Cecil Court**, the southernmost pedestrianized alleyway

between Charing Cross Road and St Martin's Lane. These short, civilized, paved alleys boast specialist bookshops, plus various antiquarian dealers selling modern first editions, old theatre posters, coins and notes, cigarette cards, maps and stamps.

## OLD COMPTON STREET

⊖ Leicester Square. MAP PP.66–67.
POCKET MAP F15–G15

If Soho has a main drag, it has to be Old Compton Street, which runs parallel to Shaftesbury Avenue. The corner shops, peep shows, boutiques and trendy cafés here are typical of the area and a good barometer of the latest Soho fads. The liberal atmosphere of Soho has also made it a permanent fixture on the **gay scene** since the last century, though nowadays it's not just gay bars, clubs and cafés jostling for position on Old Compton Street: there's a gay-run houseshare agency, a financial advice outfit and even a gay taxi service.

# Soho and Covent Garden

**ACCOMMODATION**

| | |
|---|---|
| The Fielding Hotel | 4 |
| Hazlitt's | 3 |
| Oxford Street YHA | 2 |
| Piccadilly Backpackers | 5 |
| Seven Dials Hotel | 1 |

**SHOPS**

| | |
|---|---|
| Coco de Mer | 5 |
| Davenport's Magic Shop | 8 |
| Forbidden Planet | 1 |
| Foyles | 4 |
| Mysteries | 3 |
| Neal's Yard Dairy | 6 |
| Stanfords Map and Travel Bookshop | 7 |
| Terra Plana | 2 |

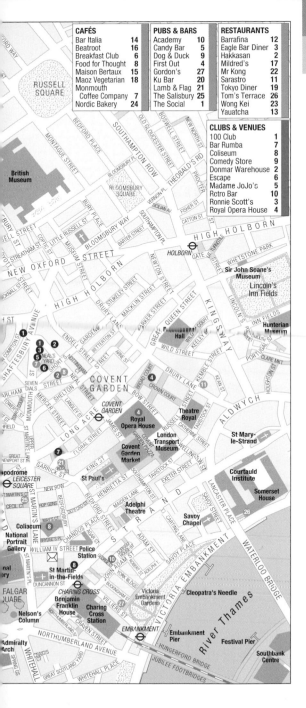

| CAFÉS | |
|---|---|
| Bar Italia | 14 |
| Beatroot | 16 |
| Breakfast Club | 6 |
| Food for Thought | 8 |
| Maison Bertaux | 15 |
| Maoz Vegetarian | 18 |
| Monmouth Coffee Company | 7 |
| Nordic Bakery | 24 |

| PUBS & BARS | |
|---|---|
| Academy | 10 |
| Candy Bar | 5 |
| Dog & Duck | 9 |
| First Out | 4 |
| Gordon's | 27 |
| Ku Bar | 20 |
| Lamb & Flag | 21 |
| The Salisbury | 25 |
| The Social | 1 |

| RESTAURANTS | |
|---|---|
| Barrafina | 12 |
| Eagle Bar Diner | 3 |
| Hakkasan | 2 |
| Mildred's | 17 |
| Mr Kong | 22 |
| Sarastro | 11 |
| Tokyo Diner | 19 |
| Tom's Terrace | 26 |
| Wong Kei | 23 |
| Yauatcha | 13 |

| CLUBS & VENUES | |
|---|---|
| 100 Club | 1 |
| Bar Rumba | 7 |
| Coliseum | 8 |
| Comedy Store | 9 |
| Donmar Warehouse | 2 |
| Escape | 6 |
| Madame JoJo's | 5 |
| Retro Bar | 10 |
| Ronnie Scott's | 3 |
| Royal Opera House | 4 |

## CARNABY STREET

⊖ Oxford Circus. MAP PP.66–67, POCKET MAP E15

Carnaby Street was famous as the fashion epicentre of London's Swinging Sixties. A victim of its own hype, it quickly declined into an avenue of overpriced tack, and so it remained for several decades. Recently, things have started to pick up again, and the shops here, and in nearby **Foubert's Place** and **Newburgh Street**, are much more interesting (and pleasant) to wander round than in neighbouring Regent Street.

## POLLOCK'S TOY MUSEUM

1 Scala St ⊖ Goodge Street ☎ 020/7636 3452, ⓦ www.pollockstoymuseum.com. Mon–Sat 10am–5pm. £3. MAP PP.66–67, POCKET MAP E12

This highly atmospheric, doll's house-like toy museum is housed above a wonderful toy shop. Its collections include a fine example of the Victorian paper theatres popularized by Benjamin Pollock, who sold them under the slogan "a penny plain, two pence coloured". The other exhibits range from vintage teddy bears to Sooty and Sweep, and from Red Army soldiers to wax dolls, filling every nook and cranny of the museum's six tiny, rickety rooms and the stairs – be sure to look out for the dalmatian, Dismal Desmond.

## COVENT GARDEN PIAZZA

⊖ Covent Garden. MAP PP.66–67, POCKET MAP H15

London's oldest planned square, laid out in the 1630s by Inigo Jones, Covent Garden Piazza was initially a great success – its novelty value alone ensured a rich and aristocratic clientele for the surrounding properties. Over the next century, though, the tone of the place fell as the fruit and vegetable **market** expanded, and theatres and coffee houses began to move in. Eventually, a large covered market was constructed in the middle of the square, but when the market closed in 1974, it was very nearly demolished to make way for an office development. Instead, the elegant Victorian market hall and its largely pedestrianized, cobbled piazza were restored to house shops, restaurants and craft stalls. The piazza is now one of London's major tourist attractions, its success prompting a wholesale gentrification of the streets all around.

## ST PAUL'S CHURCH

Bedford St ⊖ Covent Garden. MAP PP.66–67,
POCKET MAP H15

The proximity of so many
theatres has earned this church
the nickname of the "**Actors'
Church**", and it's filled with
memorials to international
thespians from Boris Karloff
to Gracie Fields. The space in
front of the church's Tuscan
portico – where Eliza Doolittle
was discovered selling violets
by Henry Higgins in George
Bernard Shaw's *Pygmalion*
– is now a legalized venue
for the piazza's buskers and
street performers, who must
audition for a slot months in
advance. Round the back, the
**churchyard** provides a tranquil
respite from the activity outside
– access is from King Street,
Henrietta Street or Bedford
Street.

## LONDON TRANSPORT MUSEUM

Covent Garden Piazza ⊖ Covent Garden
☎ 020/7379 6344, ⓦ www.ltmuseum.co.uk.
Daily 10am–6pm, Fri until 9pm. £8.
MAP PP.66–67, POCKET MAP H15

Housed in the piazza's former
flower market, the ever-popular
London Transport Museum is
a surefire hit for families with
kids under ten. To follow the
story of London's transport
chronologically, head for the
Level 2, where you'll find a
reconstructed 1829 Shillib-
eer's Horse Omnibus, which
provided the city's first regular
horse-bus service. Level 1
tells the story of the world's
first underground system and
contains a lovely 1920s Metropolitan line carriage, fitted
out in burgundy and green
with pretty, drooping lamps.
Down on the ground floor, you
can peep inside the first tube
train, from the 1890s, whose
lack of windows earned it the
nickname "the padded cell".
Most of the interactive stuff is
aimed at kids, but visitors of all
ages should check out the tube
driver simulator. The artistically
inclined can buy reproductions
of the Tube's stylish maps and
posters, many commissioned
from well-known artists, at the
shop on the way out.

## ROYAL OPERA HOUSE

Bow St ⊖ Covent Garden ☎ 020/7304 4000,
ⓦ www.roh.org.uk. MAP PP.66–67, POCKET MAP H15

The arcading in the northeast corner of the piazza was
rebuilt as part of the multi-
million pound refurbishment
of the Royal Opera House,
whose Neoclassical façade,
dating from 1811, opens onto
Bow Street (which you can
reach via a passageway in the
corner of the arcading). The
market's spectacular wrought-
iron **Floral Hall** (daily
10am–3pm) now serves as the
opera house's impressive first-
floor foyer; both this and the
glorious terrace overlooking
the piazza, beyond the
*Amphitheatre* bar/restau-
rant, are open to the public.
**Backstage tours** (Mon–Fri
10.30am, 12.30 and 2.30pm;
Sat 10.30am, 11.30am, 12.30
and 1.30pm; £9) of the opera
house are also available.

## FREEMASONS' HALL

60 Great Queen St ⊖ Covent Garden
☎ 020/7395 9257, ⓦ www.ugle.org.uk. Mon–Fri
10am–5pm. Free. MAP PP.66–67, POCKET MAP H14

It's difficult to miss the austere, Pharaonic mass of the Freemasons' Hall, built as a memorial to all the masons who died in World War I. The interior is worth a peek for the **Grand Temple** alone, whose pompous, bombastic decor is laden with heavy symbolism. To see it, you must sign up for one of the free guided tours (Mon–Fri 11am, noon, 2, 3 and 4pm) and bring some ID with you. Take a look at the shop, too, which sells masonic merchandise – aprons, wands, rings and books about alchemy and the cabbala – as do several other shops on Great Queen Street.

## BENJAMIN FRANKLIN HOUSE

36 Craven St ⊖ Charing Cross ☎ 020/7839
2006, ⓦ www.benjaminfranklinhouse.org.
Wed–Sun noon–5pm. £7. MAP PP.66–67,
POCKET MAP H16

From 1757 to 1775, **Benjamin Franklin** (1706–90) lived in London espousing the cause of the British colonies (of which the US was then one), before returning to America to help draft the Declaration of Independence and the US Constitution. Wisely, the curators have left Franklin's house pretty much empty, eschewing any attempt to install period furniture. Instead, aided by a costumed guide and a series of impressionistic audiovisuals, visitors are transported back to the time of Franklin, who lived here with his "housekeeper" in cosy domesticity while his wife and daughter languished in Philadelphia. Note that you must book usually ahead for one of the 45-minute tours.

## VICTORIA EMBANKMENT

⊖ Temple or Embankment. MAP PP.66–67,
POCKET MAP J16–H19

Built between 1868 and 1874, the Victoria Embankment was the inspiration of civil engineer **Joseph Bazalgette**, whose project simultaneously relieved congestion along the Strand, provided an extension to the underground railway and sewage systems, and created a new stretch of parkland, now dotted with statues and memorials, and a riverside walk – no longer much fun due to the volume of traffic that barrels along it, though it does afford some good views over the river.

## SOMERSET HOUSE

Victoria Embankment ⊖ Temple ☎ 020/7845
4600, ⓦ www.somerset-house.org.uk.
Courtyard & terrace daily 10am–11pm, interior
daily 10am–6pm. Free.
MAP PP.66–67, POCKET MAP J16

Sole survivor of the grand edifices which once lined this stretch of the riverfront, Somerset House's four wings enclose an elegant and surprisingly large courtyard. From March to October, a wonderful

## Cleopatra's Needle

L ondon's oldest monument, **Cleopatra's Needle** MAP PP.66–67, POCKET MAP J16 languishes little-noticed on the busy Victoria Embankment, guarded by two Victorian sphinxes (facing the wrong way). The 60-foot-high, 180-ton stick of granite actually has nothing to do with Cleopatra – it's one of a pair erected in Heliopolis in 1475 BC (the other one is in New York's Central Park) and taken to Alexandria by Emperor Augustus fifteen years after Cleopatra's suicide. This obelisk was presented to Britain in 1819 by the Turkish viceroy of Egypt, but nearly sixty years passed before it finally made its way to London. It was erected in 1878, above a time capsule containing, among other things, the day's newspapers, a box of hairpins, a railway timetable and pictures of the country's twelve prettiest women.

55-jet fountain spouts straight from the courtyard's cobbles; in winter, an ice rink is set up in its place. The monumental Palladian building itself was begun in 1776 by William Chambers as a purpose-built governmental office development, but now houses a series of exhibition spaces, and puts on events throughout the year.

In the house's north wing are the galleries of the **Courtauld Institute** (daily 10am–pm; £5, free Mon 10am–2pm; Ⓦ www.courtauld.ac.uk), chiefly known for their dazzling permanent collection of Impressionist and Post-Impressionist paintings. Among the most celebrated works are a small-scale version of Manet's nostalgic *Bar at the Folies-Bergère,* Renoir's *La Loge,* and Degas' *Two Dancers,* plus a whole heap of Cézanne's canvases, including one of his series of *Card Players.* The Courtauld also boasts a fine selection of works by the likes of Bellini, Brueghel, Rubens, van Dyck, Tiepolo and Cranach the Elder, as well as twentieth-century paintings and sculptures by, among others, Kandinksy, Matisse, Dufy, Derain, Rodin, Roger Fry and Henry Moore.

# Shops

### COCO DE MER

23 Monmouth St ⊖ Covent Garden.
Mon–Sat 11am–7pm, Thurs until 8pm, Sat
noon–6pm. MAP PP.66–67, POCKET MAP G14

Upmarket and stylish, this sex
shop for women has an inviting
boudoir feel. The lingerie
ranges from floaty to filthy, but
is always in the best possible
taste. Pick up a feather tickler
while you're here.

### DAVENPORT'S MAGIC SHOP

5–7 Charing Cross Tube Arcade, Strand
⊖ Charing Cross. Mon–Fri 9.30am–5.30pm,
Sat 10.30am–4.30pm. MAP PP.66–67,
POCKET MAP H16

The world's oldest family-run
magic business, stocking a huge
array of marvellous tricks for
amateurs and professionals.

### FORBIDDEN PLANET

179 Shaftesbury Ave ⊖ Tottenham Court
Road. Mon–Wed 10am–7pm, Thurs & Sat
10am–8pm, Fri 10am–7.30pm, Sun noon–6pm.
MAP PP.66–67, POCKET MAP G14

Two jam-packed floors of all
things science fiction- and
fantasy-related, ranging from
comics and graphic novels to
books, games and ephemera.

NEAL'S YARD DAIRY

### FOYLES

113–119 Charing Cross Rd ⊖ Tottenham
Court Road. Mon–Sat 9.30am–9pm, Sun
noon–6pm. MAP PP.66–67, POCKET MAP G14

Long-established, famous and
huge London bookshop with
a big feminist section (Silver
Moon) and Ray's Jazz Shop
and Café.

### MYSTERIES

9–11 Monmouth St ⊖ Covent Garden.
Mon–Fri 10am–7pm, Sat 10am–6pm, Sun
noon–6pm. MAP PP.66–67, POCKET MAP G14

Strangely compulsive shop that
stocks just about every occult-
related book, magazine and
crystal you can imagine, and
offers psychic readings too.

### NEAL'S YARD DAIRY

17 Shorts Gardens ⊖ Covent Garden. Mon–
Sat 10am–7pm. MAP PP.66–67, POCKET MAP G14

London's finest cheese shop,
with a huge selection of quality
cheeses from around the
British Isles, as well as a few
exceptionally good ones from
further afield. They're keen for
you to taste before you buy.

### STANFORDS MAP AND TRAVEL BOOKSHOP

12–14 Long Acre ⊖ Covent Garden. Mon–Fri
9am–7.30pm, Tues from 9.30am, Thurs till
8pm; Sat 10am–8pm; Sun noon–6pm.
MAP PP.66–67, POCKET MAP G15

The world's largest specialist
travel bookshop, stocking
pretty much any map of
anywhere, plus a huge range of
guides and travel literature.

### TERRA PLANA

64 Neal St ⊖ Covent Garden. Mon–Sat
10am–6.45pm, Sun noon–6pm.
MAP PP.66–67, POCKET MAP G14

A brilliant option for
eco-friendly shoe fetishists
that make exuberant use of
recycled materials. The innovative "barefoot" range claims to
both strengthen your feet and
increase your sex drive.

# Cafés

### BAR ITALIA

22 Frith St ⊖ Tottenham Court Road.
Nearly 24hr: closed Mon–Fri 4–6am.
MAP PP.66–67, POCKET MAP F15

This tiny café is a Soho institution, serving coffee, croissants and sandwiches more or less around the clock – as it has been since 1949.

### BEATROOT

92 Berwick St ⊖ Piccadilly Circus.
Mon–Fri 9am–9pm, Sat 11am–9pm.
MAP PP.66–67, POCKET MAP F15

Great little veggie café by the market, doling out hot savoury bakes, stews and salads (plus delicious cakes) in boxes of varying sizes from around £5.

### BREAKFAST CLUB

33 D'Arblay St ⊖ Oxford Circus. Mon–Fri
8am–6pm, Sat 9.30am–5pm, Sun 10am–4pm.
MAP PP.66–67, POCKET MAP F14

A laid-back Aussie-style place, with battered leather couches, offering substantial toasted sarnies, fresh juice, great coffee and free wi-fi.

### FOOD FOR THOUGHT

31 Neal St ⊖ Covent Garden.
Mon–Sat noon–8.30pm, Sun noon–5pm.
MAP PP.66–67, POCKET MAP G14

Long-established but minuscule bargain veggie café – the tasty and filling menu changes twice daily, and includes vegan and wheat-free options. Expect to queue, and don't expect to linger at peak times.

### MAISON BERTAUX

28 Greek St ⊖ Leicester Square or
Tottenham Court Road. Daily 8.30am–8pm.
MAP PP.66–67, POCKET MAP G15

Long-standing, old-fashioned and terribly French patisserie, with tables on two floors, plus one or two outside. A loyal

BAR ITALIA

clientele keeps the place busy all day long.

### MAOZ VEGETARIAN

43 Old Compton St ⊖ Piccadilly Circus.
Mon–Thurs 11am–1am, Fri & Sat 11am–2am,
Sun 11am–midnight. MAP PP.66–67,
POCKET MAP F15

Kosher, vegan, late-night franchise that specializes in falafel in pitta (white or wholemeal), with a good salad bar and chips to boot.

### MONMOUTH COFFEE COMPANY

27 Monmouth St ⊖ Covent Garden.
Mon–Sat 8am–6.30pm. MAP PP.66–67,
POCKET MAP G14

The marvellous aroma hits you when you walk in. Pick and mix your coffee from a fine selection, then settle into one of the cramped wooden booths and flick through the daily newspapers on hand.

### NORDIC BAKERY

14a Golden Square ⊖ Piccadilly Circus.
Mon–Sat 8am–8pm, Sat 11am–7pm, Sun
11am–6pm. MAP PP.66–67, POCKET MAP E15

Fill up on crispbreads, cinnamon rolls, rye bread sandwiches and strong coffee at this super-sharp minimalist Scandinavian café situated on a quiet Soho Square.

# Restaurants

### BARRAFINA

54 Frith St ⊖ Leicester Square or
Tottenham Court Road. Mon–Sat
noon–3pm & 5–11pm, Sun 12.30–3.30pm &
5.30–10.30pm. MAP PP.66–67, POCKET MAP F15

Barrafina means thin bar –
you'll need to get here early to
bag a seat (no bookings taken)
in this very popular, stylish and
superb tapas bar. Tapas £4–7.

### EAGLE BAR DINER

3 Rathbone Place ⊖ Tottenham Court Road
☎ 020/7637 1418. Mon–Wed noon–11pm,
Thurs & Fri noon–1am, Sat 10am–1am, Sun
11am–6pm. MAP PP.66–67, POCKET MAP F14

Elegant, modern US diner, with
cosy leather booths and a long
bar serving cocktails, martinis
and pick-me-ups. Best of all are
the burgers – Aberdeen Angus
beef, chicken, lamb, even emu
and ostrich, with brownies and
cheesecakes for afters. Come at
lunchtime if you want to avoid
the DJs (Wed–Sat).

### HAKKASAN

8 Hanway Place ⊖ Tottenham Court Road
☎ 020/7927 7000. Mon–Fri noon–3pm &
6pm–midnight, Sat noon–5pm & 6pm–
midnight, Sun 6-11pm. MAP PP.66–67,
POCKET MAP F13

Impressive, atmospheric
designer restaurant serving
novel, delicious and expensive
Chinese dishes, with a long,
fashionably crammed cocktail
bar attached. Mains £10–40.

### MILDRED'S

45 Lexington St ⊖ Oxford Circus
☎ 020/7494 1634. Mon–Sat noon–11pm.
MAP PP.66–67, POCKET MAP E15

Fresher and more stylish than
many veggie restaurants,
serving wholesome, delicious
and inexpensive stir-fries,
pasta dishes and burgers, as
well as wicked but wonderful
puddings. Mains £8–10.

### MR KONG

21 Lisle St ⊖ Leicester Square ☎ 020/7437
7341. Mon–Sat noon–2.45am, Sun
noon–1.45am. MAP PP.66–67, POCKET MAP G15

One of Chinatown's finest
places to eat, with a huge
choice of Cantonese dishes and
friendly service. There's always
something intriguing among
the specials – jellyfish, anyone?
Mains £8–25.

### SARASTRO

126 Drury Lane ⊖ Covent Garden ☎ 020/7836
0101. Daily noon–11.30pm. MAP PP.66–67,
POCKET MAP J15

Theatrically over-the-top
restaurant that's perfect for pre-
and post-theatre dining, and
also a great place to hear young
starlets perform live (Mon &
Sun), while enjoying food from
the eastern Med. Mains £8–25.

### TOKYO DINER

2 Newport Place ⊖ Leicester Square. Daily
noon–midnight. MAP PP.66–67, POCKET MAP G15

Friendly, unpretentious diner
on the edge of Chinatown,
serving fast food, Tokyo style.
Minimalist decor lets the
(tuna-free) sushi do the talking.
Mains £6–15.

## TOM'S TERRACE

Somerset House. ⊖ Temple ☎ 020/7845 4646. May–Aug only. Bar: daily 10am–late; restaurant: daily noon–3pm & 6–10pm. MAP PP.66–67, POCKET MAP J16

Alfresco dining, with views across the Thames. The menu is short and informal – think high-class steak sandwiches and grilled chicken. Mains £15–18.

## WONG KEI

41–43 Wardour St ⊖ Leicester Square. Mon–Sat noon–11.30pm, Sun noon–10.30pm. MAP PP.66–67, POCKET MAP F15

Famous for dispensing large portions of cheap Chinese washed down with free tea. The place is enormous, with communal seating. Mains £6–12.

## YAUATCHA

15 Broadwick St ⊖ Piccadilly Circus. Mon Sat noon–11.45pm, Sun 11am–10.15pm. MAP PP.66–67, POCKET MAP E15

Very popular, minimalist Chinese teahouse-restaurant serving up dim sum (£3.50–7) all day long.

# Pubs and bars

## ACADEMY

12 Old Compton St ⊖ Leicester Square. Mon Sat 4pm–midnight, Sun 4–10.30pm. MAP PP.66–67, POCKET MAP G15

Formerly known as *LAB*, this two-floor retro cocktail bar is considered one of the best in London; cocktail school graduates serve up classics and new concoctions. DJs on Fridays and every other Wednesday.

## CANDY BAR

4 Carlisle St ⊖ Tottenham Court Road. Mon–Thurs 5–11.30pm, Fri & Sat 5pm–2am, Sun 5–11pm. MAP PP.66–67, POCKET MAP F14

The crucial, cruisey vibe makes this the hottest girl-bar in central London. Pole dancing is a regular feature.

## DOG & DUCK

18 Bateman St ⊖ Tottenham Court Road. Mon–Sat 11am–11pm, Sun noon–10.30pm. MAP PP.66–67, POCKET MAP F15

Tiny Soho pub that retains much of its old character, with beautiful Victorian tiling and mosaics, plus a good range of real ales.

## FIRST OUT

52 St Giles High St ⊖ Tottenham Court Road. Mon–Sat 10am–11pm, Sun 11am–10.30pm. MAP PP.66–67, POCKET MAP G15

The West End's original gay café-bar, serving good veggie food. Upstairs is airy, downstairs dark. Girl Friday is a pre-club session for girls; gay men allowed as guests.

## GORDON'S

47 Villiers St ⊖ Embankment. Mon Sat 11am–11pm, Sun noon–10pm. MAP PP.66–67, POCKET MAP H17

Cavernous, shabby, atmospheric wine bar specializing in ports and sherries. The excellent and varied wine list, decent buffet food and genial atmosphere make this a favourite with local office workers, who spill outdoors in the summer.

ACADEMY

## KU BAR

30 Lisle St ⊖ Leicester Square.
Mon–Sat noon–3am, Sun noon–midnight.
MAP PP.66–67, POCKET MAP F15

The Lisle Street original, with a downstairs club open late, is one of Soho's largest and best-loved gay bars, serving a scene-conscious yet low-on-attitude clientele. It's now joined by a stylish sibling bar on Frith Street.

## LAMB & FLAG

33 Rose St ⊖ Leicester Square or Covent Garden. Mon–Sat 11am–11pm, Sun noon–10.30pm. MAP PP.66–67, POCKET MAP H15

Tiny and highly atmospheric old pub, hidden away down an alley between Garrick Street and Floral Street. The Poet Laureate, John Dryden, was beaten up here in 1679 by a group of thugs, hired most probably by his rival poet, the Earl of Rochester.

## THE SALISBURY

90 St Martin's Lane ⊖ Leicester Square. Mon–Thurs 11am–11.30pm, Fri 11am–midnight, Sat noon–midnight, Sun noon–10.30pm. MAP PP.66–67, POCKET MAP G16

Superbly preserved Victorian pub with cut, etched and

THE SALISBURY

engraved windows, bronze statues, red-velvet seating and a fine lincrusta ceiling, plus a wide and unusual range of ales.

## THE SOCIAL

5 Little Portland St ⊖ Oxford Circus Ⓦ www.thesocial.com. Mon–Wed noon–midnight, Thurs–Sat 1pm–midnight, Sun 5pm–midnight. MAP PP.66–67, POCKET MAP D13

Industrial club-bar and diner with great DJs playing everything from rock to rap to a truly hedonistic-cum-alcoholic crowd.

# Clubs and venues

### 100 CLUB

100 Oxford St ⊖ Tottenham Court Road ☎ 020/7636 0933, Ⓦ www.the100club.co.uk. MAP PP.66–67, POCKET MAP E14

Fun jazz venue whose history stretches back to 1942 and takes in Louis Armstrong, Glen Miller and the Sex Pistols. Now mixes mostly trad bands with DJ-led nights.

### BAR RUMBA

36 Shaftesbury Ave ⊖ Piccadilly Circus ☎ 020/7287 6933, Ⓦ www.barrumba.co.uk. Open until 3/4am. MAP PP.66–67, POCKET MAP F16

Fun, smallish West End club venue with a mix of regular nights ranging from salsa, R&B and dance to hip hop. Free before 10pm.

### COLISEUM

St Martin's Lane ⊖ Leicester Square ☎ 0871/911 0200, Ⓦ www.eno.org. MAP PP.66–67, POCKET MAP G16

Home to the English National Opera, which differs from its Royal Opera House counterpart in that all its operas are sung in English, productions tend to be more experimental, and tickets cost a lot less.

## COMEDY STORE

1a Oxendon St ⊖ Piccadilly Circus
☎ 0844/847 1728, ⓦ www.thecomedystore
.co.uk MAP PP.66–67, POCKET MAP F16

Birthplace of alternative comedy, with impro by in-house comics (Wed and Sun), and a regular stand-up bill. Weekends are busiest, with two shows – book ahead.

## DONMAR WAREHOUSE

41 Earlham St ⊖ Covent Garden
☎ 0870/060 6624, ⓦ www.donmarwarehouse
.com. MAP PP.66–67, POCKET MAP H15

Theatre noted for its new plays, top-quality reappraisals of the classics and star-studded casts.

## ESCAPE

10 Brewer St ⊖ Piccadilly Circus
☎ 020/7734 2626, ⓦ www.escapesoho
.com. Open till 3am Mon–Sat. MAP PP.66–67,
POCKET MAP F15

Trendy DJ bar in the heart of Soho, attracting a young, mixed crowd.

## MADAME JOJO'S

8–10 Brewer St ⊖ Tottenham Court Road
☎ 020/7734 3040, ⓦ www.madamejojos.com.
MAP PP.66–67, POCKET MAP F15

Louche, enjoyable Soho institution, known for its wickedly diverse range of entertainment – alongside variety and comedy, you'll find electronica, disco, rock and funk.

## RETRO BAR

2 George Court, off Strand ⊖ Charing Cross
☎ 020/7839 8760. MAP PP.66–67, POCKET MAP H16

Tucked down a quiet alleyway off the Strand, this friendly, indie/retro gay-bar plays 1970s and 80s rock, pop, goth and alternative sounds, and features regular DIY DJ nights.

## RONNIE SCOTT'S

47 Frith St ⊖ Tottenham Court Road
☎ 020/7439 0747, ⓦ www.ronniescotts.co.uk.
MAP PP.66–67, POCKET MAP F19

The most famous jazz club in London, this small and atmospheric place has smartened up its decor, upped its prices, and stretched its remit to more pop-oriented acts in recent years.

## ROYAL OPERA HOUSE

Bow St ⊖ Covent Garden ☎ 020/7304 4000,
ⓦ www.roh.org.uk. MAP PP.66–67, POCKET MAP H15

The ROH still has a deserved reputation for snobbery, and is ludicrously overpriced. Tickets are hard to come by, so queue up for one of the 67 day seats which are put on sale from 10am on the day of a performance.

## Half-price theatre tickets

The Society of London Theatre (ⓦ www.officiallondontheatre.co.uk) runs the **tkts booth** in Leicester Square (Mon–Sat 10am–7pm, Sun noon–3pm), which sells on-the-day tickets for all the West End shows, most of them at fifty percent off. On average, you're looking at £20–40 (including a service charge of £2.50 per ticket) with tickets limited to four per person.

# Bloomsbury

Bloomsbury was built in grid-plan style from the 1660s onwards, and the formal, bourgeois Georgian squares laid out then remain the area's main distinguishing feature. In the twentieth century, Bloomsbury acquired a reputation as the city's most learned quarter, dominated by the dual institutions of the British Museum and London University, and home to many of London's chief book publishers, but perhaps best known for its literary inhabitants, among them T.S. Eliot and Virginia Woolf. Only in its northern fringes does the character of the area change dramatically, as you near the busy main-line train stations of Euston, St Pancras and King's Cross.

## BRITISH MUSEUM

Great Russell St ⊖ Tottenham Court Road
☎ 020/7323 8000, ⊕ www.britishmuseum.org.
Daily 10am–5.30pm, Thurs & Fri until 8.30pm.
Free. MAP P.80, POCKET MAP G13

One of the great museums of the world, the BM contains an incredible collection of antiquities, prints, drawings and books. Begun in 1823, the building itself is the grandest of London's Greek Revival edifices, with its central **Great Court** (Mon–Wed and Sun 9am–6pm, Thurs–Sat 9am–11pm) featuring a remarkable curving glass-and-steel roof designed by Norman Foster. At the Court's centre stands the copper-domed former **Round Reading Room** of the British Library, where Karl Marx penned *Das Kapital*.

The BM's collection of **Roman and Greek antiquities** is unparalleled, and is most famous for the Parthenon sculptures, better known as the **Elgin Marbles** after the British aristocrat who walked off with the reliefs in 1801. Elsewhere, the **Egyptian collection** is

GREAT COURT, BRITISH MUSEUM

The **King's Library**, in the east wing, displays some of the museum's earliest acquisitions, brought back from the far reaches of the British Empire: everything from Javanese puppets to a model gamelan orchestra, collected by Stamford Raffles. Don't miss the museum's expanding **ethnographic collection**, including the superb African galleries in the basement. And in the north wing of the museum, closest to the back entrance on Montague Place, there are also fabulous **Asian** treasures including ancient Chinese porcelain, ornate snuffboxes, miniature landscapes and a bewildering array of Buddhist and Hindu gods.

## FOUNDLING MUSEUM

40 Brunswick Square ⊖ Russell Square ☏ 020/7841 3600, ⓦ www.foundlingmuseum .org.uk. Tues–Sat 10am–5pm, Sun 11am–5pm. £5. MAP P.80, POCKET MAP J4

This museum tells the fascinating story of the **Foundling Hospital**, London's first home for abandoned children founded in 1756 by retired sea captain Thomas Coram. As soon as it was opened, it was besieged, and soon forced to reduce its admissions drastically and introduce a ballot system. Among the most tragic exhibits are the tokens left by the mothers in order to identify the children should they ever be in a position to reclaim them: these range from a heart-rending poem to a simple enamel pot label reading "ale". The museum also boasts an impressive **art collection** including works by Hogarth, Gainsborough and Reynolds, now hung in carefully preserved eighteenth-century interiors of the original hospital.

easily the most significant outside Egypt, ranging from monumental sculptures to the ever-popular mummies and their ornate outer caskets. Also on display is the **Rosetta Stone**, which enabled French professor Champollion to finally unlock the secret of Egyptian hieroglyphs. Other highlights include a splendid series of **Assyrian reliefs** from Nineveh, and several extraordinary artefacts from **Mesopotamia** such as the enigmatic Ram in the Thicket (a goat statuette in lapis lazuli and shell) and the remarkable hoard of goldwork known as the Oxus Treasure.

The leathery half-corpse of the 2000-year-old **Lindow Man**, discovered in a Cheshire bog, and the Anglo-Saxon treasure from the **Sutton Hoo** ship burial, by far the richest single archeological find made in Britain, are among the highlights of the **Europe** collection, which ranges from the twelfth-century Lewis chessmen carved from walrus ivory to avant-garde Russian ceramics celebrating the 1917 revolution.

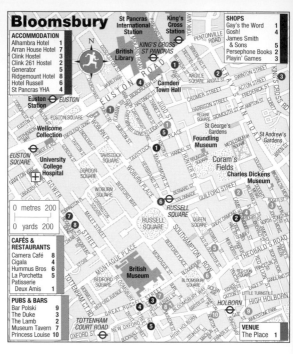

## CHARLES DICKENS MUSEUM

48 Doughty St ⊖ Russell Square
☎ 020/7405 2127, ⊗ www.dickensmuseum
.com. Mon–Sat 10am–5pm, Sun 11am–5pm.
£5. MAP P.80, POCKET MAP K4

Dickens moved to this house,
now a museum, in 1837 shortly
after his marriage to Catherine
Hogarth, and they lived here
for two years, during which
time he wrote *Nicholas Nickleby*
and *Oliver Twist*. Although
the author painted a gloomy
Victorian world in his books,
the drawing room here, in
which he entertained his
literary friends, was decorated
in a rather upbeat Regency
style. Letters, manuscripts
and first editions, the earliest
known portrait (a miniature
painted by his aunt in 1830)
and the reading copies he used
during extensive lecture tours
in Britain and the States are the
rewards for those with more

than a passing interest in the
novelist. You can also watch
a thirty-minute film about
his life.

## WELLCOME COLLECTION

183 Euston Rd ⊖ Euston or Euston Square
☎ 020/7611 2222, ⊗ www.wellcomecollection
.org. Mon–Sat 10am–6pm, Thurs until 8pm.
Sun 11am–6pm. Free. MAP P.80, POCKET MAP H4

Excellent temporary exhibitions on topical scientific issues
are staged in the ground-floor
gallery of the Wellcome Collection, originally founded by
American-born pharmaceutical
magnate Henry Wellcome
(1853–1936). Also worth a look
is the permanent collection,
on the first floor, beginning
with **Medicine Now**, which
focuses on contemporary
medical questions such as the
body, genomes, obesity and
malaria. Next door, **Medicine
Man** showcases the weird and

wonderful collection of historical and scientific artefacts amassed by Wellcome himself. These range from Florence Nightingale's moccasins to a sign for a Chinese doctor's hung with human teeth, and from erotic figurines and phallic amulets to Inuit snow goggles and a leper clapper – in other words, this section is absolute must.

## BRITISH LIBRARY

96 Euston Rd ⊖ King's Cross St Pancras ☏ 020/7412 7332, ⓦ www.bl.uk. Mon & Wed–Fri 9.30am–6pm, Tues 9.30am–8pm, Sat 9.30am–5pm, Sun 11am–5pm. Free. MAP P.80, POCKET MAP H3

The red-brick brutalism of the British Library may be horribly out of fashion, but the public exhibition galleries inside are superb. The first place to head for is the dimly lit **John Ritblat Gallery**, where a superlative selection of ancient manuscripts, maps, documents and precious books, including the Magna Carta and the richly illustrated Lindisfarne Gospels, are displayed. One of the most appealing innovations is **Turning the Pages**, a small room off the main gallery where you can "turn" the pages of selected texts on a computer terminal. The temporary exhibitions, for which there is sometimes an admission charge, are usually excellent.

## ST PANCRAS AND KING'S CROSS STATIONS

Euston Rd. MAP P.80, POCKET MAP J3

Completed in 1876, the former Midland Grand Hotel's majestic sweep of Neo-Gothic lancets, dormers and chimneypots forms the facade of **St Pancras Station**, where Eurostar trains now arrive. The adjacent **King's Cross Station**, opened in 1850, is a mere shed in comparison. King's Cross is more famous, however, as the station from which **Harry Potter** and his wizarding chums leave for school on the *Hogwarts Express* from platform 9¾. The scenes from the films are, in fact, shot between platforms 4 and 5, though a station trolley is now half-embedded in the wall beside the side platforms of 9 and 10, providing a perfect photo opportunity for passing Potter fans.

# Shops

### GAY'S THE WORD

66 Marchmont St ⊖ Russell Square.
Mon–Sat 10am–6.30pm, Sun 2–6.30pm.
MAP P.80, POCKET MAP J4

An extensive collection of lesbian and gay classics, pulps, contemporary fiction and non-fiction, plus cards, calendars and weekly lesbian discussion groups and readings.

### GOSH!

39 Great Russell St ⊖ Tottenham Court Road. Daily 10am–6pm (Thurs & Fri till 7pm). MAP P.80, POCKET MAP G13

All kinds of comics for all kinds of readers, whether you're casually curious or a serious collector.

### JAMES SMITH & SONS

53 New Oxford St ⊖ Tottenham Court Road. Mon–Fri 9.30am–5.25pm, Sat 10am–5.25pm. MAP P.80, POCKET MAP G14

A survivor from an earlier time (it was established in 1830), this beautiful and venerable shop purveys hip-flasks, portable seats and canes, but its main trade is in umbrellas.

JAMES SMITH & SONS

### PERSEPHONE BOOKS

59 Lamb's Conduit St ⊖ Russell Square.
Mon–Fri 10am–6pm. MAP P.80, POCKET MAP J12

Lovely bookshop offspring of a publishing house that specializes in neglected early twentieth-century writing, mostly by women.

### PLAYIN' GAMES

33 Museum St ⊖ Tottenham Court Road.
Mon–Sat 10am–6pm, Sun noon–6pm.
MAP P.80, POCKET MAP G13

Two floors of traditional board games (Scrabble, Cluedo and so on), plus backgammon, war games, fantasy games and more.

# Cafés and restaurants

### CAMERA CAFÉ

44 Museum St ⊖ Tottenham Court Road.
Daily 11am–7pm. MAP P.80, POCKET MAP H13

Tiny, cosy little café with free wi-fi at the back of a quality secondhand camera shop right by the British Museum. Thai food available.

### CIGALA

54 Lamb's Conduit St ⊖ Russell Square or Holborn ☎ 020/7405 1717. Daily 12.30–10.45pm. MAP P.80, POCKET MAP J12

Simple dishes, strong flavours, fresh ingredients and real passion are evident at this smart Iberian restaurant, where the menu changes daily. Mains cost £12–18 and there's a tapas menu (£2–8).

### HUMMUS BROS

37–63 Southampton Row ⊖ Holborn. Mon–Fri 11am–9pm. MAP P.80, POCKET MAP H13

Hummus and a choice of topping with a pitta bread on the side; service is efficient and they often throw in mint tea on the house.

### LA PORCHETTA

33 Boswell St ⊖ Russell Square or Holborn ☎ 020/7405 1717. Mon–Fri noon–3pm & 5–11pm, Sat 5–11pm. MAP P.80, POCKET MAP H12

Tiny, cramped, very loud, very Italian pizza and pasta place that dishes up huge portions (£6–10). Mains £6–10.

### PATISSERIE DEUX AMIS

63 Judd St ⊖ King's Cross St Pancras. Mon–Sat 9am–6pm, Sun 9am–2pm. MAP P.80, POCKET MAP J4

Small, civilized French-style bakery specializing in pastries, filled baguettes and coffee, with a great cheese shop next door.

# Pubs and bars

### BAR POLSKI

11 Little Turnstile ⊖ Holborn. Mon 4–11.30pm, Tues–Fri 12.30–11.30pm, Sat 6–11pm, Sun 6–10.30pm. MAP P.80, POCKET MAP J13

Great Polish bar hidden in an alleyway behind Holborn tube, with a wicked selection of flavoured vodkas and beers, and good, cheap Polish food.

### THE DUKE

7 Roger St ⊖ Russell Square or Holborn. Mon–Sat noon–11pm, Sun noon–10.30pm. MAP P.80, POCKET MAP J12

Lovely little neighbourhood gastropub, without the pretensions often associated with the breed, and an unusual Art Deco bent to the decor.

### THE LAMB

94 Lamb's Conduit St ⊖ Russell Square. Mon–Sat 11am–midnight, Sun noon–10.30pm. MAP P.80, POCKET MAP J12

Marvellously well-preserved Victorian pub of mirrors, polished wood and "snob" screens. Deep green leather banquettes and excellent Young's ales round things off splendidly.

THE LAMB

### MUSEUM TAVERN

49 Great Russell St ⊖ Tottenham Court Road. Mon–Sat 11am–11pm, Sun noon–10.30pm. MAP P.80, POCKET MAP G13

Large and characterful old pub, right opposite the main entrance to the British Museum, and the erstwhile drinking hole of Karl Marx. Choice range of ales.

### PRINCESS LOUISE

209 High Holborn ⊖ Holborn. Mon–Fri 11am–11pm, Sat noon–11pm. MAP P.80, POCKET MAP H13

Architecturally, this is one of London's most impressive Victorian pubs, featuring gold trimmed mirrors, gorgeous mosaics and a fine moulded ceiling. The Sam Smith's beer is very reasonably priced and there's always a lively crowd.

# Venues

### THE PLACE

17 Duke's Rd ⊖ Euston ☎ 020/7387 0031, ⊛ www.theplace.org.uk. MAP P.80, POCKET MAP H4

Small dance theatre presenting the work of new choreographers and student performers, and hosting some of the finest small-scale contemporary dance from across the globe.

# The City

The City is where London began, and its boundaries today are only slightly larger than those marked by the Roman walls and their medieval successors. However, you'll find few visible leftovers of London's early days, since four-fifths of it burned down in the Great Fire of 1666. The majority of Londoners lived and worked in or around the City up until the eighteenth century – nowadays, it's primarily one of the world's main financial centres and although 300,000 commuters work here fewer than 10,000 actually live here. The City is only really busy Monday to Friday during the day, so if you're looking for nightlife, you're best off heading for Clerkenwell, which lies on the City's northwest fringe.

## TEMPLE

Temple. MAP PP.86–87, POCKET MAP K15

Temple is the largest and most complex of the **Inns of Court**, where, since medieval times, every aspiring barrister in England and Wales has had to study in order to qualify for the bar. Despite the fact that only a few very old buildings survive here, the overall atmosphere is like that of an Oxbridge college and the maze of courtyards and passageways is fun to explore – especially after dark, when Temple is gas-lit.

Medieval students ate, attended lectures and slept in the **Middle Temple Hall** (Mon–Fri 10–11.30am and 3–4pm; free), still the Inn's main dining room. Constructed in the 1560s, the hall provided the setting for many great Elizabethan masques and plays – probably including Shakespeare's *Twelfth Night*, which is believed to have been premiered here in 1602. The hall is worth a visit for its fine hammerbeam roof, wooden panelling and decorative Elizabethan screen.

TEMPLE CHURCH

The complex's oldest building, **Temple Church** (Wed–Sun 11am–4pm; W www.temple church.com) was built in 1185 by the Knights Templar, the military monks who protected pilgrims heading for the Holy Land. Despite wartime damage, the original round church – modelled on the Holy Sepulchre in Jerusalem – still stands, with its striking Purbeck-marble piers, recumbent marble effigies of knights, and tortured grotesques grimacing in the spandrels of the blind arcading. The church features in both the book and the film of *The Da Vinci Code* by Dan Brown.

## FLEET STREET

⊖ Temple. MAP PP.86–87, POCKET MAP K6–L6

In the nineteenth century, all the major national and provincial dailies had their offices and **printing presses** in and around Fleet Street. Computer technology rendered the presses here obsolete in the 1980s, however, and within a decade or so all the newspaper headquarters had gone, leaving just a couple of landmarks to testify to five hundred years of printing history. The most remarkable is the city's first glass curtain-wall construction, the former **Daily Express** building at no. 127, with its sleek black Vitrolite facade.

## PRINCE HENRY'S ROOM

17 Fleet St ⊖ Temple W www.cityoflondon .gov.uk/phr. Mon–Sat 11am–2pm. Free. MAP PP.86–87, POCKET MAP K15

The first floor of this fine Jacobean house, with its distinctive timber-framed bay windows, now contains material relating to the diarist **Samuel Pepys** (1633–1703), who was born in nearby Salisbury Court and baptized at St Bride's. Even if you've no interest in Pepys, the wooden-panelled room itself is worth a look – it contains one of the finest Jacobean plasterwork ceilings in London, and a lot of original stained glass.

## ST BRIDE'S

Fleet St ⊖ Blackfriars or Temple. W www .stbrides.com. Mon–Fri 9am–5pm, Sat 11am–3pm. Free. MAP PP.86–87, POCKET MAP L6

To get a sense of Fleet Street in the days when the press dominated the area, head for the so-called "journalists' and printers' cathedral", St Bride's Church, which boasts Wren's tallest and most exquisite spire (said to be the inspiration for the tiered wedding cake). The crypt contains a little museum of Fleet Street's newspaper history, with information on the *Daily Courant* and the *Universal Daily Register*, which later became *The Times*, claiming to be "the faithful recorder of every species of intelligence … circulated for a particular set of readers only".

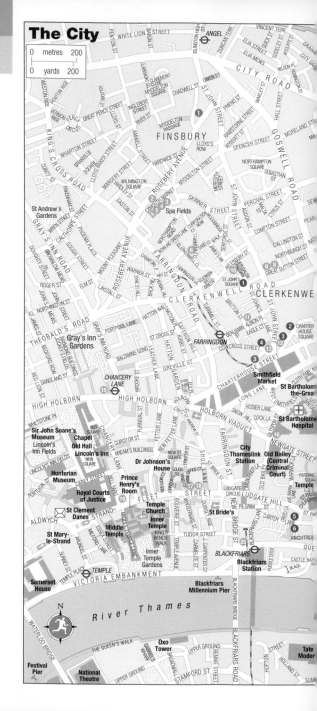

The City

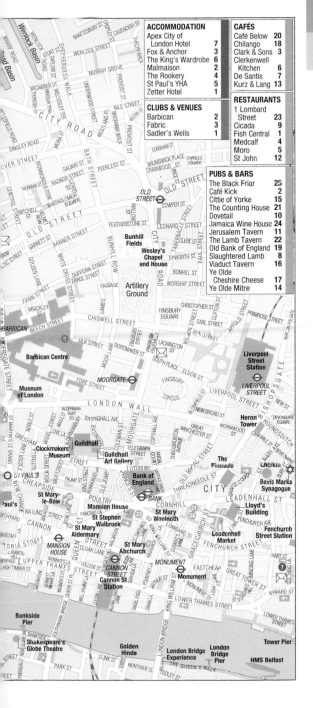

**ACCOMMODATION**
| | |
|---|---|
| Apex City of London Hotel | 7 |
| Fox & Anchor | 3 |
| The King's Wardrobe | 6 |
| Malmaison | 2 |
| The Rookery | 4 |
| St Paul's YHA | 5 |
| Zetter Hotel | 1 |

**CLUBS & VENUES**
| | |
|---|---|
| Barbican | 2 |
| Fabric | 3 |
| Sadler's Wells | 1 |

**CAFÉS**
| | |
|---|---|
| Café Below | 20 |
| Chilango | 18 |
| Clark & Sons | 3 |
| Clerkenwell Kitchen | 6 |
| De Santis | 7 |
| Kurz & Lang | 13 |

**RESTAURANTS**
| | |
|---|---|
| 1 Lombard Street | 23 |
| Cicada | 9 |
| Fish Central | 1 |
| Medcalf | 4 |
| Moro | 5 |
| St John | 12 |

**PUBS & BARS**
| | |
|---|---|
| The Black Friar | 25 |
| Café Kick | 2 |
| Cittie of Yorke | 15 |
| The Counting House | 21 |
| Dovetail | 10 |
| Jamaica Wine House | 24 |
| Jerusalem Tavern | 11 |
| The Lamb Tavern | 22 |
| Old Bank of England | 19 |
| Slaughtered Lamb | 8 |
| Viaduct Tavern | 16 |
| Ye Olde Cheshire Cheese | 17 |
| Ye Olde Mitre | 14 |

## LINCOLN'S INN

Lincoln's Inn Fields ⊖ Chancery Lane
☏ 020/7405 1393, Ⓦ www.lincolnsinn
.org.uk. Mon–Fri 9am–6pm. Free. MAP PP.86–87,
POCKET MAP K14

Lincoln's Inn was the first of the Inns of Court, and in many ways is the prettiest, having miraculously escaped the ravages of the Blitz. Every aspiring lawyer must study here in order to qualify as a barrister; famous alumni include Thomas More, Oliver Cromwell and Margaret Thatcher. The main entrance is the diamond-patterned, red-brick Tudor gateway on Chancery Lane, adjacent to which is the early seventeenth-century **chapel** (Mon–Fri noon–2pm), with its unusual fan-vaulted open undercroft and, on the first floor, a late Gothic nave, hit by a zeppelin in World War I and much restored since. The Inn's fifteenth-century **Old Hall** (appointment only), where the lawyers used to live and where Dickens set the case Jarndyce and Jarndyce in *Bleak House*, features a fine timber roof, linenfold panelling and an elaborate, early Jacobean screen.

## SIR JOHN SOANE'S MUSEUM

13 Lincoln's Inn Fields ⊖ Holborn
☏ 020/7405 2107, Ⓦ www.soane.org.
Tues–Sat 10am–5pm. Free. MAP PP.86–87,
POCKET MAP J14

The chief architect of the Bank of England, **John Soane** (1753–1837) designed this house not only as a home and office but also as a place to stash his large collection of art and antiquities. Arranged much as it was in his lifetime, the ingeniously planned house has an informal, treasure-hunt atmosphere, with countless surprises. The star exhibits are **Hogarth**'s satirical *Election* series and his merciless morality tale *The Rake's Progress,* as well as the alabaster Egyptian sarcophagus of Seti I rejected by the British Museum. Note that the museum is extremely popular on Saturdays, when there's a fascinating hour-long **guided tour** (£5) at 11am, and on the **candlelit evenings** held on the first Tuesday of the month (6–9pm).

## HUNTERIAN MUSEUM

Royal College of Surgeons, Lincoln's Inn Fields ⊖ Holborn or Temple ☏ 020/7869 6560, Ⓦ www.rcseng.ac.uk. Tues–Sat 10am–5pm. Free. MAP PP.86–87, POCKET MAP J14

Containing the unique specimen collection of the surgeon-scientist John Hunter (1728–93), the Hunterian Museum first opened in 1813. Since most of the exhibits are jars of pickled skeletons and body pieces, it's certainly not a museum for the squeamish. Among the prize exhibits are the skeletons of the Irish giant, Charles Byrne (1761–83), who was seven feet seven inches tall, and the Sicilian midget Caroline Crachami (d.1824), who was just one foot seven and a half inches when she died at the age of nine.

## DR JOHNSON'S HOUSE

17 Gough Square ⊖ Blackfriars or Temple
☏ 020/7353 3745. ⓦ www.drjohnsonshouse
.org. May–Sept Mon–Sat 11am–5.30pm;
Oct–April Mon–Sat 11am–5pm. £4.50.
MAP PP.86–87, POCKET MAP L6

Despite appearances, Dr Johnson's House is the only authentic eighteenth-century building on Gough Square. It was here the great savant, writer and lexicographer lived from 1747 to 1759 whilst compiling the 41,000 entries for the first dictionary of the English language. The grey-panelled rooms of the house are peppered with period furniture and lined with portraits and etchings, including one of Johnson's servant Francis Barber. Two first-edition copies of the great *Dictionary* are on display, while the open-plan attic, in which Johnson and his six helpers put the tome together, is now lined with explanatory panels on lexicography.

## OLD BAILEY

Newgate St ⊖ St Paul's ☏ 020/7248 3277.
ⓦ www.hmcourts-service.gov.uk. Mon–Fri
10.30am–1pm & 2–5pm. Free.
MAP PP.86–87, POCKET MAP L6

The **Central Criminal Court** is more popularly known as the Old Bailey after the street on which it stands, which used to form the outer walls of the medieval city. It was built on the site of the notoriously harsh Newgate Prison, where folk used to come to watch public hangings. The current, rather pompous Edwardian building is distinguished by its green dome, surmounted by a gilded statue of Justice, unusually depicted without blindfold, holding her sword and scales. The country's most serious criminal court cases take place here, and have included, in the past, the trials of Lord Haw-Haw, the Kray twins, and the Guildford Four and Birmingham Six "IRA bombers". You can watch the proceedings from the visitors' gallery, but bags, cameras, mobiles, personal stereos and food and drink are not allowed in, and there is no cloakroom.

## SMITHFIELD

⊖ Farringdon. MAP PP.86–87, POCKET MAP L5

For more than three centuries Smithfield was a popular venue for **public executions**: the Scottish hero, William Wallace, was hanged, disembowelled and beheaded here in 1305, and the Bishop of Rochester's cook was boiled alive in 1531, but the local speciality was burnings, which reached a peak in the mid-sixteenth century during the reign of "Bloody" Mary, when hundreds of Protestants were burned at the stake for their beliefs. These days, Smithfield is dominated by its historic **meat market**, housed in a colourful and ornate Victorian market hall on Charterhouse Street; if you want to see it in action, get here early – the activity starts around 4am and is all over by 9am or 10am.

## ST BARTHOLOMEW-THE-GREAT

Cloth Fair ⊖ Barbican ☎ 020/7606 5171, ⓦ www.greatstbarts.com. Mon–Fri 8.30am–5pm, Sat 10.30am–1.30pm, Sun

SMITHFIELD MARKET

8.30am–1pm & 2.30–8pm; mid-Nov to mid-Feb Tues–Fri closes 4pm. £4. MAP PP.86–87, POCKET MAP L5

Begun in 1123, St Bartholomew-the-Great is London's oldest and most atmospheric parish church. Its half-timbered Tudor gatehouse on Little Britain incorporates a thirteenth-century arch that once formed the entrance to the nave; above, a wooden statue of St Bartholomew stands holding the knife with which he flayed. One side of the medieval cloisters survives to the south, immediately to the right as you enter the church. The rest is a confusion of elements, including portions of the transepts and, most impressively, the chancel, where stout Norman pillars separate the main body of the church from the ambulatory. There are various pre-Fire monuments to admire, the most prominent being the tomb of Rahere, court jester to Henry I, which shelters under a fifteenth-century canopy north of the main altar.

## ST BARTHOLOMEW'S HOSPITAL MUSEUM

West Smithfield ⊖ Barbican. Tues–Fri 10am–4pm. Free. MAP PP.86–87, POCKET MAP L5

Among the medical artefacts, this hospital museum boasts some fearsome amputation instruments, a pair of leather "lunatic restrainers", some great jars with labels such as "poison – for external use only", and a cricket bat autographed by W.G. Grace, who was a student at Bart's in the 1870s. To see the magnificent **Great Hall** you must go on one of the fascinating guided tours (Fri 2pm; £5; ☎ 020/7837 0546), which take in Smithfield and the surrounding area as well; the meeting point is the Henry VIII gate.

## MUSEUM OF LONDON

London Wall ⊖ Barbican ☎ 020/7001 9844,
ⓦ www.museumoflondon.org.uk.
Daily 10am–5.50pm. Free. MAP PP.86–87.
POCKET MAP M5

Despite London's long pedigree,
very few of its ancient structures
are still standing. However,
numerous Roman, Saxon and
Elizabethan remains have
been discovered and are now
displayed at the Museum of
London. The permanent exhibition provides an imaginative
and educational trot through
London's past from prehistory
to the present day. Specific
exhibits to look out for include
the Bucklersbury Roman
mosaic; a model of Old St Paul's;
and the Lord Mayor's heavily
gilded coach (still used for state
occasions). The real strength of
the museum, though, lies in the
excellent temporary exhibitions, lectures, walks and films it
organizes throughout the year.

## GUILDHALL

Aldermanbury ⊖ Bank or Mansion House
☎ 020/7606 3030, ⓦ www.cityoflondon.gov.
uk. May–Sept daily 10am–5pm; Oct–April
Mon–Sat 10am–5pm. Free. MAP PP.86–87.
POCKET MAP M6

Situated at the geographical
centre of the City, Guildhall has
been the area's administrative
seat for over eight hundred
years. It remains the headquarters of the **City of London
Corporation**, the City's
governing body, and is used for
grand civic occasions. Architecturally, however, it's not quite
the beauty it once was, having
been badly damaged in both
the Great Fire and the Blitz,
and somewhat scarred by the
addition of a grotesque 1970s
concrete cloister and wing.

Nonetheless, the **Great Hall**,
basically a postwar reconstruction on the fifteenth-century
walls, is worth a look if there
isn't an event going on. In 1553
the venue for the high-treason
trials of Lady Jane Grey and
her husband, Lord Dudley, the
hall is home to a handful of
vainglorious late eighteenth-
and early nineteenth-century
monuments, replete with
lions, cherubs and ludicrous
allegorical figures. You might
also pop into the **Clock-
makers' Museum** (Mon–Fri
9.30am–4.30pm; free), a
collection of over six hundred
timepieces, including one
of the clocks that won John
Harrison the Longitude prize.

Also worth a visit is the
purpose-built **Guildhall Art
Gallery** (Mon–Sat 10am–5pm,
Sun noon–4pm; £2.50, free Fri
and daily after 3.30pm), which
contains one or two excep-
tional works, such as Rossetti's
*La Ghirlandata* and Holman
Hunt's *The Eve of St Agnes*, plus
a massive painting depicting
the 1782 Siege of Gibraltar,
commissioned by the Corporation. In the basement, you can
view the remains of a Roman
amphitheatre, dating from
around 120 AD, which was
discovered during the gallery's
construction.

## ST PAUL'S CATHEDRAL

St Paul's 020/7236 4128, www
.stpauls.co.uk. Mon–Sat 8.30am–4pm. £11.
MAP B6–B7, POCKET MAP M6

Designed by **Christopher Wren** and completed in 1710, St Paul's remains a dominating presence in the City despite the encroaching tower blocks. It's topped by an enormous lead-covered dome that's second in size only to St Peter's in Rome, and its showpiece west facade is particularly magnificent. However, compared to its great rival, Westminster Abbey, St Paul's is a soulless but perfectly calculated architectural set piece, a burial place for captains rather than kings.

The best place to appreciate the building's glory is from beneath the **dome**, adorned (against Wren's wishes) by trompe l'oeil frescoes. The

ST PAUL'S CATHEDRAL

most richly decorated section of the cathedral is the **chancel**, where the late Victorian mosaics of birds, fish, animals and greenery are particularly spectacular. The intricately carved oak and lime-wood choir stalls, and the imposing organ case, are the work of Wren's master carver, Grinling Gibbons.

Beginning in the south aisle, a series of stairs leads to the dome's three galleries, the first of which is the internal **Whispering Gallery**, so called because of its acoustic properties – words whispered to the wall on one side are distinctly audible over one hundred feet away on the other, though you often can't hear much above the hubbub. Of the two exterior galleries, the best views are from the tiny **Golden Gallery**, below the golden ball and cross which top the cathedral.

Although the nave is crammed full of overblown monuments to military types, burials in St Paul's are confined to the **crypt**, reputedly the largest in Europe. The whitewashed walls and bright lighting make this one of London's least atmospheric mausoleums, but **Artists' Corner** here does boast as many painters and architects as Westminster Abbey has poets, including Christopher Wren himself. The star tombs, though, are those of Nelson and Wellington, both occupying centre stage and both with more fanciful monuments upstairs.

It's well worth attending one of the cathedral's **services**, if only to hear the ethereal choir, who perform during most evensongs (Mon–Sat 5pm), and on Sundays at 10.15am, 11.30am and 3.15pm.

# City churches

The City is crowded with churches (www.cityoflondonchurches.com) – well over forty at the last count, the majority of them built or rebuilt by Wren after the Great Fire. Those particularly worth seeking out include **St Mary Abchurch** (Tues 10.30am–2.30pm; ⊖ Cannon Street; MAP PP.86–87, POCKET MAP N6) on Abchurch Lane, dominated by an unusual and vast dome fresco painted by a local parishioner and lit by oval lunettes; the superlative lime-wood reredos is by Gibbons. On Lombard Street, **St Mary Woolnoth** (Mon–Fri 9.30am–4.30pm; ⊖ Bank; MAP PP.86–87, POCKET MAP N6) is a typically idiosyncratic creation of Nicholas Hawksmoor, one of Wren's pupils, featuring an ingenious lantern lit by semicircular clerestory windows and a striking altar canopy held up by barley-sugar columns. **St Mary Aldermary** on Queen Victoria Street (Mon–Fri 11am–3pm; ⊖ Mansion House; MAP PP.86–87, POCKET MAP M6) is Wren's most successful stab at Gothic, with fan vaulting in the aisles and a panelled ceiling in the nave. Finally on Walbrook is Wren's most spectacular church interior after St Paul's, **St Stephen Walbrook** (Mon–Thurs 10am–4pm, Fri 10am–3pm; ⊖ Bank; MAP PP.86–87, POCKET MAP M6), where sixteen Corinthian columns are arranged in clusters around a central coffered dome, and the exquisite dark-wood furnishings are again by Grinling Gibbons.

## PATERNOSTER SQUARE

⊖ St Paul's. MAP PP.86–87, POCKET MAP L6

The Blitz destroyed the area immediately to the north of St Paul's, incinerating all the booksellers' shops and around six million books. In their place a modernist pedestrianized piazza was built, only to be torn down in the 1980s and replaced with post-classical office blocks in Portland stone and a Corinthian column topped by a gilded urn. One happy consequence of the square's redevelopment is that **Temple Bar**, the gateway which used to stand at the top of Fleet Street, has found its way back to London after over a hundred years of exile in a park in Hertfordshire. Designed by Wren himself, the triumphal arch, looking weathered but clean, now forms the entrance to Paternoster Square, with the Stuart monarchs, James I and Charles II, and their consorts occupying the niches.

## BANK OF ENGLAND

Threadneedle St ⊖ Bank ☎ 020/7601 5545, ⓦ www.bankofengland.co.uk. Mon–Fri 10am–5pm. Free. MAP PP.86–87, POCKET MAP M6

Established in 1694 by William III to raise funds for the war against France, the Bank of England stores the official gold reserves of many of the world's central banks. All that remains of the original building, on which John Soane spent the best part of his career (from 1788 onwards), is the windowless outer curtain wall, which wraps itself round the 3.5-acre island site. However, you can view a reconstruction of Soane's Bank Stock Office, with its characteristic domed skylight, in the **museum** (free), which has its entrance on Bartholomew Lane. The permanent exhibition here includes a scaled-down model of Soane's bank and a Victorian-style diorama of the night in 1780 when the bank was attacked by rioters. Sadly most of the gold bars are fakes, but there are specimens of every note issued by the Bank over the centuries.

## MANSION HOUSE

Mansion House Place ⊖ Bank. Tues 2pm. £6. MAP PP.86–87, POCKET MAP M6

The Lord Mayor's sumptuous Neoclassical lodgings are now open to the public by guided tour. Designed in 1753, the building's grandest room is the columned **Egyptian Hall** with its barrel-vaulted, coffered ceiling. Also impressive is the vast collection of gold and silver tableware, the mayor's 36-pound gold mace and the pearl sword given by Elizabeth I. Scattered about the rooms are an impressive array of Dutch and Flemish paintings.

## LEADENHALL MARKET

Leadenhall St ⊖ Monument. Mon–Fri 11am–2pm. MAP PP.86–87, POCKET MAP N6

Leaadenhall Market's pictur-esque cobbles and graceful Victorian cast-ironwork date from 1881. Inside, the traders cater mostly for the lunchtime City crowd, their barrows laden with exotic food and wines.

## BEVIS MARKS SYNAGOGUE

Bevis Marks ⊖ Aldgate ☎ 020/7626 1274, ⓦ www.bevismarks.org.uk. Mon, Wed & Thurs 10.30am–2pm, Tues & Fri 10.30am–1pm, Sun 10.30am–12.30pm. Guided tours Wed & Fri noon, Sun 11am. £4. MAP PP.86–87, POCKET MAP N6

Hidden behind a modern red-brick office block, the Bevis Marks Synagogue was built in 1701 by Sephardic Jews who had fled the Inquisition in Spain and Portugal. It's the country's oldest surviving synagogue, and the roomy, rich interior gives an idea of just how wealthy the worshippers were at the time. The Sephardic community has now dispersed across London and the congregation has dwindled, but the magnificent array of chandeliers ensure that it's a popular venue for candle-lit Jewish weddings.

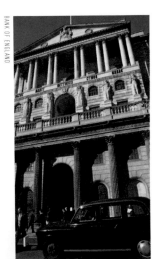
BANK OF ENGLAND

## MONUMENT

Monument St ⊖ Monument ☎ 020/7626
2717. Daily 9.30am–5.30pm. £2.
MAP PP.86–87, POCKET MAP N6

The Monument was designed by Wren to commemorate the **Great Fire of London**, which raged for five days in early September 1666 and destroyed four-fifths of the City. A plain Doric column crowned with spiky gilded flames, it stands 202ft high, making it the tallest isolated stone column in the world; if it were laid out flat it would touch the site of the bakery where the Fire started, east of the Monument. The bas-relief on the base depicts Charles II and the Duke of York in Roman garb conducting the emergency relief operation. The 311 steps to the viewing gallery once guaranteed an incredible view; nowadays it is somewhat dwarfed by the buildings surrounding it.

## City skyscrapers

Throughout the 1990s, most people's favourite modern building in the City was Richard Rogers' glitzy **Lloyd's Building** MAP PP.86–87, POCKET MAP N6 – a vertical version of Rogers' own Pompidou Centre in Paris – a startling array of glass and blue steel pipes. Lloyd's was eclipsed in the mid 2000s by its near neighbour, Norman Foster's 590ft-high, glass diamond-clad **Gherkin** MAP PP.86–87, POCKET MAP N6, which has endeared itself to Londoners thanks to its cheeky shape. Meanwhile, the City skyline is currently sprouting a whole new generation of skyscrapers, beginning with the **Heron Tower** MAP PP.86–87, POCKET MAP N5, a 663ft skyscraper with a 144ft mast at 110 Bishopsgate, designed by Kohn Pedersen Fox, and **The Pinnacle** MAP PP.86–87, POCKET MAP N6 (945ft), a swirling helter-skelter of a tower (with a restaurant on the top floor) by the same architects at 22–24 Bishopsgate, due for completion in 2012. With these two newcomers, the City has finally outreached Canary Wharf, but it is still set to be ousted for the prize of the country's tallest building by Renzo Piano's 1017ft **Shard** MAP PP.86–87, POCKET MAP N7, on the south side of London Bridge, also due for completion in 2012.

# Cafés

### CAFÉ BELOW

St Mary-le-Bow, Cheapside ⊖ St Paul's or
Mansion House. Mon–Fri 7.30am–9pm.
MAP PP.86–87, POCKET MAP M6

A rare City gem: a café, set in
a wonderful Norman church
crypt, serving excellent, good-
value bistro-style dishes plus
delicious breakfast pastries.

### CHILANGO

142 Fleet St ⊖ Blackfriars. Mon–Fri
11am–9pm. MAP PP.86–87, POCKET MAP L6

Busy, modern canteen-style
Mexican place serving up fast,
fresh, soft tortilla burritos and
tacos, salads and guacamole.

### CLARK & SONS

46 Exmouth Market ⊖ Angel or
Farringdon. Mon–Thurs 10.30am–4pm, Fri
10.30am–5.30pm, Sat 10.30am–5pm.
MAP PP.86–87, POCKET MAP K4

Despite Exmouth Market's
gentrification, this genuine
pie-and-mash shop is still
going strong, and is now the
most central one in the capital.

### CLERKENWELL KITCHEN

27–31 Clerkenwell Close ⊖ Farringdon.
Mon–Fri 8am–5pm, Thurs until 11pm.
MAP PP.86–87, POCKET MAP L4

Bright, modern airy place
decked in light wood and brick,
with an open-plan kitchen
that serves up everything from
breakfast through to afternoon
tea. The menu is short and
admirably seasonal.

### DE SANTIS

11–13 Old St ⊖ Barbican. Mon–Fri
8.30am–11pm. MAP PP.86–87, POCKET MAP L4

Swish Milanese *paninoteca* with
a terrace at the back. Home-
baked paninis with top-class
fillings, and very good coffee.

### KURZ & LANG

1 St John St ⊖ Farringdon. Mon–Wed
11am–11.30pm, Thurs 11am–1am, non-stop
Fri 11am–Sun 7am, Sun noon–8.30pm.
MAP PP.86–87, POCKET MAP L5

An *echt* German *Bratwurst*
café in a prominent corner
site off Smithfield. Choose
from a variety of sausages,
and help them down with
bread, mustard and sauerkraut.
Popular clubbers' pit-stop.

# Restaurants

### 1 LOMBARD STREET

1 Lombard St ⊖ Bank ☎ 020/7929 6611.
Mon–Fri 11am–11pm. MAP PP.86–87,
POCKET MAP N6

Former banking hall in
the heart of the City with a
spectacular glass dome above
the buzzy circular French
bar-brasserie, and a more
intimate restaurant beyond.
Brasserie mains £17–25;
restaurant mains £25–35.

### CICADA

132 St John St ⊖ Farringdon ☎ 020/7608
1550. Mon–Fri noon–2.45pm & 6–10.45pm,
Sat 6–10.45pm. MAP PP.86–87, POCKET MAP L4

CAFÉ BELOW

Part bar, part restaurant, *Cicada* offers an unusual pan-Asian menu that allows you to mix and match from small, large and side dishes ranging from fishy *tom yum* to ginger noodles or sushi. Mains £10–17.

## FISH CENTRAL

149–155 Central St ⊖ Old Street
☎ 020/7253 0229. Mon–Sat 11am–2.30pm & 5–10.30pm. MAP PP.86–87, POCKET MAP M4
Sitting on the edge of the Barbican/City and Clerkenwell's council estates, this reliable fish-and-chip restaurant attracts clientele from both. Mains £8–15.

## MEDCALF

40 Exmouth Market ⊖ Angel or Farringdon
☎ 020/7833 3533. Mon–Thurs & Sat noon–11pm, Fri noon–1am, Sun noon–6pm.
MAP PP.86–87, POCKET MAP K4
A converted hundred-year-old butcher's shop, fashionably unchic, serving modern British cuisine with fresh ingredients and excellent puds. Mains £9–15.

## MORO

34–36 Exmouth Market ⊖ Angel or Farringdon ☎ 020/7833 8336. Mon–Fri 12.30–2.30pm & 7–10.30pm, Sat 7–10.30pm.
MAP PP.86–87, POCKET MAP K4
This attractive modern restaurant is a place of pilgrimage for disciples of the restaurant's Moorish cookbooks. Food is usually excellent, service sometimes less so and you have to book well in advance. Tapas (around £4) served throughout the day. Mains £16–19.

## ST JOHN

26 St John St ⊖ Farringdon
☎ 020/7251 0848. Daily noon–midnight.
MAP PP.86–87, POCKET MAP L5
Pared-down former smokehouse close to Smithfield meat market that's become famous

THE BLACK FRIAR

for serving outstanding British dishes, often involving unfashionable animal parts. Mains £14–22.

# Pubs and bars

## THE BLACK FRIAR

174 Queen Victoria St ⊖ Blackfriars. Mon–Fri 11am–11pm, Sat 11am–11.30pm, Sun noon–10.30pm. MAP PP.86–87, POCKET MAP L6
A gorgeous pub, with Art Nouveau marble friezes of boozy monks and a highly decorated alcove – all original, dating from 1905. A lovely fireplace and an unhurried atmosphere make this a relaxing place to drink.

## CAFÉ KICK

43 Exmouth Market ⊖ Farringdon or Angel.
Mon–Sat noon–11pm, Sun noon–10.30pm.
MAP PP.86–87, POCKET MAP K4
This chaotic, very popular, French-style café/bar is great fun, the atmosphere enlivened by three busy table-football games.

## CITTIE OF YORKE

22 High Holborn ⊖ Chancery Lane. Mon–Fri 11.30am–11pm, Sat noon–11pm. MAP PP.86–87, POCKET MAP K13

A venerable London lawyers' pub now run by Sam Smith's. Head for the vaulted cellar bar or the grand quasi-medieval wine hall at the back with its rows of cosy cubicles.

## THE COUNTING HOUSE

50 Cornhill ⊖ Bank. Mon–Fri 11am–11pm. MAP PP.86–87, POCKET MAP N6

An inspired Fuller's bank conversion, the magnificent interior featuring high ceilings, marble walls, mosaic flooring and a large, oval island bar, above which is an enormous glass dome.

## DOVETAIL

9 Jerusalem Passage ⊖ Farringdon. Mon–Sat noon–11pm. MAP PP.86–87, POCKET MAP L4

Marvellous, understated Belgian bar offering 101 varieties of beer (including a dozen or so on tap). The curious decor comprises pew-style seating, green-tiled tables and kitchen-style wall tiling. First-rate Belgian food, too.

## JAMAICA WINE HOUSE

St Michael's Alley ⊖ Bank. Mon–Fri 11am–11pm. MAP PP.86–87, POCKET MAP N6

Located down a narrow alleyway, on the site of London's first coffee house (1652), this old City institution is known locally as the "Jam Pot". Despite the name, it is really just a pub, divided into four large "snugs" by original high wooden-panelled parti-tions.

## JERUSALEM TAVERN

55 Britton St ⊖ Farringdon. Mon–Fri 11am–11pm. MAP PP.86–87, POCKET MAP L5

Converted Georgian coffee house – the frontage dates from 1810 – that has retained much of its original character. Better still, the excellent draught beers are from St Peter's Brewery in Suffolk. Something of a gem in these parts.

## THE LAMB TAVERN

10–12 Leadenhall Market ⊖ Monument or Bank. Mon–Fri 11am–11pm. MAP PP.86–87, POCKET MAP N6

It's almost exclusively standing room only (both inside and out) at this super Young's pub situated in the middle of beautiful Leadenhall Market. Excellent roast beef, pork and sausage sandwiches at lunchtime.

## OLD BANK OF ENGLAND

194 Fleet St ⊖ Temple or Chancery Lane. Mon–Fri 11am–11pm. MAP PP.66–87, POCKET MAP K14

Not the actual Bank of England, but the former Law Courts' branch, this imposing High Victorian banking hall is now a magnificently opulent Fuller's ale-and-pie pub.

VIADUCT TAVERN

## SLAUGHTERED LAMB

34–35 Great Sutton St 🚇 Barbican or
Farringdon. Mon–Thurs noon–midnight,
Fri & Sat noon–1am, Sun noon–10.30pm.
MAP PP.86–87, POCKET MAP L4

Self consciously trendy former
art gallery, filled with sofas
and old furniture. Ironically
old fashioned pub grub and
lots of live music and events –
moustaches must be worn on
Saturday evenings.

## VIADUCT TAVERN

126 Newgate St 🚇 St Paul's. Mon–Fri
11am–11pm. MAP PP.86–87, POCKET MAP L5
Fuller's pub situated across
from the Old Bailey, with a
glorious Victorian interior.
The red ceiling and walls are
adorned with oils of faded
ladies representing Commerce,
Agriculture and the Arts.

## YE OLDE CHESHIRE CHEESE

Wine Office Court, 145 Fleet St 🚇 Temple.
Mon–Sat 11am–11pm, Sun noon–5pm.
MAP PP.86–87, POCKET MAP L6

A famous seventeenth-century
watering hole – chiefly because
of patrons such as Dickens
and Dr Johnson – with several
snug, dark-panelled rooms and
real fires. Popular with tourists,
but by no means exclusively so.

## YE OLDE MITRE

1 Ely Court, off Hatton Garden 🚇 Farringdon.
Mon–Fri 11am–11pm. MAP PP.86–87, POCKET MAP L5
Hidden down a tiny alleyway
off Ely Place or Hatton Garden,
this wonderfully atmospheric
pub dates back to 1546,
although it was actually rebuilt
in the eighteenth century. The
real ales are excellent.

# Clubs and venues

## BARBICAN

Silk St 🚇 Barbican ☎ 020/7638 8891, 🌐 www
.barbican.org.uk. MAP PP.86–87, POCKET MAP M5
With the outstanding resident
London Symphony Orchestra,
and top foreign orchestras and
big-name soloists in regular
attendance, the Barbican is
one of the city's outstanding
arenas for classical music. The
free music in the foyer is often
very good.

## FABRIC

77a Charterhouse St 🚇 Farringdon
☎ 020/7336 8898, 🌐 www.fabriclondon.com.
MAP PP.86–87, POCKET MAP L5
Despite big queues (arrive early
or late) and a confusing layout,
this 1600-capacity club remains
one of the world's finest. Live
bands and lengthy DJ line-ups
means you can hear a huge
variety of acts – usually underground, and almost always of
high quality.

## SADLER'S WELLS

Rosebery Ave 🚇 Angel ☎ 0044/417 4300,
🌐 www.sadlers-wells.com. MAP PP.86–87,
POCKET MAP L3
Home to Britain's best contemporary dance companies, and
host to the finest international
outfits, Sadler's Wells also
puts on theatre pieces and
children's shows.

# Hoxton and Spitalfields

Despite the area's lack of obvious aesthetic charm, over the last decade or so Hoxton has been colonized by artists, designers and architects and transformed into one of the city's most vibrant artistic enclaves, peppered with contemporary art galleries and a whole host of cool bars and clubs. Spitalfields, to the south, lies at the heart of the old East End, once the first port of call for thousands of immigrants over the centuries, and now best known for its Sunday markets and its cheap Bangladeshi curry houses.

### HOXTON SQUARE

⊖ Old Street. MAP P.102, POCKET MAP N4

The geographical focus of Hoxton's metamorphosis is Hoxton Square, a strange and not altogether happy assortment of light industrial units, many of them now converted into artists' studios arranged around a leafy, formal square. The chief landmark here is the **White Cube** gallery (Tues–Sat 10am–6pm; free; Ⓦ www .whitecube.com), a sort of miniature Tate Modern: it's an old piano factory, with a glass roof plonked on the top, and

represents the likes of Damien Hirst, Tracey Emin and Sam Taylor-Wood.

### GEFFRYE MUSEUM

Kingsland Rd ⊖ Hoxton Overground Ⓣ 020/7739 9893, Ⓦ www.geffrye-museum .org.uk. Tues–Sat 10am–5pm, Sun noon–5pm. Free. MAP P.102, POCKET MAP O3

Hoxton's chief attraction is the Geffrye Museum, housed in a grandiose enclave of eighteenth-century iron-mongers' almshouses. In 1911, at a time when the East End furniture trade was concentrated in the area, the

HOXTON SQUARE

almshouses were converted into a museum for the "education of craftsmen". The Geffrye remains, essentially, a furniture museum, with the almshouses rigged out as period living rooms of the urban middle class, ranging from the oak-panelled decor of the seventeenth century, through refined Georgian to cluttered Victorian style. Beyond lies the museum's modern extension, home to a pleasant café/restaurant and the excellent twentieth-century section. One of the **almshouses** has been restored to its original condition and can be visited (first Sat of the month and first and third Wed; £2).

## COLUMBIA ROAD FLOWER MARKET

Shoreditch High Street Overground or Hoxton Overground. Sun 8am–1pm. MAP P.102, POCKET MAP O3

**Columbia Road** is the city's most popular market for flowers and plants; it's also the liveliest, with the loud and upfront stallholders catering to an increasingly moneyed clientele. As well as seeds, bulbs, potted plants and cut flowers from the stalls, you'll also find every kind of gardening accessory from the chi-chi shops that line the street, and you can keep yourself sustained with bagels, cakes and coffee from the local cafés.

## WESLEY'S CHAPEL & HOUSE

49 City Rd ⊖ Old Street ☎ 020/7253 2262, ⓦ www.wesleyschapel.org.uk. Mon–Sat 10am–4pm, Sun 12.30–1.45pm. Free. MAP P.102, POCKET MAP N4

A place of pilgrimage for Methodists from all over the world, Wesley's Chapel was built in 1777, and heralded the coming of age of the faith founded by **John Wesley** (1703–91). The interior is uncharacteristically ornate, with powder-pink columns of French jasper and a superb, Adam-style gilded plasterwork ceiling. Predictably enough, the **Museum of Methodism** in the basement has only a passing reference to the insanely jealous 40-year-old widow Wesley married, and who eventually left him. Wesley himself spent his last two years in Wesley's House, a delightful Georgian place to the right of the main gates. On display inside are his deathbed and an early shock-therapy machine he was particularly keen on.

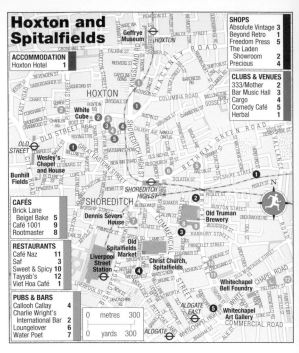

# Hoxton and Spitalfields

**ACCOMMODATION**
Hoxton Hotel 1

**SHOPS**
Absolute Vintage 3
Beyond Retro 6
Freedom Press 5
The Laden
　Showroom 2
Precious 4

**CLUBS & VENUES**
333/Mother 2
Bar Music Hall 3
Cargo 4
Comedy Café 5
Herbal 1

**CAFÉS**
Brick Lane
　Beigel Bake 5
Café 1001 9
Rootmaster 8

**RESTAURANTS**
Café Naz 11
Saf 3
Sweet & Spicy 10
Tayyab's 12
Viet Hoa Café 1

**PUBS & BARS**
Callooh Callay 4
Charlie Wright's
　International Bar 2
Loungelover 6
Water Poet 7

## BUNHILL FIELDS

City Rd ⊖ Old Street. April–Sept Mon–Fri 7.30am–7pm, Sat & Sun 9.30am–7pm; Oct–March closes 4pm. MAP P.102, POCKET MAP M4

The main burial ground for Dissenters or Nonconformists (practising Christians who were not members of the Church of England), Bunhill Fields lies across the road from Wesley's Chapel. Following bomb damage in the last war, most of the graveyard is fenced off, though you can still stroll through on the public footpaths under a canopy of giant London plane trees. The three most famous graves have been placed in the central paved area: the simple tombstone of poet and artist **William Blake** stands next to a replica of writer **Daniel Defoe**'s, while opposite lies the recumbent statue of **John Bunyan**, seventeenth-century author of *The Pilgrim's Progress*.

## PETTICOAT LANE

Middlesex St ⊖ Aldgate or Liverpool Street. Daily except Sat 9am–2pm. MAP P.102, POCKET MAP N5-Q5

Petticoat Lane may not be one of London's prettiest streets, but it has a rich history. The French Huguenot refugees sold the petticoats that gave the market its name; the authorities renamed it **Middlesex Street** in 1830 to avoid the mention of ladies' underwear. It now plays host to one of the capital's longest running **Sunday markets**, specializing in cheap (and often pretty tacky) clothing. As such, it's resolutely unfashionable, with lots of stalls selling vibrant fabrics and pungent, partially tanned leather jackets with shoulder pads.

## WHITECHAPEL ART GALLERY

80–82 Whitechapel High St ⊖ Aldgate East
☎ 020/7522 7888, ⊕ www.whitechapel.org.
Wed–Sun 11am–6pm (Thurs until 9pm). Free.
MAP P.102, POCKET MAP D5

The East End institution that draws in more outsiders than any other is the Whitechapel Art Gallery, housed in a beautiful crenellated 1899 Arts and Crafts building. The gallery puts on some of London's most innovative exhibitions of contemporary art, as well as hosting the biennial **Whitechapel Open**, a chance for local artists to get their work shown to a wider audience. The complex also has a pleasant **café** overlooking Angel Alley, where there's a stainless steel anarchist portrait gallery courtesy of the Freedom Press bookshop (see p.000).

## WHITECHAPEL BELL FOUNDRY

32–34 Whitechapel Rd ⊖ Aldgate East
☎ 020/7247 2599, ⊕ www.whitechapel
bellfoundry.co.uk. Mon–Fri 9am–4.15pm;
free. Guided tours Sat 10am & 2pm; £10.
MAP P.102

Big Ben, the Liberty Bell, the Bow Bells and numerous English church bells (including those of Westminster Abbey) all hail from this foundry, established in 1570. There's a small exhibition onsite.

## BRICK LANE

⊖ Aldgate East or Shoreditch High Street
Overground. MAP P.102, POCKET MAP D4–D5

Brick Lane lies at the heart of London's Bengali community, whose inexpensive curry houses dominate the southern end of the street. The red-brick chimney half-way up Brick Lane heralds the **Old Truman Brewery**, founded in 1666 and the largest in the world at the end of the nineteenth century. It ceased operations in 1989 and is now a multimedia centre for music, fashion, art and IT. North of the brewery and railway arch are the streets that serve as the venue for Brick Lane's **Sunday market** of bric-à-brac (Sun 8am–2pm). There are in fact virtually no stalls on Brick Lane itself any more; instead the market extends west along Sclater Street, and east down Cheshire Street. The stalls are a real mixed bag nowadays, selling cheap hardware, fruit and veg, and CDs, with services to unlock mobiles phones; the shops, though, tend to be more focused on designer accessories and interior furnishings than old-fashioned junk.

## CHRIST CHURCH, SPITALFIELDS

Commercial St ⊖ Liverpool Street
☎ 020/7247 7202, ⊛ www.christchurch
spitalfields.org. Tues 11am–4pm, Sun 1–4pm.
Free. MAP P.102, POCKET MAP O5

Built between 1714 and 1729 to
a characteristically bold design
by **Nicholas Hawksmoor**,
Christ Church features a huge
225-foot-high broach spire and
giant Tuscan portico, raised
on steps and shaped like a
Venetian window (a central
arched opening flanked by
two smaller rectangles) – a
recurring motif. Inside, there's
a forest of giant columned
bays, with a lion and a unicorn
playing peekaboo on the top
of the chancel beam and,
opposite, London's largest
Georgian organ. The church's
restoration has saved it from
falling down; sadly, it's also
removed all the atmosphere the
old decaying interior once had.

## OLD SPITALFIELDS MARKET

Commercial St ⊖ Liverpool Street.
Mon–Fri 10am–4pm, Sun 9am–5pm.
MAP P.102, POCKET MAP O5

SPITALFIELDS MARKET, BRUSHFIELD STREET

**Spitalfields Market** was the
capital's premier wholesale
fruit and vegetable market until
1991. After a decade of mixed
community use, the western
1920s half of the market was
replaced by an anonymous
glass box redevelopment
courtesy of Norman Foster,
although part of the original
facade survives on the north
side of Brushfield Street. The
market now hosts a large,
eclectic and fairly sophisticated
selection of shops and stalls
selling crafts, clothes, food and
organic fruit and vegetables
in the original red-brick and
green-gabled 1893 building, to
the east, but much of the scene
has moved east to Brick Lane.

## DENNIS SEVERS' HOUSE

18 Folgate St ⊖ Liverpool Street
☎ 020/7247 4013, ⊛ www.dennissevershouse
.co.uk. MAP P.102, POCKET MAP O5

Visiting the former home
of the American eccentric
Dennis Severs (1948–1999) is a
bizarre and uncanny theatrical
experience, which Severs once
described as "passing through
a frame into a painting". The
house is entirely candle-lit and
log-fired, and decked out as
it would have been over two
hundred years ago. Visitors are
free to explore the ten rooms
unhindered, and are left with
the distinct impression that
someone has literally just
popped out – Severs called it
a "still-life drama". The house
cat prowls, there's the smell
of gravy bubbling, and the
sound of horses' hooves on the
cobbled street outside. "The
Experience" takes place on
Sundays (noon–4pm; £8), and
on Mondays following the first
and third Sunday (noon–2pm;
£5); for the Monday evening
"Silent Night" you must book
ahead (times vary; £12).

# Shops

### ABSOLUTE VINTAGE

15 Hanbury St ⊖ Liverpool Street or
Shoreditch High Street Overground. Daily
11am–7pm. MAP P.102, POCKET MAP O5

A Spitalfields treasure-trove of
Twenties to Eighties clobber,
with one of the biggest collections of vintage shoes in the UK.

### BEYOND RETRO

110–112 Cheshire St ⊖ Shoreditch
High Street Overground. Mon Wed, Fri
& Sat 10am–7pm, Thurs 10am–8pm, Sun
10am–6pm. MAP P.102.

Cavernous warehouse of
twentieth-century classics, with
thousands of goodies including
vintage jeans, 1950s frocks,
battered cowboy boots, punk
gear and disco dolly gewgaws.

### FREEDOM PRESS

Angel Alley, 84b Whitechapel High St
⊖ Aldgate East. Mon–Sat noon 6pm, Sun
noon–4pm. MAP P.102, POCKET MAP O5

Upholding a long East End
tradition of radical politics, this
small anarchist bookshop is
packed with everything from
Bakhunin to Chomsky.

### THE LADEN SHOWROOM

103 Brick Lane ⊖ Shoreditch High Street
Overground. Mon–Fri 11am–6.30pm, Sat
11am–7pm, Sun 10.30am–6pm. MAP P.102,
POCKET MAP O4

This hip place showcases loads
of independent designers, and
is great for exuberant dressers
on a budget. There is a small
men's department.

### PRECIOUS

16 Artillery Passage ⊖ Liverpool Street
Mon–Fri 10am–6pm, Sat & Sun 11am–7pm.
MAP P.102, POCKET MAP O5

An elegant little store tucked
away in a narrow street near
Spitalfields. Cool designer
gear with a dressed-up feel,
including accessories.

Rootmaster

ROOTMASTER

# Cafés

### BRICK LANE BEIGEL BAKE

159 Brick Lane ⊖ Shoreditch High Street
Overground. Daily 24hr. MAP P.102, POCKET MAP O4

Classic no-frills bagel shop
in the heart of the East End –
unbelievably cheap, even for
fillings such as smoked salmon
with cream cheese. Stand at
the counter and munch, or
take away.

### CAFÉ 1001

1 Dray Walk, 91 Brick Lane ⊖ Shoreditch High
Street Overground. ⊕ www.cafe1001.co.uk.
Mon–Sat 6am–midnight, Sun 6am–11.30pm.
MAP P.102, POCKET MAP O5

Just off Brick Lane, this café
has a beaten-up studenty look,
with lots of sofas to crash on
and banks of seating outside in
Drays Walk, plus simple snacks
and delicious cakes to sample.
DJ sets every night; live jazz
every Wed.

### ROOTMASTER

Ely's Yard, up Dray Walk ⊖ Shoreditch High
Street Overground. Mon–Sat 11am–11pm,
Sun 11am–10.30pm. MAP P.102, POCKET MAP O5

Tasty vegan food from all over
the world, knocked up on the
ground floor of an old red
Routemaster bus; the kitchen's
on the bottom deck with seating
on the top deck and outside.

# Restaurants

### CAFÉ NAZ

46–48 Brick Lane ⊖ Aldgate East
☏ 020/7247 0234. Daily noon–midnight.
MAP P.102, POCKET MAP O5

Self-proclaimed contemporary
Bangladeshi restaurant that
cuts an imposing figure on
Brick Lane. The menu has all
the standards plus a variety of
baltis, the kitchen is open-plan,
and the prices are keen. Mains
£6–15.

### SAF

152–154 Curtain Rd ⊖ Old Street
☏ 020/7613 0007. Daily 11am–3.30pm &
6–11pm. MAP P.102, POCKET MAP N4

Modern, shiny and totally
unique vegan restaurant which
specializes in exquisitely
presented, mostly uncooked
fruit and veg dishes. Mains
£10–12.

### SWEET & SPICY

40 Brick Lane ⊖ Aldgate East. Daily
8am–10.30pm. MAP P.102, POCKET MAP O5

Very basic self-service
Bangladeshi café decorated
with pictures of wrestlers,
dishing out cheap hot curries
with a minimum of fuss.

### TAYYAB'S

83–89 Fieldgate St ⊖ Whitechapel
☏ 020/7247 9543. Daily 5–11.30pm.
MAP P.102

This smart place has been
serving good, freshly cooked,
straightforward Pakistani fare
for over thirty years. Prices
remain low, booking is essential
and service is speedy and slick.
Unlicenced but BYOB. Mains
£6–10.

### VIET HOA CAFÉ

72–74 Kingsland Rd ⊖ Hoxton Overground.
Mon–Fri noon–3.30pm & 5.30–midnight, Sat
& Sun 12.30pm–midnight. MAP P.102,
POCKET MAP O3

Large, chaotic Vietnamese café
in a street heaving with similar
places. Big portions and lots of
spicy noodle soups to choose
from.

# Pubs and bars

### CALLOOH CALLAY

65 Rivington St ⊖ Old Street. Mon–Wed
5–11pm, Thurs noon–11pm, Fri noon–1am,
Sat 6pm–1am, Sun 6–11pm. MAP P.102,
POCKET MAP N4

Hidden away off Shoreditch
High Street, this Jabberwocky-
inspired camp-kitsch bar
has a Narnia-style wardrobe
separating its wacky rooms.
Cocktails and wines are the
drinks of choice.

### CHARLIE WRIGHT'S INTERNATIONAL BAR

45 Pitfield St ⊖ Old Street. Mon–Wed
noon–1am, Thurs & Fri noon–4am, Sat
5pm–1am, Sun 5pm–2am. MAP P.102,
POCKET MAP N4

Part of old-style – rather than
trendy – Hoxton, this convivial
bar-club, serving decent Thai
food, has regular jazz nights
and a useful late licence.

CALLOOH CALLAY

### LOUNGELOVER

1 Whitby St ⬿ Shoreditch High Street Overground ⓦ www.lestroisgarcons .com. Mon–Thurs & Sun 6pm–midnight, Fri 5.30pm–1am, Sat 6pm–1am. MAP P.102, POCKET MAP 04

Behind the unprepossessing facade of this former meat-packing factory lies a bizarre array of opulently camp bric-à-brac, expertly slung together to create an extraordinary-looking and unique cocktail bar. Booking is essential, even just for a drink.

### WATER POET

9 Folgate St ⬿ Liverpool Street. Mon–Fri 11am–11pm, Sat noon–10.30pm. MAP P.102, POCKET MAP 05

Large, appealingly unorthodox pub with big bay windows, deep leather sofas and Dali-esque decor, but also a side bar with Sky TV, and a tidy little pool room with two tables. Lovely beer garden, too.

# Clubs and venues

### 333/MOTHER

333 Old St ⬿ Old Street ☎ 020/7739 5949, ⓦ www.333mother.com. MAP P.102, POCKET MAP N4

Dressed down Hoxton space combining two venues: *Mother* and the *333*, each spinning drum'n'bass, breakbeats and solid, skuzzy four/four, with *Mother* playing poppier material during the week.

### BAR MUSIC HALL

134 Curtain Rd ⬿ Old Street ☎ 020/7729 7216, ⓦ www.barmusichall.com. MAP P.102, POCKET MAP N4

Free to get in – although you'll have to queue – this draws wild club kids for electro, filthy disco and live electronica.

CARGO

### CARGO

83 Rivington St ⬿ Old Street ☎ 020/7739 3440, ⓦ www.cargo-london.com. Mon–Thurs 6pm–1am, Fri & Sat 6pm–3am, Sun 6pm–midnight. MAP P.102, POCKET MAP N4

Small and groovy venue in what was once a railway arch. Hosts a variety of live acts, including jazz, hip-hop, indie and folk, and an excellent line-up of club nights.

### COMEDY CAFÉ

66 Rivington St ⬿ Old Street ☎ 020/7739 5706, ⓦ www.comedycafe.co.uk. Wed–Sat. MAP P.102, POCKET MAP N4

Long-established, purpose-built club, often with impressive line-ups, and free admission for the new-acts slot on Wednesday nights.

### HERBAL

10–14 Kingsland Rd ⬿ Hoxton Overground ☎ 020/7613 4462, ⓦ www.herbaluk.com. MAP P.102, POCKET MAP 04

Intimate venue, with a cool New York style loft and sweaty ground-floor club – a great place to check out drum 'n' bass, breaks, dirty house and electro.

# The Tower and Docklands

One of the city's main tourist attractions, the Tower of London was the site of some of the goriest events in the nation's history, and is somewhere all visitors should try and get to see. Immediately to the east are the remains of what was the largest enclosed cargo-dock system in the world, built in the nineteenth century to cope with the huge volume of goods shipped in along the Thames from all over the Empire. No one thought the area could be rejuvenated when the docks closed in the 1960s, but since the Eighties, warehouses have been converted into luxury flats, waterside penthouse apartments have been built and a huge high-rise office development has sprung up around Canary Wharf.

## TOWER OF LONDON

⊖ Tower Hill ☎ 0844/482 7777, ⓦ www.hrp.org.uk. March–Oct Mon & Sun 10am–5.30pm, Tues–Sat 9am–5.30pm; Nov–Feb Mon & Sun 10am–5pm, Tues–Sat 9am–5pm. £17. MAP PP.110–111, POCKET MAP O7

One of the most perfectly preserved medieval fortresses in the country, the Tower of London sits beside the Thames surrounded by a wide, dry moat. Begun by William the Conqueror, the Tower is chiefly famous as a place of imprisonment and death, though it has been used variously as a royal residence, armoury, mint, menagerie, observatory and – a function it still serves – a safe-deposit box for the Crown Jewels. Before you set off, join one of the free guided tours, given by the Tower's **Beefeaters** (officially known as Yeoman Warders). As well as giving a good introduction to the history, these ex-servicemen relish hamming up the gory stories.

Visitors today enter the Tower along Water Lane, but in times gone by most prisoners were delivered through **Traitors' Gate**, on the waterfront. The nearby **Bloody Tower** saw the murders of 12-year-old Edward V and his 10-year-old brother, and was used to imprison Walter Raleigh on three separate occasions.

The central **White Tower** is the original "Tower", begun in 1076. Now home to part of the Royal Armouries, it's worth visiting if only for the beautiful Norman Chapel of St John, on

BEEFEATER, TOWER OF LONDON

the second floor. To the west of the White Tower is the execution spot on **Tower Green** where seven highly placed but unlucky individuals were beheaded, among them Henry VIII's second and fifth wives.

The **Crown Jewels** are the major reason so many people flock to the Tower, but the moving walkways which take you past the loot are disappointingly swift, allowing you just 28 seconds' viewing during peak periods. The oldest piece of regalia is the twelfth-century Anointing Spoon, but the vast majority of exhibits, including the Imperial State Crown, postdate the Commonwealth (1649–60). Among the jewels are the three largest cut diamonds in the world, including the legendary Koh-i-Noor, set into the Queen Mother's Crown in 1937.

### TOWER BRIDGE

🚇 Tower Hill 📞 020/7403 3761. 🌐 www .towerbridge.org.uk. Daily: April–Sept 10am–6.30pm; Oct–March 9.30am–6pm. £6. MAP PP.110–111, POCKET MAP Q7

Tower Bridge ranks with Big Ben as the most famous of all London landmarks. Completed in 1894, its Neo-Gothic towers are clad in Cornish granite and Portland stone, but conceal a

## Docklands Light Railway

The best way to visit Docklands is to take the Docklands Light Railway or **DLR** (📞 020/7363 9700, 🌐 www.tfl.gov.uk/dlr), whose driverless trains run on overhead tracks, and give out great views over the cityscape. DLR trains set off from Bank tube and from Tower Gateway, close to Tower Hill tube and the Tower of London.

steel frame which, at the time, represented a considerable engineering achievement. The **raising of the bascules** (from the French for "see-saw") remains an impressive sight – phone ahead to find out when the bridge is opening (📞 020/7940 3984). It's free to walk across the bridge, but you must pay to gain access to the **elevated walkways** linking the summits of the towers – closed from 1909 to 1982 due to their popularity with prostitutes and the suicidal. The views are pretty good and you get to visit the **Engine Room** on the south side of the bridge, where you can see the giant, and now defunct, coal-fired boilers and play some interactive engineering games.

TOWER BRIDGE

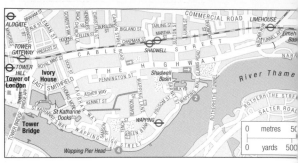

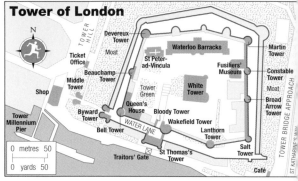

## Tower of London

## ST KATHARINE DOCKS

⊖ Tower Hill. MAP PP.110–111, POCKET MAP 07

Built in the late 1820s to relieve the congestion on the River Thames, St Katharine Docks were originally surrounded by high walls to protect the warehouses used to store luxury goods – ivory, spices, carpets and cigars – shipped in from all over the Empire. Nowadays, the docks are used as an upmarket marina, and the old warehouses house shops, pubs and restaurants. More interesting, however, are the old **swing bridges** over the basins (including one from 1828), the boats themselves – you'll often see beautiful old sailing ships and Dutch barges

ST KATHARINE DOCKS

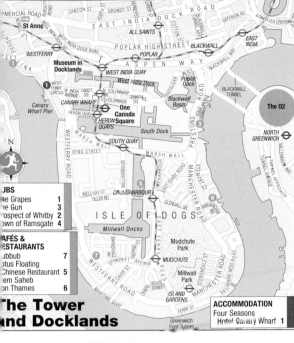

**PUBS**

The Grapes 1
The Gun 3
Prospect of Whitby 2
Town of Ramsgate 4

**CAFÉS & RESTAURANTS**

Hubbub 7
Lotus Floating 
Chinese Restaurant 5
Em Saheb 
on Thames 6

# The Tower and Docklands

– and the attractive **Ivory House** warehouse, with its clock tower, at the centre of the three basins. At its peak this warehouse received over 200 tons of ivory annually.

## WAPPING HIGH STREET

Wapping Overground. MAP PP.110–111.
Once famous for its boatyards and its three dozen riverside pubs, Wapping's Victorian atmosphere has been preserved, and as it lies just a short walk east of the Tower, this is easily the most satisfying part of Docklands to explore. Halfway along Wapping High Street is **Wapping Pier Head**, the former entrance to the London Docks, flanked by grand, curvaceous Regency terraces. Here, you'll find one of the few surviving stairs down to the river beside the **Town of Ramsgate** pub; beneath the

pub are the dungeons where convicts were chained before being deported to Australia. It was also at the *Town of Ramsgate* that "Hanging" Judge Jeffreys was captured trying to escape disguised as a collier following the victory of William of Orange in 1688.

## ST ANNE'S CHURCH

5 Newell St Westferry DLR. MAP PP.110–111.
Designed in 1714 by Nicholas Hawksmoor, and dominated by a gargantuan west tower, St Anne's boasts the highest church clock in London. Inside is a superb organ built for the Great Exhibition in 1851. In the graveyard Hawksmoor erected a pyramidal structure carved with masonic symbols, now hopelessly eroded; opposite is a war memorial with relief panels depicting the horrors of trench warfare.

## CANARY WHARF

⊖ Canary Wharf & DLR. MAP PP.110–111

The geographical and ideological heart of the new **Docklands** is Canary Wharf, once a destination for bananas (from the Canary Islands – hence the name). Now a business district, this is the one Docklands area that you can happily stroll around, taking in the architecture, looking out for the tongue-in-cheek sculptures, and having a drink overlooking one of the old wharves. Canary Wharf's name is, of course, synonymous with Cesar Pelli's landmark tower, officially known as **One Canada Square**. Britain's tallest building (for the moment) and the first skyscraper anywhere to be clad in stainless steel, it's an undeniably impressive sight, both close-up and from a distance.

## MUSEUM IN DOCKLANDS

West India Quay ⊖ West India Quay ☏ 0870/444 6856, ⓦ www.museumin docklands.org.uk. Daily 10am–6pm. £5. MAP PP.110–111

The last surviving Georgian warehouses of the West India Docks lie on the far side of a floodlit floating bridge at **West India Quay**. Amidst the dockside bars and restaurants, you'll find Warehouse No. 1, built in 1803 for storing rum,

sugar, molasses, coffee and cotton, and now home to the Museum in Docklands. Spread over several floors, the museum's exhibits chart the history of London's docks on both sides of the river from Roman times to the present day. Highlights include a model of old London Bridge, one side depicting it in 1440, the other around 1600; an eight-foot long watercolour showing the "legal quays" in the 1790s, just before the enclosed docks eased congestion; and a reconstructed warren of late nineteenth-century shops and cobbled dockland streets. Those with kids should head for Mudlarks, on the ground floor, where children can learn a bit about pulleys and ballast, drive a DLR train or simply romp around the soft play area.

## THE DOME

⊖ North Greenwich. MAP PP.110–111

Clearly visible from the east bank of the Isle of Dogs, the Dome, or **O2** as it's now known (ⓦ www.theo2.co.uk) is a 23,000-seat events arena, designed by Richard Rogers for the millennium celebrations. Over half a mile in circumference, 160ft in height and held up by a dozen, 300ft-tall yellow steel masts, it's the largest of its kind in the world.

# Cafés and restaurants

### HUBBUB

269 Westferry Rd ⊖ Mudchute DLR. Mon–Wed noon–11pm, Thurs & Fri noon–midnight, Sat 10am–midnight, Sun 10am–10.30pm.
MAP PP.110–111

A real oasis in the Docklands desert, this café-bar is housed in a former church, now arts centre, and does decent fry ups, sandwiches and tapas.

### LOTUS FLOATING CHINESE RESTAURANT

38 Limeharbour ⊖ Crossharbour DLR
☎ 020/7515 6445. Daily noon–10.30pm.
MAP PP.110–111

This floating Chinese restaurant moored in Millwall Docks specializes in steaming hot fresh dim sum (£2–3.50). Mains £5–12.

### MEM SAHEB ON THAMES

65–67 Amsterdam Rd ⊖ Crossharbour DLR
☎ 020/7538 3008. Mon–Fri noon–2.30pm & 6–11.30pm, Sat & Sun 6–11.30pm.
MAP PP.110–111

Decent riverside Indian restaurant a short walk from the business area of Docklands, with a superb view over the river. Mains £6–12.

# Pubs

### THE GRAPES

76 Narrow St ⊖ Westferry DLR. Mon–Fri noon–3.30pm & 5.30–11pm, Sat noon–11pm, Sun noon–10.30pm. MAP PP.110–111

A lovely, narrow little pub on a quiet street, with lots of seafaring paraphernalia and a great riverside balcony out back. The ales are good and there's an expensive fish restaurant upstairs.

HUBBUB

### THE GUN

27 Coldharbour ⊖ Canary Wharf or South Quay or Blackwall DLR. Mon–Sat 11am–midnight, Sun 11am–11pm. MAP PP.110–111

Legendary dockers' pub, once the haunt of Lord Nelson, and now a classy gastropub. Its cosy back bar has a couple of snugs, and the outside deck offers an unrivalled view of the Dome.

### PROSPECT OF WHITBY

57 Wapping Wall ⊖ Wapping Overground. Mon–Sat noon–11pm, Sun noon–10.30pm.
MAP PP.110–111

Steeped in history, this is London's most famous riverside pub, with a pewter bar, flagstone floor, ancient timber beams and stacks of maritime memorabilia. Decent beers and terrific views too.

### TOWN OF RAMSGATE

62 Wapping High St ⊖ Wapping Overground. Mon–Sat noon–midnight, Sun noon–10.30pm.
MAP PP.110–111

Dark, narrow, medieval pub located by Wapping Old Stairs, which once led down to Execution Dock. Admiral Bligh and Fletcher Christian were regular drinking partners here in pre-mutiny days.

# South Bank and around

The South Bank has a lot going for it. As well as the massive waterside arts centre, it's home to a host of tourist attractions including the enormously popular London Eye. With most of London's key sights sitting on the north bank of the Thames, the views from here are the best on the river, and thanks to the wide, traffic-free riverside boulevard, the whole area can be happily explored on foot. And a short walk from the South Bank lie one or two lesser-known but nonetheless absorbing sights such as the Imperial War Museum, which contains the country's only permanent exhibition devoted to the Holocaust.

## SOUTHBANK CENTRE

⊖ Waterloo. MAP P.114, POCKET MAP J17

The Southbank Centre is home to a whole variety of artistic institutions, the most attractive of which is the **Royal Festival Hall**, built in 1951 for the Festival of Britain and one of London's chief concert venues. Even the centre's most architecturally depressing parts are softened by their riverside location, the avenue of trees, fluttering banners, occasional buskers and skateboarders, and the weekend secondhand bookstalls outside the nearby **BFI Southbank**, the city's chief arts cinema. It also runs

**Mediathèque** (Tues–Sun 11am–8pm; free), where you can settle into one of the viewing stations and choose from a selective archive of British films, TV programmes and documentaries. For more on the venues within the Southbank Centre see the "Venues" listings on p.119.

## NATIONAL THEATRE

⊖ Waterloo. MAP P.114, POCKET MAP K17

Looking like a multistorey car park, the National Theatre is an institution first mooted in 1848 but sadly only realized in 1976. It has received endless flak for its architecture, but the three

SOUTH BANK FROM HUNGERFORD BRIDGE

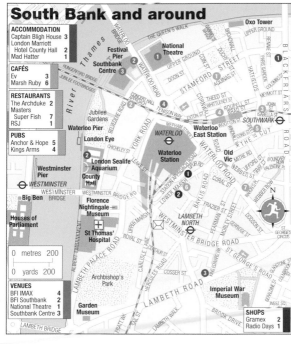

# South Bank and around

**ACCOMMODATION**
Captain Bligh House 3
London Marriott
Hotel County Hall 2
Mad Hatter 1

**CAFÉS**
Ev 3
Marsh Ruby 6

**RESTAURANTS**
The Archduke 2
Masters
Super Fish 7
RSJ 1

**PUBS**
Anchor & Hope 5
Kings Arms 4

**VENUES**
BFI IMAX 4
BFI Southbank 2
National Theatre 1
Southbank Centre 3

**SHOPS**
Gramex 2
Radio Days 1

---

auditoriums within are superb and can be visited on excellent **backstage tours** (1hr 15min; £6; ☎020/7452 3400), for which you should book in advance.

## OXO TOWER

⊖ Southwark. MAP P.114, POCKET MAP L7

The Oxo Tower started life as a Victorian power station before being converted in the 1930s into a meat-packing factory for the company that makes Oxo stock cubes – the lettering is spelt out in the windows of the main tower. The building now contains an **exhibition space** on the ground floor (Tues- Sun 11am- 6pm), plus flats for local residents, sandwiched between a series of retail workshops for designers on the first and second floors, and a swanky restaurant, bar and brasserie on the top floor. To enjoy the view,

you don't need to eat or drink here, however: you can simply take the lift to the eighth-floor **public viewing gallery** (daily 10am–10pm).

## LONDON EYE

⊖ Waterloo or Westminster ☎ 0870/500 0600, ⓦ www.ba-londoneye.com. Daily: May, June & Sept 10am–9pm; July & Aug 10am–9.30pm; Oct–April 10am–8pm. £17. MAP P.114, POCKET MAP J18

The London Eye is now one of the city's most famous landmarks. Standing an impressive 443ft high, it's the largest **Ferris wheel** in Europe, weighing over 2000 tonnes, yet as simple and delicate as a bicycle wheel. It's constantly in slow motion, which means a full-circle "flight" in one of its 32 pods should take around thirty minutes – that may seem a long time, but in fact it passes incredibly quickly. Book in advance (and online to save money) as on arrival you'll still have to queue to be loaded on.

## COUNTY HALL

⊖ Waterloo or Westminster. MAP P.114, POCKET MAP J18

The colonnaded crescent of County Hall is the only truly monumental building on the South Bank. Designed to house the now defunct London

County Council, it was completed in 1933 and enjoyed its greatest moment of fame as headquarters of the **Greater London Council**, which was abolished by Margaret Thatcher in 1986 leaving London as the only European city without an elected authority for the next sixteen years. Now in the hands of a Japanese property company, County Hall currently houses several hotels, restaurants, an amusement arcade and a bizarre clutch of tourist attractions.

## LONDON SEALIFE AQUARIUM

County Hall, Riverside Walk ⊖ Waterloo or Westminster ☎ 0871/663 1678, ⓦ www.sealife.co.uk. Mon–Fri 10am–6pm, Sat & Sun 10am–7pm. £16. MAP P.114, POCKET MAP J18

The most popular attraction in County Hall is the London Aquarium, laid out on two subterranean levels. With some super-large tanks, and everything from dog-face puffers and piranhas to robot fish (seriously), this is an attraction that's pretty much guaranteed to please kids. The Touch Pool, where children can stroke the (non-sting) rays, is particularly popular. Impressive in scale, the aquarium also has a walk-through underwater tunnel. Ask at the main desk for the times of the daily presentations.

## FLORENCE NIGHTINGALE MUSEUM

Lambeth Palace Road ⊖ Waterloo or Westminster ☎ 020/7620 0374, ⓦ www.florence-nightingale.co.uk. Daily 10am–5pm; £5.80. MAP P.114, POCKET MAP J19

Hidden among the outbuildings of **St Thomas' Hospital**, the Florence Nightingale Museum celebrates the devout woman who revolutionized the nursing profession by establishing the first school of nursing at

COUNTY HALL

IMPERIAL WAR MUSEUM

St Thomas' in 1860 and publishing her *Notes on Nursing*, which emphasized the importance of hygiene, decorum and discipline. The exhibition hits just the right note by putting the two years she spent in Istanbul during the Crimean War in the context of a lifetime of tireless social campaigning. Exhibits include the white lantern that earned her the nickname "The Lady with the Lamp"; Athena, her stuffed pet owl, and a long overdue section on the remarkable **Mary Seacole**, the Jamaican nurse who nursed soldiers in the Crimea itself.

## GARDEN MUSEUM

Lambeth Palace Rd ⊖ Westminster or Lambeth North ☎ 020/7402 8865, ⓦ www .gardenmuseum.org.uk. Daily 10.30am–5pm. £6. MAP P.114, POCKET MAP J9

Housed in the former church of **St Mary-at-Lambeth**, this unpretentious museum puts on excellent exhibitions on a horticultural theme in the ground floor galleries, and has a small permanent exhibition in the belvedere, reached by a new wooden staircase. Two interesting sarcophagi lurk among the foliage of the small

graveyard: one belongs to Captain Bligh, the commander of the *Bounty*; more unusual is the memorial to John Tradescant, gardener to James I and Charles I, depicting, among other things, a seven-headed griffin and several crocodiles.

## IMPERIAL WAR MUSEUM

Lambeth Rd ⊖ Lambeth North ⓦ www.iwm .org.uk. Daily 10am–6pm. Free. MAP P.114, POCKET MAP L9

Housed in a domed building that was, until 1930, the central portion of the infamous "Bedlam" lunatic asylum, the Imperial War Museum holds by far the best collection of militaria in the capital. The treatment of the subject matter is impressively wide-ranging and fairly sober, with the main hall's militaristic display of guns, tanks and fighter planes offset by the lower-ground-floor array of documents and images attesting to the human damage of the last century of war. In addition to the static displays, there's a walk-through **World War I trench** and a re-creation of the Blitz, in which you can wander through bomb-ravaged streets. One of the most popular exhibits is the perfectly re-created **1940s House**, a typical two-storey terraced house complete with Morrison shelter in the dining room. Entered from the third floor, the harrowing **Holocaust Exhibition** (not recommended for children under 14) pulls few punches, and has made a valiant attempt to avoid depicting the victims of the Holocaust as nameless masses by focusing on individual cases, interspersing the archive footage with eyewitness accounts from contemporary survivors.

# Shops

## GRAMEX

25 Lower Marsh ⊖ Waterloo. Mon–Sat
11am–7pm. MAP P.114, POCKET MAP K19

This new and second-hand
record store features classical
CDs and vinyl, with some jazz,
and comfy leather armchairs to
sample or discuss your finds
at leisure.

## RADIO DAYS

87 Lower Marsh ⊖ Waterloo. Mon–Sat
10am–6pm (Fri until 7pm). MAP P.114,
POCKET MAP K19

Fantastic collection of
memorabilia and accessories
from the 1930s to the 1970s,
including shoes, shot-glass
collections, cosmetics, vintage
magazines and clothes.

# Cafés

## EV

97–99 Isabella St ⊖ Southwark. Mon–Sat
noon–11.30pm, Sun noon–10.30pm. MAP P.114,
POCKET MAP L7

*Ev* is a busy, buzzy Turkish
enterprise with a lovely
spacious garden terrace. You
can choose between snacking
in the deli or going for the
full-on restaurant.

## MARSH RUBY

30 Lower Marsh ⊖ Waterloo. Mon–Fri
11.30am–3pm. MAP P.114, POCKET MAP K19

Terrific, filling lunchtime
curries for under a fiver: the
food is organic/free range and
there's a basic but cheery
communal dining area at
the back.

# Restaurants

## THE ARCHDUKE

Concert Hall Approach ⊖ Waterloo
☏ 020/7928 9370. Mon–Thurs 11am–
midnight, Fri & Sat 11am–1.30am. MAP P.114,
POCKET MAP J17

A smart modern bar-restaurant
on two levels, tucked
underneath the railway arches
near the Southbank Centre.
The menu is meaty, masculine
and modern British and there's
live jazz in the evening. Mains
£10–20.

## MASTERS SUPER FISH

191 Waterloo Rd ⊖ Waterloo ☏ 020/7928
6924. Mon 5.30–10.30pm, Tues–Sat
noon–3pm & 4.30–10.30pm. MAP P.114,
POCKET MAP L8

An old-fashioned,
unpretentious fish and chip
restaurant, which serves up
huge portions with all the
trimmings: gherkins, pickled
onions, coleslaw and a few
complimentary prawns.
Mains £7–13.

## RSJ

13a Coin St ⊖ Waterloo ☏ 020/7928 4554.
Mon–Fri noon–2.30pm & 5.30–11pm, Sat
5.30–11pm. MAP P.114, POCKET MAP K17

Regularly high standards of
Anglo-French cooking make
this a good spot for a meal after
or before an evening at a South
Bank theatre or concert hall.
Mains £11–19.

ANCHOR & HOPE

# Pubs

## ANCHOR & HOPE

36 The Cut ⊖ Southwark. Mon 5–11pm,
Tues–Sat 11am–11pm, Sun 12.30–5pm.
MAP P.114, POCKET MAP L8

Gastropub that dishes up truly
excellent, yet simple grub:
soups, salads and mains such as
slow-cooked pork with
choucroute, as well as
mouthwatering puds. You can't
book a table so the bar is
basically the waiting room.

## KINGS ARMS

25 Roupell St ⊖ Waterloo. Mon–Sat
11am–11pm, Sun noon–10.30pm. MAP P.114,
POCKET MAP K8

Terrific local on a quiet
Victorian terraced street: the
front part is a traditional
drinking area, while the
tastefully cluttered rear is a
glass and wood conservatory-
style space, featuring a large
open fire. Thai food.

# Venues

## BFI IMAX

South Bank ⊖ Waterloo ☎ 0870/787 2525,
ⓦ www.bfi.org.uk. MAP P.114, POCKET MAP K17

Remarkable glazed drum
housing Europe's largest
screen, showing 2D and 3D
films, but like all IMAX
cinemas it suffers from the fact
that very few movies are shot
on 70mm film.

## BFI SOUTHBANK

South Bank ⊖ Waterloo ☎ 020/7928 3232,
ⓦ www.bfi.org.uk. MAP P.114, POCKET MAP K17

Known for its attentive
audiences and an exhaustive,
eclectic programme that
includes directors' seasons and
thematic series. Around six
films daily are shown in the
vast NFT1 and the smaller
NFT2 and NFT3.

THE KINGS ARMS

## NATIONAL THEATRE

South Bank ⊖ Waterloo ☎ 020/7452 3000,
ⓦ www.nationaltheatre.org.uk. MAP P.114,
POCKET MAP K17

The NT consists of three
separate theatres – the
1100-seater Olivier, the
proscenium-arched Lyttelton
and the experimental Cottesloe
– and puts on a programme
ranging from Greek tragedies
to Broadway musicals. Some
productions sell out months in
advance, but £10 day seats go
on sale at 9.30am on the
morning of each performance
– get there by 8am for the
popular shows.

## SOUTHBANK CENTRE

South Bank ⊖ Waterloo ☎ 0871/663 2500,
ⓦ www.southbankcentre.co.uk. MAP P.114,
POCKET MAP J17

The SBC has three concert
venues. The gargantuan Royal
Festival Hall (RFH) is
tailor-made for large-scale
choral and orchestral works,
and is home to the
Philharmonia and the London
Philharmonic. The lugubrious
Queen Elizabeth Hall (QEH) is
used for chamber concerts, solo
recitals and contemporary
work, while the Purcell Room
is the most intimate venue.

# Bankside and Southwark

In Tudor and Stuart London, the chief reason for crossing the Thames to Southwark was to visit the then disreputable Bankside entertainment district around the south end of London Bridge. Four hundred years on, Londoners have rediscovered the area, thanks to wholesale regeneration that has engendered a wealth of new attractions along the riverside between Blackfriars and Tower bridges and beyond – with the charge led by the mighty Tate Modern. And with a traffic-free, riverside path connecting most of the sights, this is easily one of the most enjoyable areas of London in which to hang out.

## MILLENNIUM BRIDGE

⊖ Southwark. MAP PP.122–123, POCKET MAP L6-L7
The first new bridge to be built across the Thames since Tower Bridge opened in 1894, the sleek, stainless-steel Millennium Bridge is London's sole pedestrian-only river crossing. A suspension bridge of innovative design, it famously bounced up and down when it first opened and had to be closed immediately for another two years for repairs. It still wobbles a bit, but most people are too busy enjoying the spectacular views across to St Paul's Cathedral and Tate Modern to notice.

## TATE MODERN

Bankside ⊖ Southwark ☎ 020/7887 8008, ⓦ www.tate.org.uk. Daily 10am–6pm (Fri & Sat until 10pm). Free. MAP PP.122–123, POCKET MAP L7
Bankside is dominated by the austere power station transformed by the Swiss duo Herzog & de Meuron into Tate Modern, where the Tate shows off its vast collection of international twentieth-century art. The best way to enter is down the ramp from the west, so you get the full effect of the stupendously large **turbine hall**, used to display one huge, mind-blowing installation. Given that Tate Modern is the

TATE MODERN

world's largest modern art gallery, you need to devote the best part of a day to do it justice – or be very selective. It's easy enough to find your way around: pick up a plan (and, for an extra £2, an audioguide), and take the escalator to level 3. This, and level 5, display the **permanent collection**; level 4 is used for fee-paying temporary exhibitions, and level 7 has a rooftop café with a great view over the Thames.

The curators have eschewed the usual chronological approach and gone instead for hanging (and rehanging) works according to -isms. On the whole this works very well, though the early twentieth-century canvases, in their gilded frames, do struggle when made to compete with the attention-grabbing conceptual stuff.

Although the displays change every six months or so, you're still pretty much guaranteed to see at least some works by **Monet** and Bonnard, Modigliani, Cubist pioneers **Picasso** and Braque, Surrealists such as **Dalí**, abstract artists like **Mondrian**, Bridget Riley and Jackson Pollock, and Pop supremos **Warhol** and Lichtenstein. There are seminal works such as a replica of the **Duchamp**'s urinal entitled *Fountain* and signed "R. Mutt", Yves Klein's totally blue paintings, and Carl André's infamous "Bricks" (officially entitled *Equivalent VIII*). And such is the space here that several artists get whole rooms to themselves, among them **Joseph Beuys** and his shamanistic wax and furs, and **Mark Rothko**, whose abstract *Seagram Murals*, originally destined for a posh restaurant in New York, have their own shrine-like room in the heart of the collection. There's usually a few surprises, too, such as sections on Soviet graphics or Vienna's violent *Aktionismus* movement, plus plenty of video installations by contemporary artists. You'll also find quite a bit of overlap with Tate Britain, with works by British artists such as Stanley Spencer, Francis Bacon, David Hockney, Barbara Hepworth, Henry Moore and Lucian Freud.

## Tate to Tate

The **Tate Boat** shuttles between Tate Britain and Tate Modern every forty minutes; journey time is twenty minutes (£5).

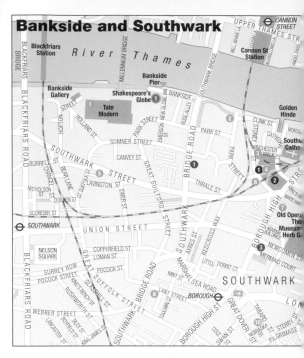

# Bankside and Southwark

## SHAKESPEARE'S GLOBE THEATRE

21 New Globe Walk ⊖ Southwark or London Bridge ☎ 020/7902 1400, ⓦ www
.shakespeares-globe.org. Daily: mid-April to mid-Sept 9am–noon & 12.30–5pm; mid-Oct to mid-April 10am–5pm. Exhibition £10.50. MAP PP.122–123, POCKET MAP M7

Dwarfed by the Tate Modern, but equally remarkable in its own way, Shakespeare's Globe Theatre is a more or less faithful reconstruction of the polygonal playhouse where most of the Bard's later works were first performed. Sporting the first new thatched roof in central London since the 1666 Great Fire, the theatre puts on plays (May–Sept) by Shakespeare and his contemporaries (see p.127). To find out more about Shakespeare and Bankside, visit the Globe's stylish **exhibition**, whose imaginative hands-on displays really hit the spot.

Visitors also get taken on an informative half-hour **guided tour** round the theatre itself, except in the afternoons during the summer season, when you can only visit the exhibition (for a reduced fee).

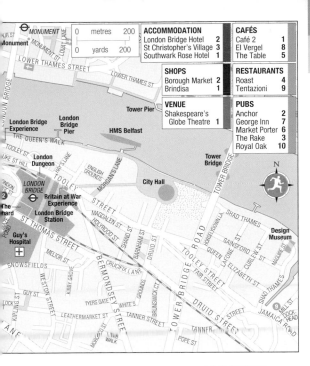

| ACCOMMODATION | | CAFÉS | |
|---|---|---|---|
| London Bridge Hotel | 2 | Café 2 | 1 |
| St Christopher's Village | 3 | El Vergel | 8 |
| Southwark Rose Hotel | 1 | The Table | 5 |

| SHOPS | | RESTAURANTS | |
|---|---|---|---|
| Borough Market | 2 | Roast | 4 |
| Brindisa | 1 | Tentazioni | 9 |

| VENUE | | PUBS | |
|---|---|---|---|
| Shakespeare's Globe Theatre | 1 | Anchor | 2 |
| | | George Inn | 7 |
| | | Market Porter | 6 |
| | | The Rake | 3 |
| | | Royal Oak | 10 |

## GOLDEN HINDE

St Mary Overie Dock, Cathedral St
⊖ London Bridge ☎ 020/7403 0123.
Ⓦ www.goldenhinde.com. Mon–Sat
10am–5.30pm. £6. MAP PP.122–123.
POCKET MAP M7

An exact replica of the galleon in which **Francis Drake** sailed around the world from 1577 to 1580, this modern version of the *Golden Hinde* circumnavigated the globe for some twenty years before eventually settling permanently in Southwark. The ship is surprisingly small, and its original crew of eighty-plus must have been cramped to say the least. There's a lack of interpretive panels, so it's worth booking yourself on a guided tour, during which costumed guides show you the ropes, so to speak, and demonstrate activities such as firing a cannon or using the ship's toilet.

## SOUTHWARK CATHEDRAL

Cathedral St ⊖ London Bridge ☎ 020/7367
6700, Ⓦ www.southwark.anglican.org
/cathedral. Mon–Fri 7.30am–6pm, Sat & Sun
8.30am–6pm. Free. MAP PP.122–123.
POCKET MAP M7

Of the original thirteenth-century Augustinian priory church of St Mary Overie, only the choir and retrochoir now remain, separated by a tall and beautiful stone Tudor screen; they're thought to be the oldest Gothic structures left in London. The nave was rebuilt in the nineteenth century, but the cathedral contains numerous interesting monuments, from a thirteenth-century oak effigy of a knight to an early twentieth-century memorial to Shakespeare (his brother is buried here). Above the memorial is a stained-glass window featuring a whole cast of characters from the plays.

123

## OLD OPERATING THEATRE, MUSEUM AND HERB GARRET

9a St Thomas St ⊖ London Bridge
☎ 020/7188 2679, ⓦ www.thegarret.org.uk.
Daily 10.30am–5pm. £5.60. MAP PP.122–123,
POCKET MAP N7

By far the most educational – and strangest – of Southwark's museums, the Old Operating Theatre is as stomach-churning as the London Dungeon, despite being entirely gore-free. Visitors must climb up to the attic of a former church tower, which houses an old hospital **apothecary**, with displays explaining the painful truth about pre-anaesthetic operations. These took place in the adjacent women's **operating theatre**, designed in 1821 "in the round", literally like a theatre, so that students (and members of high society) could view the proceedings. The surgeons had to concentrate on speed and accuracy (most amputations took less than a minute), but there was still a thirty percent mortality rate, with many patients simply dying of shock, and many more from bacterial infection, about which very little was known.

## LONDON DUNGEON

28–34 Tooley St ⊖ London Bridge
☎ 020/7403 7221, ⓦ www.thedungeons
.com. Daily: March to mid-July & Sep–Oct 10am–5.30pm; mid-July to Aug 9.30am–7.30pm; Nov–March 10.30am–5pm.
£17 online, £22 on the door. MAP PP.122–123,
POCKET MAP N7

Young teenagers and the credulous probably get the most out of the life-sized waxwork tableaux of folk being hanged, drawn, quartered and tortured, the general hysteria being boosted by actors dressed in period garb. Visitors are led into the labyrinth, an old-fashioned mirror maze, before being herded through a series of live-action scenarios, starting with an eighteenth-century courtroom, passing through the exploitative "Jack the Ripper Experience" and ending with a walk through a revolving tunnel of flames.

## LONDON BRIDGE EXPERIENCE

2–4 Tooley St ⊖ London Bridge ☎ 020/7403
7221, ⓦ www.thelondonbridgeexperience.com.
Mon–Fri 10am–5pm; Sat & Sun 10am–6pm.
£17 online, £22 on the door. MAP PP.122–123,
POCKET MAP N7

This place is divided into two sections. The first part tells the story of the construction of old London Bridge, which used to have houses all the way along its length. Special effects and live actors are used to try and sex up the whole affair. The aim of the second section – the London Tombs – is to whip up the same sort of Gothic horror hysterics as the London Dungeon.

## BRITAIN AT WAR EXPERIENCE

64–66 Tooley St ⊖ London Bridge
☎ 020/7403 3171, ⓦ www.britainatwar
.co.uk. Daily: April–Oct 10am–5pm;
Nov–March 10am–4.30pm. £11.45.
MAP PP.122–123, POCKET MAP N7

HMS BELFAST

CITY HALL

For an illuminating insight into London's stiff-upper-lip mentality during the World War II Blitz, head for Winston Churchill's Britain at War Exhibition, where you'll find hundreds of fascinating wartime artefacts, from ration books to babies' gas masks. You can sit in darkness in an Anderson shelter, hear the chilling sound of the V1 "doodlebugs" and tune in to contemporary radio broadcasts. The final set piece is a walk through the chaos of a just-bombed street.

## HMS BELFAST

Morgan's Lane, Tooley St ⊖ London Bridge ☎ 020/7940 6300, Ⓦ hmsbelfast.iwm.org.uk. Daily: March–Oct 10am–6pm; Nov–Feb 10am–5pm. £10.70. MAP PP.122–123, POCKET MAP N7

An 11,550-ton **Royal Navy cruiser**, HMS *Belfast* saw action both in World War II and in the Korean War, and has been permanently moored on the Thames since 1971. The most enjoyable aspect of a visit is exploring the maze of cabins and scrambling up and down the vertiginous ladders. If you want to know more about the ship's history, head for the Exhibition Flat in Zone 5; in the adjacent Life at Sea room, you can practise your Morse code and knots and listen to accounts of naval life on board.

## CITY HALL

The Queen's Walk ⊖ London Bridge or Tower Hill ☎ 020/7983 4000, Ⓦ www .london.gov.uk. Mon–Fri 8am–8pm, plus occasional weekends. Free. MAP PP.122–123, POCKET MAP N7

Bearing a striking resemblance to a giant car headlight, Norman Foster's startling glass-encased City Hall is the headquarters for the **Greater London Authority** and the Mayor of London. Visitors are welcome to stroll up the helical walkway, visit the café and watch proceedings from the second floor. Contact in advance for access to "London's Living Room" on the ninth floor, which boasts the best views over the Thames.

## DESIGN MUSEUM

28 Shad Thames ⊖ Tower Hill ☎ 0870/833 9955, Ⓦ www.designmuseum.org. Daily 10am–5.45pm. £7. MAP PP.122–123, POCKET MAP Q8

A Bauhaus-like conversion of an old 1950s riverside warehouse, the stylish white Design Museum is the perfect showcase for mass-produced industrial design, from classic cars to Tupperware. Nothing is on permanent display, but the museum hosts a series of temporary exhibitions on important designers, movements or single products.

# Shops

## BOROUGH MARKET

8 Southwark St ⊖ London Bridge Fruit & veg
daily until 9am; food stalls Thurs 11am–5pm,
Fri noon–6pm & Sat 9am–4pm. MAP PP.122–123,
POCKET MAP M7

Borough Market is one of the
few wholesale fruit and vegetable
markets in London still trading
under its original Victorian
wrought-iron shed. However, it's
now best known as a foodie
hotspot, with gourmet daytime
market stalls (Thurs–Sat).

## BRINDISA

Borough Market ⊖ London Bridge. Tues–Thurs
10am–5.30pm, Fri 10am–6pm, Sat
8.30am–4pm. MAP PP.122–123, POCKET MAP M7

If you're missing pimientos,
manchego, *habas fritas* and
chorizo, this superb and stylish
Spanish deli is the place for you.

# Cafés

## CAFÉ 2

Tate Modern ⊖ Southwark or London
Bridge. Mon–Thurs & Sun 10am–5.30pm,
Fri & Sat 10am–9.30pm. MAP PP.122–123, POCKET
MAP L7

Tate Modern's Level 2 café
offers sophisticated British

cuisine for around £10 a main
course, though you can snack
for less. Kids' menu's good, too.

## EL VERGEL

8 Lant St ⊖ Borough. Mon–Fri 8.30am–3pm.
MAP PP.122–123, POCKET MAP M8

Small, very busy café that does
all the usual lunchtime
takeaways, but you're really
here to sample the Latin
American specialities such as
empanadas (pasties filled with
meat and spices or spinach and
feta cheese).

## THE TABLE

83 Southwark St ⊖ London Bridge.
Mon–Fri 7am–5pm, Sat & Sun 9am–3pm.
MAP PP.122–123, POCKET MAP L7

Tucked behind the Tate, this
self-service place has an
excellent salad bar and chunky
canteen tables. It's owned and
designed by neighbouring
architects, with a nice
industrial-style decked outside
space.

# Restaurants

## ROAST

Borough Market ⊖ London Bridge ☎ 020/
7940 1300. Mon–Fri 7–11am, noon–2.30pm &
5.30–11pm, Sat 8am–3.30pm & 6–11pm, Sun
11.30am–3.45pm. MAP PP.122–123, POCKET MAP M7

With a game and offal section
on the menu, this is a place for
those seeking truly British
meat dishes. The glamorous
contemporary dining room
looks down on the bustle of
Borough Market. It's also open
for breakfast. Mains £14–19.

## TENTAZIONI

2 Mill St ⊖ Bermondsey or Tower Hill
☎ 020/7237 1100. Mon–Fri noon–2.45pm &
6.30–10.45pm. MAP PP.122–123, POCKET MAP O8

Smart, busy Italian restaurant
serving high-quality,
imaginative peasant fare.
Mains £11–19.

# Pubs

### ANCHOR

Bankside ⊖ London Bridge. Mon–Sat
11am–11pm, Sun noon–10.30pm.
MAP PP.122–123, POCKET MAP M7

First built in 1770, this
sprawling pub retains only a
few vestiges of the past, but it
does boast a rare central
riverside terrace – inevitably it's
often mobbed by tourists.

### GEORGE INN

77 Borough High St ⊖ London Bridge.
Mon–Thurs 11am–11pm, Fri & Sat
11am–midnight, Sun noon–10.30pm.
MAP PP.122–123, POCKET MAP M7

London's only surviving
galleried coaching inn, dating
from the seventeenth century,
and now owned by the
National Trust. Expect lots of
wonky flooring, half-timbering,
a good range of real ales and a
fair smattering of tourists.

### MARKET PORTER

9 Stoney St ⊖ London Bridge. Mon–Fri
6–8.30am & 11am–1pm, Sat noon–11pm, Sun
noon–10.30am. MAP PP.122–123, POCKET MAP M7

Handsome semicircular pub by
Borough Market, with an
interesting range of real ales
and decent food. Outrageously
popular, as evidenced by the
masses that spill out onto the
surrounding pavements.

### THE RAKE

14 Winchester Walk ⊖ London Bridge.
Mon–Fri noon–11pm, Sat 10am–11pm.
MAP PP.122–123, POCKET MAP M7

Sleek, bright little bar whose
enthusiastic staff are happy to
advise on half a dozen (very
strong and very expensive)
draught beers from Germany,
America, Belgium and Holland,
as well as over 100 bottled
beers from around the globe.
There's also a pleasant decked
terrace.

ROYAL OAK

### ROYAL OAK

44 Tabard St ⊖ Borough. Mon–Fri
11am–11pm, Sat 6–11pm, Sun noon–6pm.
MAP PP.122–123, POCKET MAP M8

Beautiful, lovingly restored
Victorian pub that eschews
jukeboxes and one-armed
bandits, and opts simply for
serving a superb stock of real
ales (mild, pale and old) from
Harvey's Brewery in Sussex
and some good old-fashioned
pub grub.

# Venues

### SHAKESPEARE'S GLOBE THEATRE

21 New Globe Walk ⊖ Southwark or London
Bridge ☏ 020/7902 1400, ⓦ www
.shakespeares-globe.org. Mid-May to
mid Sept. MAP PP.122–123, POCKET MAP M7

This thatch-roofed replica of
the famous Elizabethan theatre
(see p.122) uses only natural
light and the minimum of
scenery, and puts on fun,
historically authentic and, more
often than not, critically
acclaimed plays by Shakespeare
and his contemporaries, with
"groundling" tickets
(standing-room only) for
around a fiver.

# Kensington and Chelsea

London's wealthiest district, the Royal Borough of Kensington and Chelsea is particularly well-to-do in the area south of Hyde Park. The moneyed feel here is evident in the flash shops and swanky bars as well as the plush houses and apartments. The most popular area for tourists, meanwhile, is South Kensington, where three of London's top museums stand side by side. Further south, Chelsea still has a slightly more bohemian pedigree, although these days, it's really just another wealthy west London suburb. To the north, Notting Hill is rammed solid with trendy – but wealthy – media folk, yet retains a strong Moroccan and Portuguese presence, as well as vestiges of the African-Caribbean community who initiated – and still run – Carnival, the city's (and Europe's) largest street party.

## WELLINGTON ARCH

Hyde Park Corner ⊖ Hyde Park Corner
☎ 020/7930 2726, ⓦ www.english-heritage
.org.uk. Wed–Sun: April–Oct 10am–5pm;
Nov–March 10am–4pm. £3.50. MAP PP.130–131,
POCKET MAP B18

Standing in the midst of one of London's busiest traffic interchanges, Wellington Arch was erected in 1828 to commemorate Wellington's victories in the Napoleonic Wars. In 1846, it was topped by an equestrian statue of the Duke himself, which was later replaced by Peace driving a four-horse chariot. Inside, you can view an informative exhibition on London's outdoor sculpture and take a lift to the top of the monument, where the exterior balconies offer a bird's-eye view of the surrounding area.

## APSLEY HOUSE

Hyde Park Corner ⊖ Hyde Park Corner
☎ 020/7499 5676, ⓦ www.english-heritage
.org.uk. Wed–Sun: April–Oct 11am–5pm;
Nov–March 11am–4pm. £5.70. MAP PP.130–131,
POCKET MAP B18

The former London residence of the "Iron Duke", Apsley House has housed the **Wellington Museum** since 1952. However unless you're a keen fan of the Duke (or the building's architect, Benjamin Wyatt), the highlight here is the **art collection**, much of which used to belong to the King of Spain. Among the best pieces,

WELLINGTON ARCH

displayed in the Waterloo Gallery on the first floor, are works by de Hooch, van Dyck, Velázquez, Goya, Rubens and Murillo. The famous, more than twice life-size, nude statue of Napoleon by Antonio Canova stands at the foot of the main staircase. It was disliked by the sitter, not least for the figure of Victory in the emperor's hand, which appears to be trying to fly away.

## HYDE PARK

Ⓦ www.royalparks.gov.uk. Daily 5am–midnight.
MAP PP.130–131, POCKET MAP E7

Seized from the Church by Henry VIII to satisfy his desire for yet more hunting grounds, Hyde Park was first opened to the public by James I, when refreshments available included "milk from a red cow". Hangings, muggings and duels, the 1851 Great Exhibition and numerous public events have all taken place here – and it's still a popular gathering point or destination for political demonstrations. For the most part, however, Hyde Park is simply a leisure ground – a wonderful open space that allows you to lose all sight of the city beyond a few persistent tower blocks.

At the treeless northeastern corner is **Marble Arch**, erected in 1828 as a triumphal entry to Buckingham Palace but now stranded on a ferociously busy traffic island at the west end of Oxford Street. This is the most historically charged spot in Hyde Park, as it marks the site of Tyburn gallows, the city's main location for public executions until 1783, when the action moved to Newgate. It's also the location of **Speakers' Corner**, a peculiarly English Sunday tradition, featuring an assembly of soap-box orators, religious extremists and hecklers.

At the centre of the park is the curvaceous lake of the **Serpentine**. Rowing boats and pedalos can be rented (March–Oct daily 10am–6.30pm or dusk; £4 per hour) from the boathouse on the north bank, while the lake's popular **Lido** (mid-June to mid-Sept daily 10am–6pm; £3.50) is situated on the south bank. Nearby is the **Diana Memorial Fountain** (daily: March and Oct 10am–6pm; April–Aug 10am–8pm; Sept 10am–7pm; Nov–Feb 10am–4pm; free), less of a fountain, and more of a giant oval-shaped mini-moat, in which kids can dabble their feet.

# Kensington and Chelsea

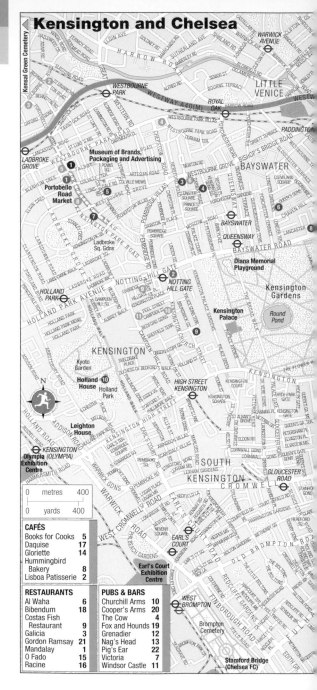

**Kensal Green Cemetery**

WARWICK AVENUE

LITTLE VENICE

PADDINGTON

Museum of Brands, Packaging and Advertising

BAYSWATER

LADBROKE GROVE

Portobello Road Market

BAYSWATER

QUEENSWAY

BAYSWATER

Ladbroke Sq. Gdns

Diana Memorial Playground

Kensington Gardens

HOLLAND PARK

NOTTING HILL GATE

Kensington Palace

Round Pond

KENSINGTON

Kyoto Garden

Holland House

Holland Park

HIGH STREET KENSINGTON

KENSINGTON

Leighton House

Olympia (OLYMPIA) Exhibition Centre

SOUTH KENSINGTON

GLOUCESTER ROAD

CROMWELL

N

| 0 | metres | 400 |
| 0 | yards | 400 |

EARL'S COURT

Earl's Court Exhibition Centre

WEST BROMPTON

Brompton Cemetery

Stamford Bridge (Chelsea FC)

## CAFÉS
| | |
|---|---|
| Books for Cooks | 5 |
| Daquise | 17 |
| Gloriette | 14 |
| Hummingbird Bakery | 8 |
| Lisboa Patisserie | 2 |

## RESTAURANTS
| | |
|---|---|
| Al Waha | 6 |
| Bibendum | 18 |
| Costas Fish Restaurant | 9 |
| Galicia | 3 |
| Gordon Ramsay | 21 |
| Mandalay | 1 |
| O Fado | 15 |
| Racine | 16 |

## PUBS & BARS
| | |
|---|---|
| Churchill Arms | 10 |
| Cooper's Arms | 20 |
| The Cow | 4 |
| Fox and Hounds | 19 |
| Grenadier | 12 |
| Nag's Head | 13 |
| Pig's Ear | 22 |
| Victoria | 7 |
| Windsor Castle | 11 |

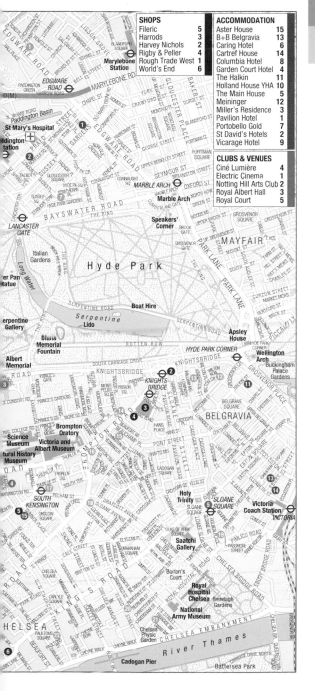

| SHOPS | |
|---|---|
| Fileric | 5 |
| Harrods | 3 |
| Harvey Nichols | 2 |
| Rigby & Peller | 4 |
| Rough Trade West | 1 |
| World's End | 6 |

| ACCOMMODATION | |
|---|---|
| Aster House | 15 |
| B+B Belgravia | 13 |
| Caring Hotel | 6 |
| Cartref House | 14 |
| Columbia Hotel | 8 |
| Garden Court Hotel | 4 |
| The Halkin | 11 |
| Holland House YHA | 10 |
| The Main House | 5 |
| Meininger | 12 |
| Miller's Residence | 3 |
| Pavilion Hotel | 1 |
| Portobello Gold | 7 |
| St David's Hotels | 2 |
| Vicarage Hotel | 9 |

| CLUBS & VENUES | |
|---|---|
| Ciné Lumière | 4 |
| Electric Cinema | 1 |
| Notting Hill Arts Club | 2 |
| Royal Albert Hall | 3 |
| Royal Court | 5 |

## KENSINGTON GARDENS

Queensway, Lancaster Gate or High Street Kensington ⓦ www.royalparks.gov.uk. Daily 6am–dusk. MAP PP.130–131, POCKET MAP C7

The more tranquil, leafier half of Hyde Park, Kensington Gardens is home to **Long Water**, the pretty upper section of the Serpentine and the **Italian Gardens**, a group of five fountains laid out symmetri-cally in front of an Italianate loggia.

One of the park's best-loved monuments is **Peter Pan**, the fictional character who enters London along the Serpentine in the eponymous tale. The book's author, J.M. Barrie, used to walk his dog in Kensington Gardens, and it was here that he met the five pretty, upper-class Llewellyn Davies boys, who wore "blue blouses and bright red tam o'shanters". They were the inspiration for the book's "Lost Boys", and he eventually became their guardian. Barrie himself paid for the statue, which was erected in secret during the night in 1912. More fun for kids (and also inspired by Peter Pan), is the nearby excellent **Diana Memorial Playground**.

To the south of Peter Pan is the **Serpentine Gallery** (daily 10am–6pm; free; ⓦ www .serpentinegallery.org), which has a reputation for lively and often controversial contemporary art exhibitions. The gallery also commissions a leading architect each year to design a summer **teahouse pavilion**.

The park's most impressive monument by far, however, is the **Albert Memorial**, erected in 1876. It's as much a hymn to the glorious achievements of the British Empire as to its subject, Queen Victoria's husband (he died of typhoid in 1861), whose gilded image sits under its central canopy, clutching a catalogue for the 1851 Great Exhibition. If you want to learn more about the 169 life-sized depictions of long-gone artists (all men) around the pediment, and the various other allegorical sculptures, join one of the monthly guided tours (March– Dec first Sun of month 2pm and 3pm; 45min; £4.50).

## KENSINGTON PALACE

Kensington Gardens Queensway or High Street Kensington ☏ 020/3166 6000, ⓦ www.hrp.org.uk. March–Oct daily 10am–6pm; Nov–Feb 10am–5pm. £12.50. MAP PP.130–131, POCKET MAP B8

ALBERT MEMORIAL

Bought by William and Mary in 1689, the modestly proportioned Jacobean brick mansion of Kensington Palace was the chief royal residence for the next fifty years. KP, as it's fondly known in royal circles, is best known today as the place where **Princess Diana** lived from her marriage until her death in 1997. It was, in fact, the official London residence of both Charles and Di until the couple formally separated and Charles moved to St James's Palace. In the weeks following Diana's death, literally millions of flowers, mementoes, poems and gifts were deposited at the gates to the south of the palace.

Diana's former apartments, where various minor royals still live, are closed to the public. Instead, **guided tours** take in some of the frocks worn by Diana, as well as several of the Queen's, and then the sparsely furnished state apartments. The highlights are the trompe-l'oeil ceiling paintings by William Kent, particularly those in the Cupola Room, and the paintings in the King's Gallery by, among others, Tintoretto. Also of interest in the King's Gallery is the wind dial above the fireplace, connected to the palace weather vane, which was built for William III and is still fully functioning. En route, you also get to see the tastelessly decorated rooms in which the future Queen Victoria spent her unhappy childhood. According to her diary, her best friends were the palace's numerous "black beetles", though it's clear from the Indian clubs that she was also into keep-fit.

## BROMPTON ORATORY

Brompton Rd ⊖ South Kensington
☎ 020/7808 0900, ⓦ www.bromptonoratory
.com. MAP PP.130–131, POCKET MAP D9
London's most flamboyant Roman Catholic church, Brompton Oratory was completed in 1886 and modelled on the Gesù church in Rome. The ornate Italianate interior is filled with gilded mosaics and stuffed with sculpture, much of it genuine Italian Baroque, while the pulpit is a superb piece of Neo-Baroque from the 1930s; note the high cherub count on the tester. And true to its architecture, the church practises "smells and bells" Catholicism, with daily Mass in Latin.

## NATURAL HISTORY MUSEUM

Cromwell Rd ⊖ South Kensington
☎ 020/7942 5000, ⊛ www.nhm.ac.uk. Daily
10am–5.50pm. Free. MAP PP.130–131,
POCKET MAP D9

With its 675-foot terracotta
facade, Alfred Waterhouse's
purpose-built mock-
Romanesque 1881 colossus
ensures the Natural History
Museum's status as London's
most handsome museum. The
collections are as much an
important resource for serious
zoologists as they are a
popular attraction.

The main entrance leads to
the vast **Central Hall**
dominated by an 85ft-long
plaster cast of a Diplodocus
skeleton. To one side, you'll
find the **Dinosaur** gallery,
where a raised walkway leads
straight to the highlight for
many kids, the grisly life-sized
animatronic dinosaur tableau,
currently a roaring
Tyrannosaurus rex. Other
child-friendly sections include
the **Creepy-Crawlies** room,
which features a live colony of
leaf-cutter ants and the old-
fashioned **Mammals** gallery
with its life-size model of a
blue whale.

For a visually exciting romp
through evolution, head for the
**Red Zone** (once the Geology
Museum); popular sections
include the slightly tasteless
Kobe earthquake simulator,
and the spectacular display
of gems and crystals in the
Earth's Treasury.

Visitors can also view a
selection of zoological bits and
bobs in the giant, glass-
encased, concrete Cocoon in
the museum's new **Darwin
Centre** (Orange Zone), which
houses 200 scientists, 28
million insect and 6 million
plant specimens. Among the
more bizarre items pickled in
the glass jars are a 50-year-old
piece of algae from Mauritius, a
partially digested human head
from a sperm whale's stomach
and a brown rat found during
the building's construction. To
visit the Cocoon, you need to
book ahead online or by phone.

## SCIENCE MUSEUM

Exhibition Rd ⊖ South Kensington
☎ 0870/870 4868, ⊛ www.sciencemuseum
.org.uk. Daily 10am–6pm. Free. MAP PP.130–131,
POCKET MAP D9

The Science Museum is
undeniably impressive, filling
seven floors with items drawn
from every conceivable area of
science, including space travel,
telecommunications, time

measurement, chemistry, photography and medicine. The museum also puts on lively daily demonstrations to show that not all science teaching has to be deathly dry.

First off, ask at the information desk in the Power Hall for details of the day's (usually free) events and demonstrations. Most people will want to head for the four-floor **Wellcome Wing**, with its interactive computers and IMAX cinema (tickets £8). To get there, you must pass through the **Making the Modern World**, a display of iconic inventions from Robert Stephenson's *Rocket* steam train of 1829 to the Ford Model T, the world's first mass-produced car.

If you've got kids, head for the **Launch Pad**, the museum's chief interactive gallery where they can experiment with water, waves, light and sound and build a catenary arch (and knock it down again); "explainers" are on hand to try and impart some educational input.

## VICTORIA AND ALBERT MUSEUM

Cromwell Rd ⊖ South Kensington
☎ 020/7942 2000, ⓦ www.vam.ac.uk. Daily
10am–5.45pm (Fri until 10pm). Free.
MAP PP130–131, POCKET MAP D9

In terms of sheer variety and scale, the **V&A** is the greatest museum of applied arts in the world. Beautifully but haphazardly displayed across a seven-mile, four-storey maze of halls and corridors, the V&A's treasures are impossible to survey in a single visit. Floor plans from the information desks can help you decide which areas to concentrate on.

The most celebrated of the V&A's exhibits are the **Raphael Cartoons**, seven vast biblical paintings that served as designs for a set of tapestries destined for the Sistine Chapel. Close by, you can view highlights from the UK's largest dress collection and theatre exhibition, and the world's biggest collection of Indian art outside India. In addition, there are extensive Chinese, Islamic and Japanese galleries; a gallery of twentieth-century **objets d'art** to rival the Design Museum; and more Constable **paintings** than Tate Britain. And the V&A's temporary shows – for which you have to pay – are among the best in Britain.

Wading through the huge collection of European sculpture, you come to the surreal **plaster casts** gallery, filled with copies of European art's greatest hits, from Michelangelo's *David* to Trajan's Column from the forum in Rome (sawn in half to make it fit). Before you leave, make sure you check out the museum's trio of original refreshment rooms (now back to their original use), the **Morris, Gamble & Poynter Rooms**, at the back of the main galleries.

CAST COURTS, V&A

## HOLY TRINITY CHURCH

Sloane Square ⊖ Sloane Square ☎ 020/7730 7270, ⓦ www.holytrinitysloanesquare.co.uk. Free. MAP PP.130-131, POCKET MAP F9

An architectural masterpiece created in 1890, Holy Trinity is probably the finest **Arts and Crafts** church in London. The east window is the most glorious of the furnishings, a vast, 48-panel extravaganza designed by Edward Burne-Jones, and the largest ever made by Morris & Co. Holy Trinity is very High Church, filled with the smell of incense and statues of the Virgin Mary, and even offering confession.

## SAATCHI GALLERY

King's Rd ⊖ Sloane Square ☎ 020/7823 2363, ⓦ www.saatchi-gallery.co.uk. Daily 10am–6pm. Free. MAP PP.130-131, POCKET MAP E10

On the south side of King's Road, a short stroll from Sloane Square, are the former **Duke of York's Barracks**, now housing upmarket shops and cafés. The main building, erected in 1801 and fronted by a solid-looking Tuscan portico, is home to the privately-run Saatchi Gallery. Its fifteen whitewashed rooms – "a study in blandness" according to one art critic – host changing exhibitions of contemporary art.

## ROYAL HOSPITAL CHELSEA

Royal Hospital Rd ⊖ Sloane Square ☎ 020/7881 5200, ⓦ www .chelsea-pensioners.co.uk. April–Sept daily 10am–noon & 2–4pm; Oct–March closed Sun. Free. MAP PP.130-131, POCKET MAP F10

Founded as a retirement home for army veterans by Charles II in 1682 and still going strong, the Wren-designed Royal Hospital is worth a visit for the vast, barrel-vaulted **chapel**, with its colourful apse fresco, and the equally grand, wood-panelled **dining hall**, opposite, with its allegorical mural of Charles II and his hospital. In the Secretary's Office, on the east side of the hospital, there's a small **museum**, displaying Pensioners' uniforms, medals and two German bombs.

## NATIONAL ARMY MUSEUM

Royal Hospital Rd ⊖ Sloane Square ☎ 020/7730 0717, ⓦ www.national-army -museum.ac.uk. Daily 10am–5.30pm. Free. MAP PP.130-131, POCKET MAP E11

Appropriately housed in a sort of concrete bunker, the National Army Museum harbours interesting historical artefacts, plus an impressive array of uniforms and medals (though for a more balanced view of war, you're better off visiting the Imperial War

Museum; see p.117). Highlights include a vast spot-lit model of the Battle of Waterloo (at 7pm before the Prussians arrived to save the day); the skeleton of Marengo, Napoleon's charger at the battle; the saw used to amputate the Earl of Uxbridge's leg; a paper lantern used by Florence Nightingale; and Richard Caton-Woodville's famous painting of *The Charge of the Light Brigade*.

## CHELSEA PHYSIC GARDEN

Royal Hospital Rd ⊖ Sloane Square
☎ 020/7352 5646, ⓦ www.chelseaphysic
garden.co.uk. April–Oct Wed–Fri noon–5pm,
Sun noon–6pm. £8. MAP PP.130-131, POCKET
MAP E11

Hidden from the road by a high wall, Chelsea Physic Garden is a charming little inner-city escape. Founded in 1673, it's the second oldest botanic garden in the country: England's first rock garden was constructed here in 1773, and the walled garden contains Britain's oldest olive tree. Unfortunately, it's also rather small, and a little too close to Chelsea Embankment to be a peaceful oasis, but keen botanists will enjoy it nevertheless. There's also a teahouse, which serves afternoon tea and delicious home-made cakes.

## PORTOBELLO ROAD MARKET

⊖ Notting Hill Gate or Ladbroke Grove. Main
market Mon–Wed, Fri & Sat 8am–6.30pm,
Thurs 8am–1pm; antiques Sat 6am–4pm.
MAP PP.130-131, POCKET MAP A6

Situated in one of the wealthiest, celebrity-saturated parts of town, Portobello Road Market is probably London's trendiest, yet it's always a great spot for a browse and a bargain. Things kick off, at the intersection with Chepstow Villas, with junky antique stalls and classier, pricier antique

PORTOBELLO ROAD MARKET

shops. After a brief switch to fruit and veg around the Electric Cinema, the market gets a lot more fun and funky at Portobello Green under the Westway flyover, where the emphasis switches to retro clothes and jewellery, odd trinkets, records and books. Further up again, the secondhand material becomes pure boot-sale, laid out on rugs on the road. Beyond Portobello Green, **Golborne Road market** (same times as Portobello) is cheaper and less crowded, with some very attractive antique and retro furniture.

## MUSEUM OF BRANDS, PACKAGING AND ADVERTISING

Colville Mews, off Lonsdale Rd ⊖ Notting
Hill Gate ☎ 020/7908 0880 ⓦ www
.museumofbrands.com. £5.80. MAP PP.130-131,
POCKET MAP A6

Despite its rather unwieldy title, it's definitely worth popping into this museum, which is based on the private collection of Robert Opie, a Scot whose compulsive collecting disorder has left him with ten thousand yoghurt pots alone. From Victorian ceramic pots of anchovy paste to the alcopops of the 1990s, the displays provide a fascinating social commentary on the times.

## LEIGHTON HOUSE

12 Holland Park Rd ⊖ High Street Kensington Ⓦ www.rbkc.gov.uk/leightonhouse museum. MAP PP.130-131, POCKET MAP A9

Leighton House was built by the architect George Aitchison for Frederic Leighton, President of the Royal Academy and the only artist ever to be made a peer (albeit on his deathbed). "It will be opulence, it will be sincerity", the artist opined before construction commenced in the 1860s. The big attraction is its domed **Arab Hall**. Based on the banqueting hall of a Moorish palace in Palermo, it has a central black marble fountain, and is decorated with Saracen tiles, gilded mosaics and latticework drawn from all over the Islamic world. The other rooms are less spectacular but in compensation are hung with excellent paintings by Lord Leighton and his Pre-Raphaelite friends Edward Burne-Jones, Lawrence Alma-Tadema and John Everett Millais.

## HOLLAND PARK

⊖ Holland Park or High Street Kensington. MAP PP.130-131, POCKET MAP A8

Holland Park is laid out in the former grounds of the Jacobean mansion of Holland House – sadly only the east wing survived the war, but it's enough to give an idea of what the place looked like. Several formal gardens are laid out before the house, drifting down in terraces to a café, a restaurant (the former Garden Ballroom) and an art gallery. The most unusual of the gardens is the **Kyoto Garden**, a Japanese-style sanctuary to the northwest of the house, peppered with modern sculpture and complete with koi carp and peacocks.

## KENSAL GREEN CEMETERY

Harrow Rd ⊖ Kensal Green ☎ 020/8960 1030, Ⓦ www.kensalgreen.co.uk. MAP PP.130-131.

Opened in 1833, Kensal Green Cemetery was the first of the city's commercial graveyards, and contains some of London's most extravagant Gothic tombs. Hemmed in by railway, gasworks and canal, the cemetery is vast, so it makes a lot of sense to join one of the **guided tours** that take place every Sunday at 2pm (£5), and include a visit to the catacombs (bring a torch) on the first and third Sunday of the month. Graves of the more famous incumbents – Thackeray, Trollope, Siemens and the Brunels – are less interesting architecturally than those on either side of the **Centre Avenue**, which leads from the easternmost entrance on Harrow Road. Worth looking out for are Major-General Casement's bier, held up by four grim-looking turbaned Indians; circus manager Andrew Ducrow's conglomeration of beehive, sphinx and angels; and artist William Mulready's neo-Renaissance extravaganza.

# Shops

## FILERIC

57 Old Brompton Rd ⊖ South Kensington.
Mon–Sat 9am–8pm, Sun 9am–4pm.
MAP PP.130–131, POCKET MAP D10

A beautiful French food shop
without the extravagant prices
you might imagine. Oils,
preserves, meats, terrines,
cheeses and wines, plus dishes
to take away.

## HARRODS

87–135 Brompton Rd ⊖ Knightsbridge.
Mon–Sat 10am–8pm, Sun noon–6pm.
MAP PP.130–131, POCKET MAP E8

London's most famous
department store is an
enduring landmark of quirks
and pretensions – don't wear
shorts, a sleeveless T-shirt or a
backpack, or you may fall foul
of the draconian dress code.
Harrods has everything, but is
most notable for its Art
Nouveau tiled food hall, its
Dodi & Di fountain shrine and
statue, the huge toy department
and its range of designer labels.

## HARVEY NICHOLS

109–125 Knightsbridge ⊖ Knightsbridge.
Mon–Sat 10am–8pm, Sun noon–6pm.
MAP PP.130–131, POCKET MAP A19

Absolutely fabulous, darling,
with all the latest designer
collections and shop assistants
who look like models. The
gorgeous cosmetics department
is frequented by A- and
Z-listers alike, while the
fifth-floor food hall offers
frivolous goodies at high prices.

## RIGBY & PELLER

2 Hans Rd ⊖ Knightsbridge. Mon–Sat
9.30am–6pm (Wed until 7pm), Sun noon–6pm.
MAP PP.130–131, POCKET MAP E9

Corsetières to HM the Queen,
if that can be counted as a
recommendation, this
old-fashioned store stocks a

HARRODS

wide range of beautiful lingerie
and swimwear, with designer
names as well as its own range,
for all shapes and sizes. The
personal fitting service is
deemed to be London's best.

## ROUGH TRADE WEST

130 Talbot Rd ⊖ Ladbroke Grove. Mon–Sat
10am–6.30pm, Sun 1–5pm. MAP PP.130–131,
POCKET MAP A6

Legendary indie music
specialist shop, first opened in
1976 at the height of punk/new
wave, with knowledgeable,
friendly staff and a dizzying
array of genres from indie pop
and electronica to country and
beyond.

## WORLD'S END

430 King's Rd ⊖ Sloane Square. Mon–Sat
10am–6pm. MAP PP.130–131, POCKET MAP D11

This is Vivienne Westwood's
outlet, halfway down the King's
Road, from which she sells
clothes from her Anglomania
label. In a previous incarnation,
when it was co-owned by
Malcolm McLaren, it sold
proto-punk fetishist gear, and
became a magnet for the young
punks who went on to form the
Sex Pistols.

# Cafés

## BOOKS FOR COOKS

4 Blenheim Crescent ⊖ Ladbroke Grove.
Tues–Sat 10am–6pm.

Tiny café/restaurant within
London's top cookery
bookshop. Conditions are
cramped, but this is an
experience not to be missed.
Just wander in and have a
coffee while browsing, or get
there in time to grab a table
for the set-menu lunch
(noon–1.30pm).

## DAQUISE

20 Thurloe St ⊖ South Kensington. Daily
11.30am–11pm. MAP PP.130–131, POCKET MAP D9

This old-fashioned Polish café
right by the tube is something
of a South Ken institution. It
stands little changed since
1947, serving Polish home
cooking or simple coffee, tea
and cakes depending on the
time of day.

## GLORIETTE

128 Brompton Rd ⊖ Knightsbridge. Mon–Fri
7am–8pm, Sat 8am–8pm, Sun 9am–6pm.
MAP PP.130–131, POCKET MAP E9

Long-established Viennese café
serving coffee and outrageous
cakes as well as sandwiches,
Wiener schnitzel, pasta dishes,
goulash and fish and chips.

## HUMMINGBIRD BAKERY

133 Portobello Rd ⊖ Notting Hill Gate.
Mon–Sat 10.30am–5.30pm, Sun 11am–5pm.
MAP PP.130–131, POCKET MAP A6

A cute and kitsch place selling
quality American home baking,
from prettily garish cupcakes to
sumptuous Brooklyn Blackout
Cake. The tables outside make
for great people-watching.

## LISBOA PATISSERIE

57 Golborne Rd ⊖ Ladbroke Grove. Daily
8am–8pm. MAP PP.130–131

Authentic Portuguese
*pastelaria,* with the best *pasteis
de nata* (custard tarts) this side
of Lisbon – also coffee, cakes
and a friendly atmosphere.

# Restaurants

## AL WAHA

75 Westbourne Grove ⊖ Bayswater or
Queensway ☎ 020/7229 0806. Daily noon–
midnight. MAP PP.130–131, POCKET MAP B6

Arguably London's most
authentic Lebanese restaurant;
courteous service and delicious
meze, but also mouth-watering
main course dishes such as
grilled chicken and lamb, sea
bass and red mullet. Mains
£10–17.

## BIBENDUM

Michelin House, 81 Fulham Rd ⊖ South
Kensington ☎ 020/7589 1480. Mon–Sat
noon–10.30pm, Sun noon–10pm.
MAP PP.130–131, POCKET MAP D9

A glorious tiled affair built in
1911, this former garage is a
great place to eat shellfish. You
can snack in the café for under
a fiver, splash out on a *plateau
de fruits de mer* for £30 a head
at the oyster bar or enjoy a
three-course lunch in the
restaurant, also for around £30.
Mains £15–27.

DAQUISE

## MANDALAY

444 Edgware Rd ⊖ Edgware Road
☎ 020/7258 3696. Mon–Sat noon–2.30pm &
6–10.30pm. MAP PP.130–131, POCKET MAP D5

Pure and unexpurgated
Burmese cuisine – a melange of
Thai, Malaysian and a lot of
Indian. The portions are huge,
the service friendly and the
prices low. Booking essential in
the evening. Mains £4–8.

## O FADO

50 Beauchamp Place ⊖ Knightsbridge
☎ 020/7589 3002. Daily noon–3pm &
7pm–1am. MAP PP.130–131, POCKET MAP E9

Probably the oldest Portuguese
restaurant in London, which
speaks volumes for its
authenticity. It can get rowdy,
what with the live fado ballads
(Mon–Sat) and family parties,
but that's half the enjoyment.
You'll need to reserve a table.
Mains £15–18.

## COSTAS FISH RESTAURANT

18 Hillgate St ⊖ Notting Hill Gate
☎ 020/7727 4310. Tues–Sat noon–2.30pm &
5.30–10.30pm. MAP PP.130–131, POCKET MAP A7

One of the best fish-and-chips
experiences in London can be
had at this old-fashioned
Greek-Cypriot outfit. Head past
the takeaway counter and grab
a seat. Mains £8–10.

## GALICIA

323 Portobello Rd ⊖ Ladbroke Grove or
Westbourne Park ☎ 020/8969 3539. Tues–Sat
noon–3pm & 7–11.30pm, Sun noon–3pm &
7–10.30pm. MAP PP.130–131

Pleasant Spanish restaurant
without pretension and with a
regular Iberian clientele who
enjoy the straightforward
traditional tapas (£3–7) at the
bar. Mains £8–14.

## RACINE

239 Brompton Rd ⊖ Knightsbridge or South
Kensington ☎ 020/7584 4477. Daily noon–3pm
& 6–10.30pm. MAP PP.130–131, POCKET MAP D9

The food here is French – not
just any old French, but
familiar, delicious, nostalgic
dishes from the glory days of
French cooking, with friendly
service. Booking is imperative.
Mains £12–20.

## GORDON RAMSAY

68 Royal Hospital Rd ⊖ Sloane Square
☎ 020/7352 4441, ⓦ www.gordonramsay.com.
Mon–Fri noon–2.30pm & 6.30–11pm.
MAP PP.130–131, POCKET MAP E11

The great man may be
nowhere to be seen, but his
small Chelsea restaurant is a
class act through and through
– book well in advance and
dress up. Three-course lunch
£45, dinner £90.

BIBENDUM

# Pubs and bars

## CHURCHILL ARMS

119 Kensington Church St ⊖ Notting Hill Gate. Mon–Wed 11am–11pm, Thurs–Sat 11am–midnight, Sun noon–10.30pm. MAP PP.130–131, POCKET MAP B7

Justifiably popular, flower-festooned pub serving Fuller's beers, superb Guinness and good Thai food.

## COOPER'S ARMS

87 Flood St ⊖ Sloane Square. Mon–Sat 11am–11pm, Sun noon–10pm. MAP PP.130–131, POCKET MAP E11

Very fine, popular, easy-going neighbourhood pub, offering first-rate beer and food. The attractively understated, spacious interior features vintage travel posters and grandfather clocks.

## THE COW

89 Westbourne Park Rd ⊖ Westbourne Park or Royal Oak. Mon–Thurs noon–11pm, Fri & Sat noon–midnight, Sun noon–10.30pm. MAP PP.130–131, POCKET MAP B5

Owned by Tom Conran, son of gastro-magnate Terence, this pub pulls in the beautiful W11 types, thanks to its spectacular

THE COW

food, which includes a daily supply of fresh oysters.

## FOX AND HOUNDS

27 Passmore St ⊖ Sloane Square. Mon–Sat 11am–11pm, Sun noon–10.30pm. MAP PP.130–131, POCKET MAP F10

On a quiet street near Sloane Square, this tiny Young's pub provides a perfect winter retreat. With an open fire, faux books, oil paintings and a flagstone floor, plus plenty of hunting memorabilia, it feels as if you've stumbled into a country squire's living room.

## GRENADIER

18 Wilton Row ⊖ Hyde Park Corner or Knightsbridge. Mon–Sat noon–11pm, Sun noon–10.30pm. MAP PP.130–131, POCKET MAP B19

Located in a private mews, this quaint little pub was Wellington's local (his horse mounting block survives outside) and his officers' mess; the original pewter bar survives, while there's plenty of military paraphernalia to gawp at. Classy but pricey bar food.

## NAG'S HEAD

53 Kinnerton St ⊖ Hyde Park Corner or Knightsbridge. Mon–Sat 11am–11pm, Sun noon–10.30pm. MAP PP.130–131, POCKET MAP A19

A convivial, quirky and down-to-earth little pub in a posh cobbled mews, with dark wood-panelling, nineteenth-century china handpumps and old prints on a hunting, fishing and military theme. The unusual sunken backroom has a flagstone floor and fires in winter.

## PIG'S EAR

35 Old Church St ⊖ Sloane Square. Mon–Sat noon–11pm, Sun noon–10.30pm. MAP PP.130–131, POCKET MAP O11

Deep in Chelsea village, *The Pig's Ear* is a sympathetically converted and stylish panelled pub, where you can enjoy a leisurely board game, a pint of Pig's Ear or some classy pub grub.

## VICTORIA

10a Strathearn Place ⊖ Lancaster Gate or Paddington. Mon–Sat 11am–11pm, Sun noon–10.30pm. MAP PP.130–131, POCKET MAP D6

Fabulously ornate corner pub, with two open fires, much Victorian brass and tilework, and gold trimmed mirrors. The Fuller's beer is excellent, too.

## WINDSOR CASTLE

114 Campden Hill Rd ⊖ Notting Hill Gate. Mon–Sat noon–11pm, Sun noon–10.30pm. MAP PP.130–131, POCKET MAP A7

Popular, pretty, early Victorian wood-panelled pub with a great courtyard – the kind of place you might find in the country rather than tucked away in the backstreets of one of London's poshest residential neighbourhoods.

# Clubs and venues

## CINÉ LUMIÈRE

17 Queensberry Place ⊖ South Kensington ☎ 020/7073 1350, ⓦ www.institut-francais .org.uk. MAP PP.130–131, POCKET MAP D9

Predominantly, but by no means exclusively, French films, both old and new (sometimes with subtitles), put on by the Institut Français.

## ELECTRIC CINEMA

191 Portobello Rd ⊖ Ladbroke Grove ☎ 020/7908 9696, ⓦ www.the-electric.co.uk. MAP PP.130–131, POCKET MAP A6

One of the oldest cinemas in the country (opened 1910), the Electric has been filled out with luxury leather armchairs, footstools, two-seater sofas and an excellent bar.

NOTTING HILL ARTS CLUB

## NOTTING HILL ARTS CLUB

21 Notting Hill Gate ⊖ Notting Hill Gate ☎ 020/7460 4459, ⓦ www.nottinghillartsclub .com. MAP PP.130–131, POCKET MAP B7

Groovy, arty basement club that's popular for everything from Latin-inspired funk, jazz and disco through to soul, house and indie.

## ROYAL ALBERT HALL

Kensington Gore ⊖ South Kensington or High Street Kensington ☎ 020/7589 8212, ⓦ www.royalalberthall.com. MAP PP.130–131, POCKET MAP C8

Splendid red-brick, terracotta and marble concert hall built in 1871 that serves as the main venue for the annual BBC Proms summer festival of classical music (ⓦ www.bbc .co.uk/proms), and also the place for a whole range of spectacular popular shows from opera to pop concerts. Guided tours are also available (daily except Wed 10.30am–3.30pm; £8).

## ROYAL COURT

Sloane Square ⊖ Sloane Square ☎ 020/7565 5000, ⓦ www.royalcourttheatre .com. MAP PP.130–131, POCKET MAP F10

One of the best places in London to catch radical new writing, either in the proscenium arch Theatre Downstairs, or the smaller-scale Theatre Upstairs studio space.

# Regent's Park and Camden

Framed by dazzling Nash-designed, magnolia-stuccoed terraces, and home to London Zoo, Regent's Park is a very civilized and well-maintained spot. Nearby Camden, by contrast, has a scruffy feel to it, despite its many well-to-do residential streets. This is partly due to the chaos and fall-out from the area's perennially popular weekend market, centred around Camden Lock on the Regent's Canal. A warren of stalls with an alternative past still manifest in its quirky wares, street fashion, books, records and ethnic goods, the market remains one of the city's best-known off-beat attractions.

## REGENT'S PARK

⊖ Regent's Park, Great Portland Street or Baker Street ⓦ www.royalparks.org.uk. MAP P.145, POCKET MAP E4–F4

It was under the Prince Regent (later George IV) that Regent's Park began to take its current form – hence its official title – and the public weren't allowed in until 1845 (and even then for just two days of the week). According to John Nash's 1811 masterplan, the park was to be girded by a continuous belt of terraces, and sprinkled with a total of 56 villas, including a magnificent pleasure palace for the prince himself. The plan was never fully realized, but enough was built to create something of the idealized garden city that Nash and the Prince Regent envisaged. Pristine, mostly Neoclassical terraces form a near-unbroken horseshoe around the Outer Circle, which marks the park's perimeter along with a handful of handsome villas.

By far the prettiest section of the park is **Queen Mary's Gardens**, within the central Inner Circle. As well as a pond replete with exotic ducks, and a

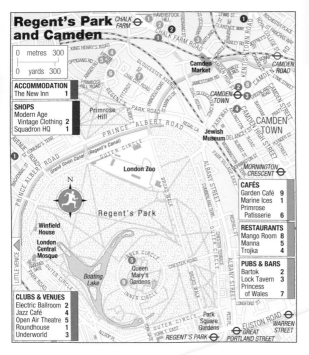

# Regent's Park and Camden

| | |
|---|---|
| 0 metres 300 | |
| 0 yards 300 | |

**ACCOMMODATION**
The New Inn 1

**SHOPS**
Modern Age
Vintage Clothing 2
Squadron HQ 1

**CLUBS & VENUES**
Electric Ballroom 2
Jazz Café 4
Open Air Theatre 5
Roundhouse 1
Underworld 3

**CAFÉS**
Garden Café 9
Marine Ices 1
Primrose
Patisserie 6

**RESTAURANTS**
Mango Room 8
Manna 5
Trojka 4

**PUBS & BARS**
Bartok 2
Lock Tavern 3
Princess
of Wales 7

handsomely landscaped giant rockery, a large slice of the gardens is taken up with a glorious rose garden, featuring some 400 varieties surrounded by a ring of ramblers. Along the eastern edge of the park, the tree-lined **Broad Walk** forms a stately approach (much appreciated by rollerbladers) to the park's most popular attraction, London Zoo.

## LONDON CENTRAL MOSQUE

146 Park Rd, Regent's Park ⊖ St John's Wood or Baker Street ☎ 020/7725 2213, ⓦ www.iccuk.org. MAP P.145, POCKET MAP E4

Prominent on the Regent's Park skyline is the shiny copper dome and minaret of the London Central Mosque, an entirely appropriate addition to the park given the Prince Regent's taste for the Orient. Non-Muslim visitors are welcome to look in at the information centre, and glimpse at the beautiful chandelier inside the hall of worship, which is packed out with a diversity of communities for the Friday lunchtime prayers.

LONDON CENTRAL MOSQUE

# Regent's Canal by boat

Three companies run daily boat services on the Regent's Canal between Camden and Little Venice, passing through the Maida Hill tunnel. The narrowboat **Jenny Wren** (April–Oct only; ☎ 020/7485 4433, ⦿ www.walkersquay.com) starts off at Camden, goes through a canal lock (the only company to do so) and heads for Little Venice, while **Jason's** narrowboats (☎ 020/7286 3428, ⦿ www.jasons.co.uk) start off at Little Venice; the **London Waterbus Company** (April–Sept daily; Oct Thurs–Sun only; Nov–March Sat and Sun only, weather permitting; ☎ 020/7482 2660, ⦿ www.londonwaterbus.com) sets off from both places and calls in at London Zoo en route. Whichever you choose, you can board at either end; tickets cost around £9 return, and journey time is 45 minutes one-way.

## REGENT'S CANAL

⊖ Warwick Avenue or Camden Town.
MAP P.145, POCKET MAP J2–A4

The Regent's Canal, completed in 1820, was constructed as part of a direct link from Birmingham to the newly built London Docks. After an initial period of heavy usage it was overtaken by the railway, and never really paid its way as its investors had hoped. By some miracle, however, it survived, and its nine miles, 42 bridges, twelve locks and two tunnels stand as a reminder of another age. The lock-less stretch of the canal between **Little Venice** and Camden Town is the busiest, most attractive section, tunnelling through to Lisson Grove, skirting Regent's Park, offering views of London Zoo, and passing straight through the heart of Camden Market. It's also the one section that's served by scheduled narrowboats (see box above). Alternatively, you can cycle, walk or jog along the towpath.

## LONDON ZOO

Outer Circle, Regent's Park ⊖ Camden Town
☎ 020/7722 3333, ⦿ www.zsl.org/zsl-london-zoo. Daily: March–Oct 10am–5.30pm; Nov–Feb 10am–4pm. £14.
MAP P.145, POCKET MAP F3

The northeastern corner of Regent's Park, is occupied by London Zoo. Founded in 1826 with the remnants of the royal menagerie, the enclosures here are as humane as any inner-city zoo could make them, and kids usually enjoy themselves. In particular they love **Animal Adventure**, the children's zoo (and playground) where they can actually handle the animals, and the regular "Animals in Action" live shows. The invertebrate house, now known as **BUGS**, the **Gorilla Kingdom**, the **African Bird Safari** and the walk-through rainforest and monkey

REGENT'S CANAL

enclosure are also guaranteed winners. The zoo boasts some striking architectural features, too, such as the 1930s modernist, spiral-ramped concrete former **penguin pool** (where Penguin Books' original colophon was sketched), designed by the Tecton partnership, led by Berthold Lubetkin, who also made the zoo's Round House. The **Giraffe House**, by contrast, was designed in Neoclassical style by Decimus Burton, who was also responsible for the mock-Tudor Clock Tower. Other landmark features are the mountainous **Mappin Terraces**, from just before World War I, and the colossal tetrahedral aluminium-framed tent of Lord Snowdon's modern **aviary**.

GORILLA KINGDOM, LONDON ZOO

## CAMDEN MARKET

⊖ Camden Town ⓦ www.camdenlock.net. Most stalls open daily 9.30am–5.30pm. MAP P.145, POCKET MAP F1–G2

For all its tourist popularity, Camden Market (in actual fact, a conglomeration of markets) remains a genuinely offbeat place. The tiny crafts market, which began in the 1970s in the cobbled courtyard by **Camden Lock**, has since mushroomed out of all proportion, with everyone trying to grab a piece of the action on both sides of Camden High Street and Chalk Farm Road. More than 100,000 shoppers turn up here each weekend, and some stalls now stay open all week long, alongside a crop of shops, cafés and bistros. The overabundance of cheap leather goods, hats, trainers, incense and naff jewellery is compensated for by the sheer variety of what's on offer: everything from bootleg tapes to furniture and mountain bikes, alongside a mass of clubwear and street-fashion stalls. And there are plenty of takeaway food outlets ready to fuel hungry shoppers with wok-fried noodles, bowls of paella, burgers, kebabs, cakes and smoothies.

## JEWISH MUSEUM

129 Albert St ⊖ Camden Town ⓣ 020/7284 7384, ⓦ www.jewishmuseum.org.uk. Mon–Wed & Sun 10am–5pm, Thurs 10am–9pm, Fri 10am–2pm. £7. MAP P.145, POCKET MAP G2

Despite having no significant Jewish associations, Camden is home to London's Jewish Museum. The displays aim both to tell the history of Jewish settlement in Britain, and also the rudiments of Judaism as a religion. One of the most remarkable exhibits is the medieval mikveh (ritual bath) excavated from the City. The Holocaust gallery tells the story of the Shoah through the life of Leon Greenman, one of the few British Jews who experienced the horror of Auschwitz. The museum's temporary exhibitions are always thought-provoking and there's a café onsite.

# Shops

## MODERN AGE VINTAGE CLOTHING

65 Chalk Farm Rd ⊖ Chalk Farm. Daily 10.30–6pm. MAP P.145, POCKET MAP F1

Splendid clobber (mostly menswear) for lovers of 1940s and 1950s American-style gear. The best bargains are on the rails outside.

## SQUADRON HQ

121 Kentish Town Rd ⊖ Camden Town. Mon–Sat 10am–5.30pm, Sun noon–5pm. MAP P.145, POCKET MAP G1

London's best army surplus shop also stocks lab coats, thermals, heavy-duty waterproofs and lots of hats.

# Cafés

## GARDEN CAFÉ

Inner Circle, Regent's Park ⊖ Baker Street. Daily 9am to dusk. MAP P.145, POCKET MAP F4

Classic 1960s modernist building with a copper-domed roof. The food is as retro as the decor, with mains such as fish pie and ribeye steak, and Bakewell tart or crumble for afters.

## MARINE ICES

8 Haverstock Hill ⊖ Chalk Farm. Tues–Sat noon–11pm, Sun noon–10pm. MAP P.145, POCKET MAP F1

This is a splendid and justly famous old-fashioned Italian ice-cream parlour; pizza and pasta are served in the adjacent kiddie-friendly restaurant.

## PRIMROSE PATISSERIE

136 Regent's Park Rd ⊖ Chalk Farm. Daily 8am–10pm. MAP P.145, POCKET MAP E2

Very popular pastel-pink and sky-blue patisserie in fashionable Primrose Hill, offering superb East European cakes and pastries.

# Restaurants

## MANGO ROOM

10 Kentish Town Rd ⊖ Camden Town ☏ 020/7482 5065. Daily noon–11pm. MAP P.145, POCKET MAP G2

An engaging, laid-back, Camden-cool Caribbean place whose cooking is consistent and whose presentation is first class. Mains £10–13.

## MANNA

4 Erskine Rd ⊖ Chalk Farm ☏ 020/7722 8028. Tues–Fri 6.30–10.30pm, Sat & Sun noon–3pm & 6.30–10.30pm. MAP P.145, POCKET MAP E1

Smart restaurant serving large portions of very good veggie and vegan food from around the world. Mains £10–13.

## TROJKA

101 Regent's Park Rd ⊖ Chalk Farm ☏ 020/7483 3765. Daily 9am–10.30pm. MAP P.145, POCKET MAP E1

The East European food is inexpensive, filling and tasty: blinis and caviar, schnitzel and stroganoff, pierogi and pelmeni. Service can be a bit East European as well. Live Russian music Fri and Sat eve. Mains £6–9.

MARINE ICES

# Pubs and bars

### BARTOK

78–79 Chalk Farm Rd ⊖ Chalk Farm.
Mon–Thurs 5pm–1am, Fri 5pm–4am, Sat
noon–4am, Sun noon–3am. MAP P.145,
POCKET MAP F1

Stylish bar with a superb and
quite unusual programme of
live music, from jazz and world
to classical and opera. Acoustic
evenings and DJ sets, too.

### LOCK TAVERN

35 Chalk Farm Rd ⊖ Chalk Farm.
Mon–Thurs noon–midnight, Sun noon–11pm.
MAP P.145, POCKET MAP F1

Rambling pub with comfy
sofas, a leafy terrace upstairs
and beer garden below, posh
pub grub and DJs playing
anything from punk funk and
electro to rock. Effortless cool.

### PRINCESS OF WALES

?? Chalcot Rd ⊖ Chalk Farm. Mon–Thurs
& Sun noon–11pm, Fri & Sat noon–midnight.
MAP P.145, POCKET MAP F2

Smart, popular Victorian pub
with excellent if pricey food.
Get here early to eat in the pub,
or book a table in the
restaurant or lovely garden.

# Clubs and venues

### ELECTRIC BALLROOM

184 Camden High St ⊖ Camden Town
☏ 020/7485 9006, ⓦ www.electricballroom
.co.uk. MAP P.145, POCKET MAP G2

Long-running and large club
that hosts rock and metal (most
Fri) and disco nights (Sat), plus
several gigs a week.

### JAZZ CAFÉ

5 Parkway ⊖ Camden Town ☏ 020/7485
6834, ⓦ www.jazzcafelive.com. Daily 7pm–2am.
Entry from £10. MAP P.145, POCKET MAP G2

BARTOK

Buzzing venue whose
adventurous music policy
explores Latin, funk and
hip-hop. If you fancy a
sit-down book a seat at the
restaurant tables. Clubbier late
sessions start at 11pm on Fri
and Sat.

### OPEN AIR THEATRE

Regent's Park, Inner Circle ⊖ Baker Street
☏ 020/7486 2431, ⓦ www.openairtheatre.org.
MAP P.145, POCKET MAP F4

This beautiful space in Regent's
Park hosts a tourist-friendly
summer programme of
Shakespeare, musicals, plays
and concerts; perfect when the
weather's good.

### ROUNDHOUSE

Chalk Farm Rd ⊖ Chalk Farm ☏ 0844/482
8008, ⓦ www.roundhouse.org.uk. MAP P.145,
POCKET MAP F1

Camden's barn-like former
engine shed puts on theatrical
spectacles and circus stuff
interspersed with live gigs.

### UNDERWORLD

174 Camden High St ⊖ Camden Town
☏ 020/7482 1932, ⓦ www.theunder
worldcamden.co.uk. MAP P.145, POCKET MAP G2

This popular, scruffy warren
under the *World's End* pub is a
great place to check out metal,
hardcore and heavy rock
bands.

# Hampstead and Highgate

The high points of north London, both geographically and aesthetically, the elegant, largely eighteenth-century developments of Hampstead and Highgate have managed to cling on to their village origins. Of the two, Highgate is slightly sleepier and more aloof, Hampstead busier and buzzier, with high-profile intelligentsia and discerning pop stars among its residents. Both benefit from direct access to one of London's wildest patches of greenery, Hampstead Heath, where you can enjoy stupendous views over London, as well as outdoor concerts and high art in and around the country mansion of Kenwood House.

## HAMPSTEAD HEATH

Gospel Oak or Hampstead Heath Overground, or ⊖ Hampstead or Golders Green.
MAP PP.152-153

Hampstead Heath is the city's most enjoyable public park, with a wonderful variety of bucolic scenery across its 800 acres. At the park's southern end are the rolling green pastures of **Parliament Hill**, north London's premier spot for kite-flying. On either side are numerous **ponds**, three of which – one for men, one for women and one mixed – you can swim in (daily 7am–9pm or dusk). The thickest woodland is to be found in the West Heath, also the site of the most formal section, **Hill Garden**, a secretive and romantic little gem with eccentric balustraded terraces and a ruined pergola. Beyond lies **Golders Hill Park**, where you can gaze at pygmy goats and fallow deer, and inspect the impeccably maintained aviaries, home to flamingos, cranes and other exotic birds.

The Heath's most celebrated sight is the whitewashed Neoclassical mansion of **Kenwood House** (daily 11.30am–4pm; free; ⓦ www.english-heritage.org.uk), set in its own magnificently landscaped grounds at the high point of the Heath. The

house is home to a superlative collection of seventeenth- and eighteenth-century art, including masterpieces by Vermeer, Rembrandt, Boucher, Gainsborough and Reynolds. Of the period interiors, the most spectacular is Robert Adam's sky-blue and gold library, its book-filled apses separated from the central entertaining area by paired columns.

## KEATS HOUSE

Keats Grove ⊖ Hampstead or Hampstead Heath Overground ☎ 020/7435 2062, ⓦ www .keatshouse.cityoflondon.gov.uk. Tues–Sun 1–5pm. £6. MAP PP.152–153

An elegant, whitewashed Regency double villa, Keats House is a shrine to Hampstead's most lustrous figure. Inspired by the tranquillity of the area and by his passion for girl-next-door Fanny Brawne (whose house is also part of the museum), Keats wrote some of his most famous works here before leaving for Rome, where he died of consumption in 1821 aged just 25. The neat, rather staid interior contains books and letters, Fanny's engagement ring and the four-poster bed in which the poet first coughed up blood.

## 2 WILLOW ROAD

⊖ Hampstead or Hampstead Heath Overground ☎ 020/7435 6166, ⓦ www .nationaltrust.org.uk. March & Nov Sat 11am–5pm; April–Oct Thurs & Fri noon–5pm, Sat 11am–5pm. £5.30. MAP PP.152–153

An unassuming red-brick terraced house built in the 1930s by the Hungarian-born architect **Ernö Goldfinger** (1902–87), 2 Willow Road gives a fascinating insight into the modernist mindset. This was a state-of-the-art pad when Goldfinger moved in, and as he changed little during the

FENTON HOUSE

following fifty years, what you see today is a 1930s avant-garde dwelling preserved in aspic, a house at once both modern and old-fashioned. An added bonus is that the rooms are packed with **works of art** by the likes of Max Ernst, Duchamp, Henry Moore and Man Ray. Before 3pm, visits are by hour-long guided tour only (noon, 1 and 2pm); after 3pm the public has unguided, unrestricted access.

## FENTON HOUSE

Windmill Hill ⊖ Hampstead ☎ 020/7435 3471, ⓦ www.nationaltrust.org.uk. March Sat & Sun 2–5pm; April–Oct Wed–Fri 2–5pm, Sat & Sun 11am–5pm. £5.70. MAP PP.152–153

Decorated in the eighteenth-century taste, grand Fenton House is home to a collection of European and Oriental ceramics, as well as a superb collection of **early musical instruments**. Experienced keyboard players are occasionally let loose on some of the instruments during the day and you can sign up for one of the occasional **demonstration tours** (£10). Tickets for the house also allow you to take a stroll in the beautiful orchard, kitchen garden and formal **garden** (garden only; £1), which features some top-class topiary and herbaceous borders.

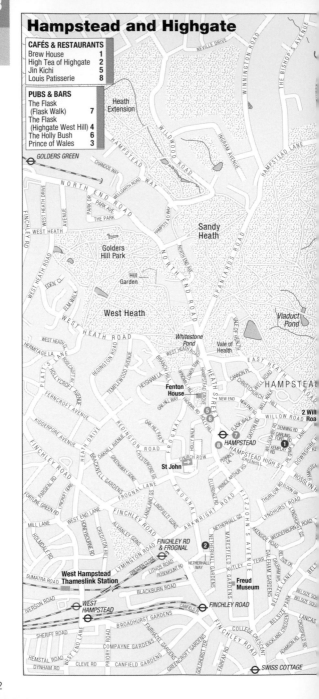

# Hampstead and Highgate

**CAFÉS & RESTAURANTS**

| | |
|---|---|
| Brew House | 1 |
| High Tea of Highgate | 2 |
| Jin Kichi | 5 |
| Louis Patisserie | 8 |

**PUBS & BARS**

| | |
|---|---|
| The Flask (Flask Walk) | 7 |
| The Flask (Highgate West Hill) | 4 |
| The Holly Bush | 6 |
| Prince of Wales | 3 |

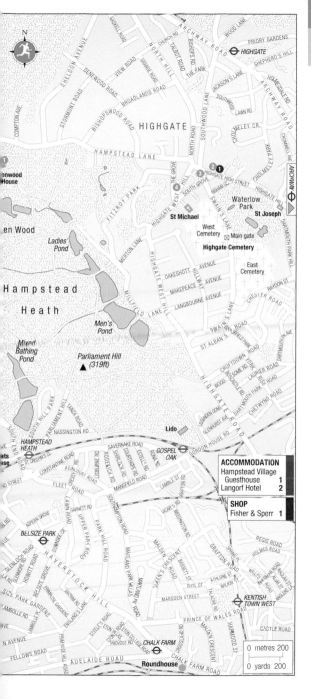

**ACCOMMODATION**
| | |
|---|---|
| Hampstead Village Guesthouse | 1 |
| Langorf Hotel | 2 |

**SHOP**
| | |
|---|---|
| Fisher & Sperr | 1 |

## FREUD MUSEUM

20 Maresfield Gardens ⊖ Finchley Road.
☎ 020/7435 2002, ⓦ www.freud.org.uk. Wed–
Sun noon–5pm. £5. MAP PP.152–153

Hidden away in the leafy
streets of south Hampstead, the
Freud Museum is one of the
most poignant of London's
museums. Having lived in
Vienna for his entire adult life,
**Sigmund Freud** was forced to
flee the Nazis, and arrived in
London during the summer of
1938 as a semi-invalid (he died
within a year). The
ground-floor study and library
look exactly as they did when
Freud lived here – the
collection of erotic antiquities
and the famous couch,
sumptuously draped in Persian
carpets, were all brought here
from Vienna. Upstairs, home
movies of family life in Vienna
are shown continually, and a
small room is dedicated to his
daughter, Anna, herself an
influential child analyst, who
lived in the house until her
death in 1982.

## HIGHGATE CEMETERY

Swain's Lane ⊖ Archway ☎ 020/8340 1834.
ⓦ www.highgate-cemetery.org. MAP PP.152–153.

Receiving far more visitors
than Highgate itself, Highgate
Cemetery is London's most
famous graveyard. The most
illustrious incumbent of the
**East Cemetery** (April–Oct
Mon–Fri 10am–5pm, Sat and
Sun 11am–5pm; Nov–March
closes 4pm; £3) is **Karl Marx**.
Erected by the Communist
movement in 1954, his vulgar
bronze bust surmounting a
granite plinth is a far cry from
the unfussy memorial he had
requested; close by lies the
much simpler grave of the
author George Eliot. The East
Cemetery's lack of atmosphere
is in part compensated for by
the fact that you can wander at
will through its maze of
circuitous paths.

On the other side of Swain's
Lane, the overgrown **West
Cemetery**, with its spooky
Egyptian Avenue and terraced
catacombs, is the ultimate
Hammer Horror graveyard,
and one of the city's most
impressive sights. Visitors can
only enter by way of a **guided
tour** (March–Nov Mon–Fri
2pm, Sat and Sun hourly
11am–4pm; Dec–Feb Sat and
Sun hourly 11am–3pm; £5; no
under 8s) – get there early on
summer Sundays. Among the
prominent graves usually
visited are those of artist Dante
Gabriel Rossetti, and of lesbian
novelist Radclyffe Hall.

# Shops

### FISHER & SPERR

46 Highgate High St. Bus #210 from
⊖ Archway. Mon–Sat 10.30am–5pm.
MAP PP.152–153.

Bookshop with several
rooms, one entirely dedicated
to books about London, plus
a few expensive antiquarian
jewels and a wide range of
titles covering travel,
literature, history and
philosophy.

# Cafés and restaurants

### BREW HOUSE

Kenwood House, Hampstead Heath. Bus
#210 from ⊖ Archway. Daily 9am–6pm.
MAP PP.152–153

Everything from full English
breakfast to lunches, cakes and
teas, either served in the old
laundry at Kenwood, or
enjoyed in the sunny garden
courtyard.

### HIGH TEA OF HIGHGATE

50 Highgate High St. Bus #210 from
⊖ Archway. Tues–Sun 11am–5pm.
MAP PP.152–153

Half-modern, half-retro
tearoom run by the lovely
Georgina, serving proper
loose-leaf tea and gorgeous
home-made cakes.

### JIN KICHI

73 Heath St ⊖ Hampstead ☎ 020/7794
6158. Tues–Fri 6–11pm, Sat 12.30–2pm &
6–11pm, Sun 12.30–2pm & 6–10pm.
MAP PP.152–153

Cramped, homely and very
busy (so book ahead), Jin Kichi
has a vast menu with almost
every Japanese dish, though it
specializes in grilled skewers of
meat. Mains £6–12.

### LOUIS PATISSERIE

32 Heath St ⊖ Hampstead. Daily 9am–6pm.
MAP PP.152–153

Tiny, understated, old-fashioned
Hungarian tearoom serving
sticky cakes, tea and coffee to a
mixed crowd.

# Pubs

### THE FLASK

14 Flask Walk ⊖ Hampstead. Mon–Sat
11am–11pm, Sun noon–10.30pm.
MAP PP.152–153

Convivial Young's pub, tucked
down one of Hampstead's more
atmospheric lanes, that retains
much of its original Victorian
interior.

### THE FLASK

77 Highgate West Hill. Bus #210 from
⊖ Archway. Mon–Sat noon–11pm, Sun
noon–10.30pm. MAP PP.152–153

Ideally situated at the heart of
Highgate village green, this pubs
has a rambling, low-ceilinged
interior and a summer terrace –
as a result, it's very, very popular
on the weekend.

### THE HOLLY BUSH

22 Holly Mount ⊖ Hampstead. Mon–Sat
noon–11pm, Sun noon–10.30pm. MAP PP.152–153

A lovely old pub, with a real fire
in winter, tucked away in the
steep backstreets of Hampstead
village. Some fine real ales on
offer, as well as decent food
(particularly the sausages and
pies), though it can get a bit too
mobbed at weekends.

### PRINCE OF WALES

53 Highgate High St ⊖ Archway. Mon–Thurs
noon–11pm, Fri & Sat noon–midnight, Sun
noon–10.30pm. MAP PP.152–153

If The Flask is mobbed, this is a
great alternative: a cosy, tiny
local with good real ales, Thai
food and a nice terrace out
the back.

# Greenwich

Greenwich is one of London's most beguiling spots. Its nautical associations are trumpeted by the likes of the magnificent *Cutty Sark* tea clipper and the National Maritime Museum; its architecture, especially the Old Royal Naval College and the Queen's House, is some of the finest on the river; and its Observatory is renowned throughout the world. With the added attractions of riverside pubs and walks, a large and well-maintained park with superb views across the river and to Docklands, plus a popular weekend arts and crafts market, you can see why Greenwich is the one place in southeast London that draws large numbers of visitors.

## OLD ROYAL NAVAL COLLEGE

Romney Rd ⊖ Cutty Sark DLR ☎ 020/8269 4747, ⓦ www.oldroyalnavalcollege.org. Daily 10am–5pm. Free. MAP P.158

It's entirely appropriate that the Old Royal Naval College is the one London building that makes the most of its riverbank location. Initially intended as a royal palace, Wren's beautifully symmetrical Baroque ensemble was eventually converted into a hospital for disabled seamen in the eighteenth century. From 1873 until 1998 it was home to the Royal Naval College, but now houses the University of Greenwich and the Trinity College of Music.

The two grandest rooms, situated underneath Wren's twin domes, are magnificently opulent and well worth visiting. The **Chapel**'s exquisite pastel-shaded plasterwork and spectacular decorative ceiling detail were designed by James "Athenian" Stuart, after a fire in 1799 destroyed the original interior. The magnificent **Painted Hall** features trompe-l'oeil fluted pilasters, and James Thornhill's gargantuan allegorical ceiling painting depicting William and Mary handing down Peace and Liberty to Europe, with a vanquished Louis XIV clutching a broken sword below them.

OLD ROYAL NAVAL COLLEGE

## NATIONAL MARITIME MUSEUM AND QUEEN'S HOUSE

Romney Rd ⊖ Cutty Sark DLR ☏ 020/8858 4422, ⓦ www.nmm.ac.uk. Daily 10am–5pm; June–Aug closes 6pm. Free. MAP P.158.

The excellent **National Maritime Museum** houses a vast collection of boats and nauticalia, imaginatively displayed in modern, interactive galleries designed to appeal to visitors of all ages. The glass-roofed central courtyard houses the museum's largest artefacts, among them the splendid 63ft-long gilded **Royal Barge**, designed in Rococo style for Prince Frederick, the much unloved eldest son of George II.

The numerous themed galleries of the museum proper are superbly designed to appeal to visitors of all ages, but if you have kids in tow, head for Level 2, which boasts two hands-on galleries: **The Bridge**, where you can navigate a catamaran, a paddle-steamer and a rowing boat to shore; and **All Hands**, where children can have a go at radio transmission, loading miniature cargo, firing a cannon, learning to use Morse Code and so forth.

A bright white Palladian villa flanked by colonnades, the **Queen's House** is the focal point of Greenwich's riverside architectural ensemble and an integral part of the Maritime Museum. Inside, one or two features survive from Stuart times, most notably the cuboid Great Hall, and the beautiful cantilevered Tulip Staircase. The rooms now provide a permanent home for the museum's vast maritime **art collection**, including works by Reynolds, Hogarth, Gainsborough and Turner.

## Getting to Greenwich

The most scenic and leisurely way to reach Greenwich is to take a **boat** from one of the piers in central London. Greenwich can also be reached by **train** from Charing Cross, Waterloo East or London Bridge (every 15–30min), or by **Docklands Light Railway** (DLR) from Bank or Tower Gateway direct to Cutty Sark. For the best view of the Wren buildings, get out at Island Gardens station to admire the view across the river, and then take the Greenwich Foot Tunnel under the Thames.

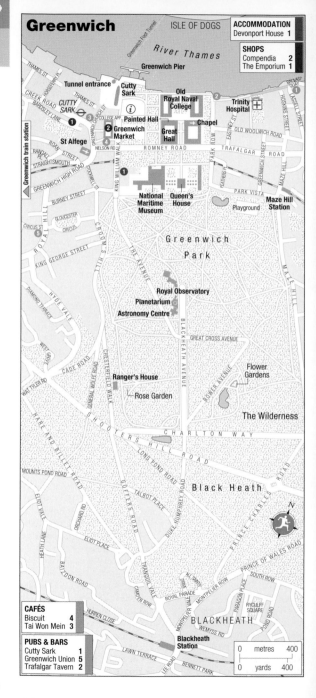

# Greenwich

ISLE OF DOGS

**ACCOMMODATION**
Devonport House **1**

**SHOPS**
Compendia **2**
The Emporium **1**

*River Thames*

Greenwich Foot Tunnel

Greenwich Pier

BALLAST QUAY

RUSSELL STREET

HOSKINS STREET

THAMES ST

HORSEFERRY PL

Tunnel entrance

**Cutty Sark**

Old Royal Naval College

**Trinity Hospital**

CREEK ROAD

BARNSLEY LANE

THAMES ST

*CUTTY SARK*

**1**

**3**

COLLEGE APP

i **Painted Hall**

**2**

**Greenwich Market**

PARK ROW

EASTNEY ST

OLD WOOLWICH ROAD

PARK VISTA

**Chapel**

**Great Hall**

TRAFALGAR ROAD

CHARLOTTE STREET

MAZE HILL

**St Alfege**

**4**

NELSON RD

ROMNEY ROAD

ROAN STREET

STRAIGHTSMOUTH

RANDALL PL

Greenwich train station

GREENWICH HIGH ROAD

STOCKWELL ST

KING WILLIAM WALK

**1**

FEATHERS PL

PARK ROW

FEATHERS PL

**National Maritime Museum**

**Queen's House**

Playground

PARK VISTA

**Maze Hill Station**

BURNEY STREET

CROOM'S HILL

GLOUCESTER CIRCUS

CIRCUS ST

**5**

ROYAL HILL

KING GEORGE STREET

HYDE VALE

DIAMOND TERRACE

WEST GROVE

CADE ROAD

CHESTERFIELD WALK

CROOM'S HILL

THE AVENUE

G r e e n w i c h

P a r k

**Royal Observatory**

**Planetarium**

**Astronomy Centre**

BLACKHEATH AVENUE

GREAT CROSS AVENUE

BOWER AVENUE

**Flower Gardens**

MAZE HILL

**Ranger's House**

**Rose Garden**

**The Wilderness**

WAT TYLER RD

HARE AND BILLET ROAD

GENERAL WOLFE ROAD

SHOOTER'S HILL ROAD

C H A R L T O N   W A Y

MOUNTS POND ROAD

GOFFER'S ROAD

LONG POND ROAD

TALBOT PLACE

**Black Heath**

PRINCE CHARLES ROAD

ELIOT VALE

HEATH LANE

ORCHARD RD

ELIOT PLACE

TRANQUIL VALE

DUKE HUMPHREY ROAD

ALL SAINTS

ROYAL PARADE

MONTPELIER ROW

SOUTH ROW

PARAGON PLACE

PRINCE OF WALES ROAD

PAGODA POND RD

BAIZDON ROAD

CAMDEN ROW

MONTPELIER VALE

WEMYSS RD

RYCULFF SQUARE

**BLACKHEATH**

HURREN CLOSE

**Blackheath Station**

LAWN TERRACE

LEE ROAD

BENNETT PARK

N

**CAFÉS**
Biscuit **4**
Tai Won Mein **3**

**PUBS & BARS**
Cutty Sark **1**
Greenwich Union **5**
Trafalgar Tavern **2**

| 0 | metres | 400 |
| 0 | yards | 400 |

## CUTTY SARK

King William Walk ⊖ Cutty Sark DLR
☎ 020/8858 2698, ⓦ www.cuttysark.org.uk.
Due to re-open 2011. MAP P.158.

Wedged in a dry dock by the
Greenwich Foot Tunnel is the
majestic *Cutty Sark*, the world's
last surviving **tea clipper**.
Launched from the Clydeside
shipyards in 1869, the *Cutty
Sark* was more famous in its
day as a wool clipper, returning
from Australia in just 72 days.
The vessel's name comes from
Robert Burns' *Tam O'Shanter*,
in which Tam, a drunken
farmer, is chased by Nannie, an
angry witch in a short Paisley
linen dress, or "cutty sark"; the
clipper's figurehead shows her
clutching the hair from the tail
of Tam's horse.

## GREENWICH PARK

⊖ Cutty Sark DLR ⓦ www.royalparks.gov.uk.
Daily dawn–dusk. MAP P.158.

A welcome escape from the
traffic and crowds, Greenwich
Park is a great place to have a
picnic or collapse under the
shade of one of the giant plane
trees. The chief delight, though,
is the superb view from the
steep hill crowned by the Royal
Observatory (see p.160), from
which Canary Wharf looms
large over Docklands and the
Dome. The park is also
celebrated for its rare and
ancient trees, its royal deer
enclosure in "The Wilderness"
and its semicircular rose garden.

## RANGER'S HOUSE

Chesterfield Walk ⊖ Cutty Sark or
Greenwich DLR ☎ 020/8853 0035, ⓦ www
.english-heritage.org.uk. Mon–Wed guided
tours 11.30am & 2.30pm, Sun 11am–5pm.
£5.70. MAP P.158.

An imposing red-brick
Georgian villa, the Ranger's
House was built as a private
residence, later becoming the
park ranger's official home. It
now shelters an art collection
amassed by **Julius Wernher**
(1850–1912), the German-born
millionaire who made his
money from South Africa's
diamond deposits. His taste
was eclectic, ranging from
medieval ivory miniatures to
Iznik pottery, though he was
definitely a man who placed
technical virtuosity above
artistic merit. Upstairs, the
high points of the collection are
Memlinc's *Virgin and Child*,
and a pair of sixteenth-century
majolica dishes decorated with
mythological scenes for Isabella
d'Este; downstairs, take note of
the Reynolds portraits and
de Hooch interior.

## ROYAL OBSERVATORY

Greenwich Park ⊖ Cutty Sark DLR
☎ 020/8312 6565, ⓦ www.nmm.ac.uk. Daily
10am–5pm. Free. MAP P.158

Established in 1675 by Charles II to house the first Astronomer Royal, John Flamsteed, the Royal Observatory perches on the crest of Greenwich Park's highest hill. The oldest part of the complex is the rather dinky Wren-built red-brick building, whose northeastern turret sports a bright-red time-ball that climbs the mast at 12.58pm and drops at 1pm GMT precisely; it was added in 1833 to allow ships on the Thames to set their clocks. On the house's balcony overlooking the Thames, you can take a look at a **Camera Obscura**, of the kind which Flamsteed used to make safe observations of the sun.

Flamsteed's chief task was to study the night sky in order to discover an astronomical method of finding the **longitude** of a ship at sea, the lack of which was causing enormous problems for the emerging British Empire. Greenwich's greatest claim to fame, nowadays, is as the home of **Greenwich Mean Time** (GMT) and the Prime Meridian. Since 1884, Greenwich has occupied zero longitude – hence the world sets its clocks by GMT.

Astronomers continued to work here until the postwar smog forced them to decamp; the old observatory, meanwhile, is now a very popular **museum**. Along the Meridian route, you can see Flamsteed's restored apartments and the Octagon Room, where the king used to show off to his guests. The Time galleries beyond display four of the fabulous marine clocks designed by **John Harrison**, including "H4", which helped win the Longitude Prize in 1763. In the Meridian Building, you get to see several meridians, including the present-day Greenwich Meridian fixed by the cross hairs in Airy's "Transit Circle", the astronomical instrument that dominates the last room.

The astronomy route includes a visit to the new **Astronomy Centre**, housed in the fanciful, domed terracotta South Building. The high-tech galleries here give a brief rundown of the Big Bang theory of the universe, allow you to conduct some hands-on experiments to explain concepts such as gravity and spectroscopy, and then invite you to consider the big questions of astronomy today. You can also choose to watch one of the thirty-minute presentations in the state-of-the-art **Planetarium** (daily 11am–4pm; £6), introduced by a Royal Observatory astronomer.

ROYAL OBSERVATORY

# Shops

## COMPENDIA

10 Greenwich Market ⊖ Cutty Sark DLR.
Daily 11am–5.30pm. MAP P.158
Old-fashioned games shop in
Greenwich market, selling
traditional board games from
all over the globe, as well as
pub favourites like bagatelle,
shove ha'penny and skittles.

## THE EMPORIUM

330–332 Creek Rd ⊖ Cutty Sark DLR.
Tues–Sun 10.30am–6pm. MAP P.158
Swanky retro store specializing
in 1940s to 1960s clothes for
men and women, and featuring
kitsch and well-preserved bras,
stockings, compacts and
cigarette-holders.

# Cafés

## DISCUIT

3–4 Nelson Rd ⊖ Cutty Sark DLR. Mon–Sat
11am–6pm, Sun 11am–5pm. MAP P.158
This quirky modern café,
serving soup, toast and cakes, is
great for those with kids: you
can paint your own design on
their blank ceramics and they'll
fire it for you within a week.

## TAI WON MEIN

39 Greenwich Church St ⊖ Cutty Sark DLR.
Daily 11.30am–11.30pm. MAP P.158
Good-quality fast-food noodle
bar that gets very busy at
weekends. Decor is functional
and minimalist; choose between
rice, soup or various fried
noodles, all for under a fiver.

# Pubs and bars

## CUTTY SARK

Ballast Quay, off Lassell St ⊖ Cutty Sark
DLR. Mon–Sat 11am–11pm, Sun
noon–10.30pm. MAP P.158

TRAFALGAR TAVERN

This Georgian pub is the best
one along Greenwich's
riverside, with friendly staff, an
appropriately nautical flavour, a
good range of real ales and pub
grub served all day.

## GREENWICH UNION

56 Royal Hill ⊖ Greenwich DLR & train
station. Mon–Fri 11am–11pm; Sat
10am–11pm, Sun noon–6pm. MAP P.158
A modern, laid-back place with
a youthful, unpretentious feel,
fine gastro grub and a nice
garden. Go for free samples of
blonde ale, raspberry beer,
chocolate stout or the house
Union before committing
yourself to a pint.

## TRAFALGAR TAVERN

5 Park Row ⊖ Cutty Sark DLR. Mon–Thurs
noon–11pm, Fri & Sat noon–midnight, Sun
noon–10.30pm. MAP P.158
Frequented by the likes of
Dickens (and mentioned in
*Our Mutual Friend*), William
Thackeray and Wilkie Collins,
this Regency-style inn is a firm
tourist favourite. It has a great
riverside position and serves
good whitebait and other
snacks.

# Kew and Richmond

The wealthy suburbs of Kew and Richmond like to think of themselves as apart from the rest of London, and in many ways they are. Both have a distinctly rural feel: Kew, thanks to its outstanding botanic gardens; Richmond, owing to its picturesque riverside setting and its gigantic park. Taking the leafy towpath from Richmond Bridge to one of the nearby stately homes, or soaking in the view from Richmond Park, you'd be forgiven for thinking you were in the countryside. Both Kew and Richmond are an easy tube ride from the centre, but the most pleasant way to reach them is to take one of the boats that plough up the Thames from Westminster.

## SYON PARK

Twickenham Rd. Syon Lane train station from Waterloo ☎ 020/8560 0881, Ⓦ www .syonpark.co.uk. House: Easter–Oct Wed, Thurs & Sun 11am–5pm. Gardens: March–Oct daily 10.30am–5pm, Nov–Feb closes 4pm. House & gardens £9; gardens only £4.50. MAP P.163

From its rather plain, castellated exterior, you'd never guess that **Syon House** boasts London's most opulent eighteenth-century interior. The splendour of Robert Adam's refurbishment is immediately revealed in the pristine Great Hall, an apsed double cube with a screen of Doric columns at one end and classical statuary dotted around the edges. There are several more Adam-designed rooms to admire, and a smattering of works by van Dyck, Lely, Gainsborough and Reynolds adorn the walls. While Adam beautified Syon House, Capability Brown laid out its **gardens** around an artificial lake, surrounding the water with oaks, beeches, limes and cedars. The gardens' real highlight, however, is the crescent-shaped Great Conservatory.

GREAT CONSERVATORY, SYON HOUSE

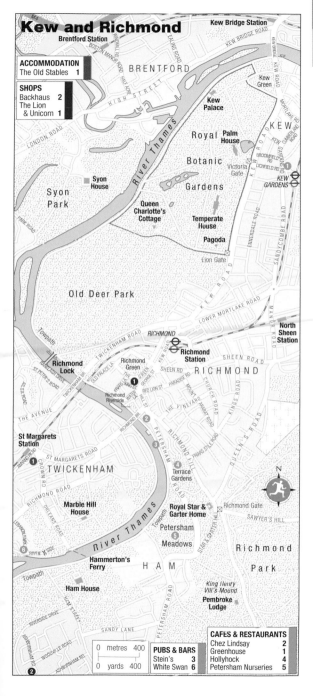

## KEW GARDENS

Kew Gardens ☎ 020/8332 5000, ⊕ www
.kew.org. Daily 9.30am–6.30pm or dusk. £13.
MAP P.163

PALM HOUSE, KEW GARDENS

Established in 1759, Kew's **Royal Botanic Gardens** have grown from their original eight acres into a 300-acre site in which more than 33,000 species are grown in plantations and glasshouses. The display attracts over a million visitors every year, who come to enjoy the beautiful landscaped parkland and steamy palmhouses. There's always something to see, whatever the season, but to get the most out of the place, come sometime between spring and autumn, bring a picnic and stay for the day.

The majority of people arrive at Kew Gardens tube and train station, a few minutes' walk east of the Victoria Gate. Immediately opposite the Victoria Gate, the **Palm House** is by far the most celebrated of the glasshouses, a curvaceous mound of glass and wrought-iron designed by Decimus Burton in the 1840s. Its drippingly humid atmosphere nurtures most of the known palm species, while there's a small but excellent tropical aquarium in the basement. South of here is the largest of the glasshouses, the **Temperate House**, which contains plants from every continent, including the sixty-foot Chilean Wine Palm, one of the largest indoor palms in the world.

Elsewhere in the park, Kew's origins as an eighteenth-century royal pleasure garden are evident in the diminutive royal residence, **Kew Palace** (Easter–Sept Mon 11am–5pm, Tues–Sun 10am–5pm; £5), bought by George II as a nursery for his umpteen children. There are numerous follies dotted about the gardens, the most conspicuous of which is the ten-storey, 163-foot-high **Pagoda**, visible to the south of the Temperate House. A sure way to lose the crowds is to head for the thickly wooded, southwestern

## River transport

From April to October, **Westminster Passenger Services** (☎ 020/7930 2062, ⊕ www.wpsa.co.uk) runs a scheduled service from Westminster Pier to Kew, Richmond and Hampton Court. The full trip takes three hours one-way, and costs £13.50 single, £19.50 return. In addition, **Turks** (☎ 020/8546 2434, ⊕ www.turks.co.uk) runs a regular service from Richmond to Hampton Court (April to mid-Sept Tues–Sun), which costs £6.70 single or £8.20 return. For the latest on boat services on the Thames, see ⊕ www.tfl.gov.uk.

section of the park around **Queen Charlotte's Cottage** (July and Aug Sat and Sun 10am–4pm; free), a tiny thatched summerhouse built in the 1770s as a royal picnic spot for George III's queen.

## RICHMOND

Richmond & Richmond train station. MAP P.163

Pedestrianized, terraced and redeveloped in the 1980s, Richmond's **riverside** is a neo-Georgian pastiche for the most part, and a popular one at that. The real joy of the waterfront, though, is **Richmond Bridge**, an elegant span of five arches made from Purbeck stone in 1777 and cleverly widened in the 1930s, thus preserving what is London's oldest extant Thames bridge. From April to October you can rent rowing boats from the nearby jetties, or take a boat trip to Hampton Court or Westminster. Alternatively, simply head south down the towpath, past the terraced gardens which give out great views over the river – quite quickly, you'll leave the rest of London far behind. On either side are the wooded banks of

the Thames: to the left cows graze on Petersham Meadows; beyond lies Ham House.

## HAM HOUSE

Ham St. Bus #371 or #65 from Richmond & Richmond train station 020/8940 1950, www.nationaltrust.org .uk/hamhouse. April–Oct Mon–Wed, Sat & Sun 1–5pm. £9.90. MAP P.163

Expensively furnished in the seventeenth century but little altered since then, Ham House boasts one of the finest Stuart interiors in the country, from the stupendously ornate Great Staircase to the Long Gallery, featuring six "Court Beauties" by Peter Lely. Elsewhere, there are several fine Verrio ceiling paintings, some exquisite parquet flooring, lavish plasterwork and silverwork, and paintings by van Dyck and Reynolds. Another bonus is the formal seventeenth-century **gardens** (all year Mon–Wed, Sat and Sun 11am–6pm; £3.30), especially the Cherry Garden, with a pungent lavender parterre surrounded by yew hedges and pleached hornbeam arbours. The Orangery, overlooking the original kitchen garden, currently serves as a tearoom.

RICHMOND RIVERSIDE

## MARBLE HILL HOUSE

Marble Hill Park, Richmond Rd. St Margarets train station from Waterloo ☎ 020/8892 5115, ⓦ www.english-heritage.org.uk. April–Oct Sat 10am–2pm, Sun 10am–5pm. £4.40. MAP P.163

This stuccoed Palladian villa, set in rolling green parkland, was built in 1729 for the **Countess of Suffolk**, mistress of George II for some twenty years and, conveniently, also a lady-in-waiting to his wife, Queen Caroline. She was renowned for her wit and intelligence and she entertained the Twickenham Club of Pope, Gay and Horace Walpole. The few original furnishings are slowly being added to with reproductions and the place is beginning to have the feel once again of an eighteenth-century villa. **The Great Room**, on the piano nobile, is a perfect cube whose coved ceiling carries on up into the top-floor apartments. Copies of van Dycks decorate the walls as they did in Lady Suffolk's day, but the highlight is **Lady Suffolk's Bedchamber**, with its Ionic columned recess – a classic Palladian device – where she died in 1767 at the age of 79. In the grounds, there are occasional **open-air concerts** on summer evenings.

## RICHMOND PARK

Bus #371 from ⊖ Richmond ☎ 020/8948 3209, ⓦ www.royalparks.gov.uk. Daily: March–Sept 7am–dusk; Oct–Feb 7.30am–dusk. Free. MAP P.163

Richmond's greatest attraction is its enormous park, at the top of Richmond Hill – 2500 acres of undulating grassland and bracken, dotted with coppiced ancient woodland. Eight miles across at its widest point, this is Europe's largest city park, famed for its red and fallow deer, which roam freely, and for its venerable oaks. For the most part untamed, the park does have a couple of deliberately landscaped areas. The most popular spot is **Isabella Plantation**, a carefully landscaped woodland park, with a little rivulet running through it, two small artificial ponds, and spectacular rhododendrons and azaleas in the spring. For refreshment, head for **Pembroke Lodge**, once the childhood home of the philosopher Bertrand Russell, and now a teahouse at the park's highest point, affording wonderful views up the Thames valley. Tradition has it that Henry VIII waited here for the flare that signalled the execution of his second wife, Anne Boleyn.

RICHMOND PARK

# Shops

### BACKHAUS

175 Ashburnham Rd, Richmond. Bus #371 from ⊖ Richmond. Mon–Fri 7.30am–5pm, Sat 7.30am–4pm. MAP P.163

Top German bakery making authentic cheesecakes, Stollen and to-die-for rye breads, with an adjacent deli selling sausages and cheese.

### THE LION & UNICORN

19 King St, Richmond ⊖ Richmond. Mon–Fri 9.30am–5.30pm, Sat 9.30am–6pm, Sun 11am–5pm. MAP P.163

Wonderful, busy children's bookshop that regularly organizes visits by popular children's writers on Saturdays.

# Cafés and restaurants

### CHEZ LINDSAY

11 Hill Rise ⊖ Richmond ☎ 020/8948 7473. Mon–Sat noon–10.45pm, Sun noon–10pm. MAP P.163

There's a wide choice of galettes, crepes or more formal French main courses, including lots of fresh fish and shellfish, at this bright, authentic Breton *creperie*. Mains £10–19.

### GREENHOUSE

1 Station Parade ⊖ Kew Gardens. Daily 8am–dusk. MAP P.163

A deliciously old-fashioned and pretty place near Kew Gardens, with cream teas and home-made tarts.

### HOLLYHOCK

Terrace Gardens ⊖ Richmond. Daily 9am–dusk. MAP P.163

Laidback, fair-trade veggie café, perfect for tea and cakes on the terrace overlooking the gardens and the river.

STEIN'S

### PETERSHAM NURSERIES

Off Petersham Rd. Bus #371 or #65 from Richmond ☎ 020/8605 3627, Wed–Sun noon–2.45pm. MAP P.163

Expect fresh, organic, expensive food at this restaurant, hidden behind the exotic ferns, profuse vines and Indian antiques of a posh garden centre. Mains £19–26.

# Pubs

### STEIN'S

Richmond Towpath ⊖ Richmond. May to mid-Oct Mon–Fri noon–10pm, Sat & Sun 10am–10pm; mid-Oct to April Fri–Sun noon–10pm. MAP P.163

An authentic Bavarian beer garden, serving up wurst and sauerkraut washed down with *echt* beers (no beer without food). Outdoor seating only, so closed in wet weather.

### WHITE SWAN

Riverside. Twickenham train station from Waterloo. Mon–Sat 11am–11pm, Sun noon–10.30pm. MAP P.163

Filling pub food, draught beer and a quiet riverside location – except on rugby match days – make this a good halt on any towpath ramble. The excellent summer Sunday barbecues are a big draw.

# Hampton Court

Hampton Court Palace is the finest of England's royal abodes and well worth the trip out from central London. A wonderfully imposing, sprawling red-brick ensemble on the banks of the Thames, it was built in 1516 by the upwardly mobile Cardinal Wolsey, Henry VIII's Lord Chancellor, only to be purloined by Henry himself after Wolsey fell from favour. Charles II laid out the gardens, inspired by what he had seen at Versailles, while King William III and Queen Mary II had large sections of the palace remodelled by Wren. With so much to see, both inside and outside the palace, you're best off devoting the best part of a day to the place, taking a picnic with you to have in the grounds.

## STATE APARTMENTS

☎ 0870/751 5175, ⊕ www.hrp.org.uk.
April–Oct daily 10am–6pm; Nov–March
closes 4.30pm. £14. MAP P.169

The palace's Tudor west front may no longer be moated but it positively prickles with turrets, castellations, chimneypots and pinnacles. Its impressive **Great Gatehouse** would have been five storeys high in its day. King Henry lavished more money on Hampton Court than any other palace, yet the only major survival from Tudor times in **Henry VIII's Apartments** is his Great Hall, which features a glorious double hammerbeam ceiling. The **Haunted Gallery** is home to the ghost of Henry's fifth wife, 19-year-old Catherine Howard, who ran down the gallery to plead for the king's mercy – only to be dragged kicking and screaming back to her chambers. Another highlight is the superbly ornate **Chapel Royal**, one of the most memorable sights in the whole palace, with its colourful plasterwork vaulting, heavy with pendants of gilded music-making cherubs.

HAMPTON COURT PALACE

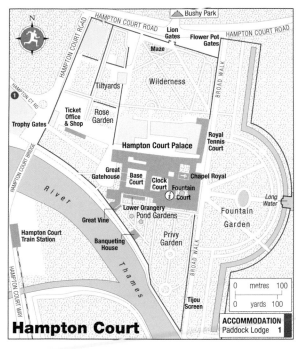

**Hampton Court**

**Mary II's Apartments**
boast wonderful trompe-l'oeil
frescoes on the grandiose
Queen's Staircase and in the
Queen's Drawing Room, where
Anne's husband is depicted
riding naked and wigless on
the back of a "dolphin". The
gem of the **Georgian Private
Apartments** is in fact the
Wolsey Closet, a tiny Tudor
room that gives a tantalizing
glimpse of the splendour of the
original palace. Next door is
the **Communication Gallery**,
linking the King's and Queen's
apartments, now lined with
Lely's "Windsor Beauties",
flattering portraits of the
best-looking women in the court
of Charles II. **William III's
Apartments**, built at the
same time as Mary II's, are
even more grand, particularly
the militaristic trompe-l'oeil
paintings on the King's

Staircase and the King's Great
Bedchamber, which boasts a
superb vertical Gibbons frieze
and ceiling paintings by Verrio.

Several early Tudor rooms,
with striking linenfold panelling
and gilded strapwork ceilings,
are now used to display **Young
Henry VIII's Story**. This is a
worthy attempt by the palace to
portray Henry in his virile
youth, during his happy,
twenty-year marriage to his first
wife, Catherine of Aragon. Last,
but not least, are the earthy and
evocative **Henry VIII's
Kitchens**, large sections of
which have survived to this day
and have been restored and
embellished with historical
reconstructions. To make the
most of this route, you really do
need to use the free
**audioguide**, which helps to
bring the scene to life with
contemporary accounts.

## Getting to and around the palace

**T**rains from Waterloo take around half an hour to reach Hampton Court train station, which is just across the river from the palace.

The State Apartments are divided into six thematic **walking tours**, which are numbered and colour-coded. There's not a lot of information in any of the rooms, but **guided tours** (book at the info desk in Clock Court), each lasting half an hour or so, are available at no extra charge for the State Apartments; all are led by period-costumed historians, who do a fine job of bringing the place to life. In addition, **audioguides** are available (for all except the Wolsey Rooms and the Queen's State Apartments) from the information centre on the east side of Clock Court. If your energy is lacking – and Hampton Court is a huge complex – the most rewarding sections are Henry VIII's Apartments, William III's Apartments and Henry VIII's Kitchens. And be sure not to miss out on the Maze.

### THE GARDENS AND THE MAZE

MAP P.169

If you're coming from the State Apartments, you'll probably emerge onto the magnificent Broad Walk, which runs along Wren's austere east front and is lined with superbly maintained herbaceous borders. Halfway along is the indoor **Royal Tennis Court**, established here by Henry VIII – if you're lucky, you might catch a game of this arcane precursor of modern tennis.

Fanning out from the Broad Walk is the **Fountain Garden**, a grand, semicircular parterre featuring conical dwarf yew trees. To the south of the palace is the more formal **Privy Garden** (£4.60; free with palace ticket) which features magnificent wrought-iron riverside railings by Jean Tijou. The **Pond Gardens**, originally constructed as ornamental fish ponds stocked with freshwater fish for the kitchens, feature some of the gardens' most spectacularly colourful flowerbeds. Further along, protected by glass, is the palace's celebrated **Great Vine**, grown from a cutting in 1768 by Capability Brown and averaging about seven hundred pounds of Black Hamburg grapes per year (sold at the palace in September).

HAMPTON COURT MAZE

## Booking a room

Demand for beds is so great that London doesn't really have a low season, though things do slacken off a little in January and February. Look online well in advance to get the best price – you may be able to shave £50–100 off room rates at some of the more upmarket hotels.

London's **tourist offices** (see p.193) operate a room-booking service, for which a small fee is levied (they also take the first night's fee in advance). There are also **British Hotel Reservation Centre** (BHRC; 24hr helpline ☎ 020/7592 3055, 🌐 www.bhrc.co.uk) desks at Heathrow and Gatwick airports, and Paddington, King's Cross and Victoria stations. BHRC desks are open daily from 6am till midnight, and there's no booking fee – they can also get big discounts at the more upmarket hotels.

You can book accommodation for free **online** at 🌐 www.londontown .com; payment is made directly to the hotel on checking out and they offer discounts of over fifty percent. Other useful websites include 🌐 www .accommodationlondon.net and 🌐 www.hotelsengland.com, and for last-minute offers: 🌐 www.laterooms.com and 🌐 www.lastminute .com. 🌐 www.londonbb.com sources classy **B&B** options, while 🌐 www .couchsurfing.org puts travellers in touch with people to stay or hang out with.

eighteenth-century stables. The hotel's *American Bar* was founded to provide cocktails for pioneering American visitors in the early 1930s, and its courtyard terrace remains a delight. **£250–300**

## Mayfair and Marylebone

**CENTRAL YHA** > 104 Bolsover St ⊖ Great Portland Street ☎ 0845/371 9154, 🌐 www.yha.org.uk. MAP P.59, POCKET MAP D12. YHA's newest hostel is in a quiet location, and yet walking distance from the West End. Free wi-fi, kitchen and a 24hr café-bar. No groups. Dorms only (4–8 beds). **Dorms £25**

**CLARIDGE'S** > Brook St ⊖ Bond Street ☎ 020/7629 8860, 🌐 www.claridges .co.uk. MAP P.53, POCKET MAP C15. This famous and glamorous Art Deco Mayfair hotel is the chosen abode of visiting heads of state and media megastars. For your money you get wardrobes bigger than most bathrooms, showerheads the size of dinner plates and decor as plush as any vacationing potentate could wish for. **£330**

**EDWARD LEAR HOTEL** > 28–30 Seymour St ⊖ Marble Arch ☎ 020/7402 5401, 🌐 www.edlear.com. MAP P.59,

POCKET MAP A14. Lear's former home enjoys a great location close to Oxford Street and Hyde Park, lovely flower boxes and a plush foyer. Rooms themselves need a bit of a makeover, but the low prices reflect both this and the fact that most only have shared facilities. **£80**

**LINCOLN HOUSE HOTEL** > 33 Gloucester Place ⊖ Marble Arch or Baker Street ☎ 020/7486 7630, 🌐 www .lincoln-house-hotel.co.uk. MAP P.59, POCKET MAP A14. Dark wood panelling gives this Georgian B&B in Marylebone a ship's-cabin feel. All the rooms are en suite and well equipped; rates vary according to the size of the bed and length of stay. Breakfast not included. **£75**

**WIGMORE COURT HOTEL** > 23 Gloucester Place ⊖ Marble Arch or Baker Street ☎ 020/7935 0928, 🌐 www .wigmore-court-hotel.co.uk. MAP P.59, POCKET MAP A14. The ruched curtains and floral decor may not be to everyone's taste, but this Georgian townhouse is a better-than-average B&B, boasting a high tally of returning clients. Comfortable rooms with en-suite facilities, plus two cheaper doubles with shared facilities. No lift, but there's a laundry and basic kitchen for guests' use. **£89**

## Budget chain hotels

Chain hotels have pretty much got the budget hotel market sewn up. B&Bs may be able to offer a more personal touch and more character in the decor, but the franchises are often in unbeatable central locations. Although they will never really be more than perfunctory places to stay, on the whole they can be guaranteed to provide clean if anonymous rooms.

Bumping along at the bottom are **easyHotel** (W www.easyhotel.com), whose prices start at just £25 for an en-suite double – if you want a window, TV use or room cleaning, it's extra; there are branches in Victoria, South Ken, Paddington and Earl's Court. Serious bargains can also be had at **Travelodge**, which has some very handily situated hotels in Covent Garden, Farringdon, Marylebone and Southwark; rooms are utilitarian, but if you book online well in advance, en-suite doubles can cost less than £50. **Premier Inn** is the other real budget option. It's generally considered a cut above Travelodge (and it doesn't have quite the online bargains); centrally located branches exist at the back of County Hall, near Tate Modern and by the Tower of London. The rest of the chain gang aren't worth considering as you can get better value elsewhere.

Look out, however, for **nitenite** (W www.nitenite.com), a "micro boutique" hotel chain which offers luxury "cabins" for as little as £50, and should have several London branches by 2011; ditto **Yotel** (W www.yotel.com), a Japanese-style capsule chain, where rooms can be rented by the hour.

## Soho and Covent Garden

**THE FIELDING HOTEL >** 4 Broad Court, Bow St ⊖ Covent Garden ☎ 020/7836 8305, W www.the-fielding-hotel.co.uk. MAP PP.66–67, POCKET MAP H15. Quietly situated on a traffic-free, gas-lit court, this excellent hotel is one of Covent Garden's hidden gems. Its en-suite rooms are a firm favourite with visiting performers, since it's just a few yards from the Royal Opera House. No lift and no breakfast. £130

**HAZLITT'S >** 6 Frith St ⊖ Tottenham Court Road ☎ 020/7434 1771, W www .hazlittshotel.com. MAP PP.66–67, POCKET MAP F14. Located off the south side of Soho Square, this early eighteenth-century building is a hotel of real character and discreet charm, offering en-suite rooms exquisitely decorated with period furniture. There's a small sitting room, but no dining room; breakfast (served in the rooms) is not included. £230

**OXFORD STREET YHA >** 14 Noel St ⊖ Oxford Circus or Tottenham Court Road ☎ 0845/371 9133, W www .yha.org.uk. MAP PP.66–67, POCKET MAP E14. The Soho location and modest size mean this hostel tends to be full year-round. It's also seen better days. No groups, no under 16s, no towels, no lift and no café, but a large kitchen and laundry facilities. Dorms (4–6 beds) and twins only. Dorms £25; doubles £60

**PICCADILLY BACKPACKERS >** 12 Sherwood St ⊖ Piccadilly Circus ☎ 020/7434 9009, W www .piccadillybackpackers.com. MAP PP.66–67, POCKET MAP E16. Vast, 700-bed hostel with small, cramped rooms and an institutional feel. Not the quietest place to crash out, nor the cleanest, but it's incredibly cheap and central. You can pay more for pod bunks and en-suite facilities. Breakfast not included; laundry but no kitchen. Dorms £12; doubles £65

**SEVEN DIALS HOTEL >** 7 Monmouth St ⊖ Covent Garden ☎ 020/7681 0791, W www.sevendialshotellondon .com. MAP PP.66–67, POCKET MAP G14. Pleasant family-run B&B hotel on a lovely street in the heart of the West End. The staircase is narrow and winding (no lift) and the rooms are small, but all are en suite, with TV, tea/coffee-making facilities and free wi-fi and the staff are very helpful. **£80.**

## Bloomsbury

**ALHAMBRA HOTEL** > 17 Argyle St ⊖ King's Cross St Pancras ☎ 020/7631 4115, ⓦ www.alhambrahotel.com. MAP P.80, POCKET MAP J3. Clean, modern, functional place just a stone's throw from St Pancras. Cheapest rooms have shared facilities and there's no lift, but free wi-fi is available. **£60**

**ARRAN HOUSE HOTEL** > 77–79 Gower St ⊖ Goodge Street ☎ 020/7535 2186, ⓦ www.arranhotel-london.com. MAP P.80, POCKET MAP F12. Comfortable and clean B&B, with pink furnishings. All doubles are en suite, but there are a few bargain singles with shared facilities. **£82**

**CLINK HOSTEL** > 78 King's Cross Rd ⊖ King's Cross St Pancras ☎ 020/7183 9400, ⓦ www.clinkhostel.com. MAP P.80, POCKET MAP K3. This 300-bed place is run by Ashlee House, but has funkier decor, bargain pod beds, and plenty of period features from the days when it was a Victorian courthouse, like the spacious internet courtroom – you can even stay in one of the old prison cells. Breakfast included; kitchen facilities from noon; 4–16 bed dorms available. **Dorms from around £10; doubles £40**

**CLINK 261 HOSTEL** > 261–265 Gray's Inn Rd ⊖ King's Cross St Pancras ☎ 020/7833 9400, ⓦ www.ashleehouse .co.uk. MAP P.80, POCKET MAP J3. A clean and friendly 170-bed hostel in a converted office block near King's Cross station, with laundry and kitchen facilities. Breakfast included. Dorms (4–16 beds) available. **Dorms from £14; doubles £50**

**GENERATOR** > Compton Place, off Tavistock Place ⊖ Russell Square ☎ 020/7388 7666, ⓦ www .generatorhostels.com. MAP P.80, POCKET MAP J4. A huge hostel, with over 800 beds, in a converted police barracks tucked away down a cobbled street. The neon and UV lighting and post-industrial decor may not be to everyone's taste, but this is without doubt the best bargain in Bloomsbury. There's a young, party atmosphere with themed nights in the late-night bar. Laundry, but no kitchen; breakfast included, plus cheap café; 4–12 bed dorms available. **Dorms from £15; doubles £50**

**RIDGEMOUNT HOTEL** > 65–67 Gower St ⊖ Goodge Street ☎ 020/7636 1141, ⓦ www.ridgemounthotel .co.uk. Map P.80, POCKET MAP F12. Very friendly, old-fashioned, family-run place, with small rooms (half with shared facilities), a garden and free hot drinks machine. A reliable, basic bargain. **£60**

**HOTEL RUSSELL** > 1–8 Russell Square ⊖ Russell Square ☎ 020/7837 6470, ⓦ www.londonrussellhotel .co.uk. MAP P.80, POCKET MAP G12. From its grand 1898 exterior to its opulent interiors of marble, wood and crystal, this late-Victorian landmark fully retains its period atmosphere in all its public areas – if not in the rooms themselves. Service could often be better, and the rack rates are pretty high, but online you can get good deals. Breakfast not included. **£125–230**

**ST PANCRAS YHA** > 79–81 Euston Rd ⊖ King's Cross St Pancras ☎ 0845/371 9344, ⓦ www.yha.org.uk. MAP P.80, POCKET MAP J4. Modern hostel opposite the Eurostar terminal on the busy Euston Road; rooms are very clean, bright, triple-glazed and air-conditioned. All doubles, and some dorms, are en suite and family rooms are available, all with TVs. **Dorms from £25; doubles £50**

## The City

**APEX CITY OF LONDON HOTEL** > 1 Seething Lane ⊖ Tower Hill ☎ 020/7977 9593, ⓦ www.apexhotels .co.uk. MAP PP.86–87, POCKET MAP N6. A swish hotel on a secluded City street, designed for corporate clientele – the rooms are very masculine, in black, grey and burgundy, with the pricier ones enjoying more light and better views. Rates vary enormously according to availability so book early. The gym, sauna and steam room are free for guests. **£60–130**

**FOX & ANCHOR** > 115 Charterhouse St ⊖Farringdon or Barbican ☎0845/347 0100, Ⓦ www.foxandanchor.com. MAP PP.86–87, POCKET MAP L5. This traditional Clerkenwell pub has six small but luxuriously furnished rooms, up a narrow flight of stairs, with all the mod cons you could desire. The only issue is noise from nearby clubs so ask for a room at the back. Check-in is at Malmaison (see below). **£95–165**

**THE KING'S WARDROBE** > 6 Wardrobe Place, Carter Lane ⊖St Paul's ☎020/7792 2222, Ⓦ www .bridgestreet.com. MAP PP.86–87, POCKET MAP L6. In a quiet courtyard just behind St Paul's Cathedral, this place is part of an international chain that caters largely for a business clientele. The apartments offer fully equipped kitchens and workstations, a concierge service and housekeeping. Though the building is Georgian and occupies the site of the medieval Royal Wardrobe, the interior is modern. **£130–210**

**MALMAISON** > 18–21 Charterhouse Square ⊖Farringdon or Barbican ☎020/7012 3700, Ⓦ www .malmaison-london.com. MAP PP.86–87, POCKET MAP L5. Set in a quiet, cobbled square in Clerkenwell, close to the Barbican, this is the London branch of a slowly expanding chain of very successful British boutique hotels. The tone is dark, modern and quite clubby in deference to the nearby City. Service and facilities are difficult to fault. **£125–250**

**THE ROOKERY** > 12 Peter's Lane, Cowcross St ⊖Farringdon ☎020/7336 0931, Ⓦ www.rookeryhotel.com. MAP PP.86–87, POCKET MAP L5. Rambling Georgian townhouse on the edge of the City that makes a fantastically discreet little hideaway. Each room has been individually designed in a deliciously camp, modern take on the Baroque period, and all have super bathrooms with lots of character, plus air-conditioning and free wi-fi. Breakfast served in your room or in the conservatory. **£220**

**ST PAUL'S YHA** > 36 Carter Lane ⊖St Paul's ☎0845/371 9012, Ⓦ www.yha.org.uk. MAP PP.86–87,

POCKET MAP L6. Large 190-bed hostel in a superb location opposite St Paul's Cathedral. Breakfast included and a café for dinner, but no kitchen. Small groups only. Dorms (4–8 beds) and twins. **Dorms £25; doubles £50**

**ZETTER HOTEL** > 86–88 Clerkenwell Rd ⊖Farringdon ☎020/7324 4444, Ⓦ www.thezetter.com. MAP PP.86–87, POCKET MAP L4. A warehouse converted with real style and a dash of 1960s glamour. Rooms are simple and minimalist, with fun touches such as lights that change colour and decorative floral panels; ask for a room at the back, overlooking quiet, cobbled St John's Square. Water for guests is supplied from *The Zetter's* own well, beneath the building. **£170**

# Hoxton and Spitalfields

**HOXTON HOTEL** > 81 Great Eastern St ⊖Old Street ☎020/7550 1000, Ⓦ www.hoxtonhotels.com. MAP P.102, POCKET MAP N4. Fittingly trendy hotel in über-hip Hoxton, with contemporary art on the walls and fashionably lugubrious decor in the rooms, plus flat-screen TVs and duck-down duvets. The tiny breakfast is delivered to your room. Free wi-fi and cheap phone calls. Price depends entirely on availability; rooms are occasionally even sold for £1. **£30–165**

# Tower and Docklands

**FOUR SEASONS HOTEL CANARY WHARF** > 46 Westferry Circus ⊖Canary Wharf ☎020/7510 1999, Ⓦ www.fourseasons.com. MAP PP.110–111. A spectacular riverfront setting, funky modern interiors and good links to the City have made this hotel very popular with business folk, but weekend rates, which bring prices down, mean that it's an equally good base for sightseeing. Several rooms have superb Thames views. Pool, fitness centre, spa and tennis courts, and there's also the option of taking a boat into town. **£150–190**

# South Bank and around

**CAPTAIN BLIGH HOUSE** > 100 Lambeth Rd ⊖ Lambeth North ☎ 020/8769 3500, ⓦ www .captainblighhouse.co.uk. MAP P.115, POCKET MAP K9. The former home of Captain Bligh (of *Bounty* fame) is now a nautically flavoured Georgian B&B, a short walk from the South Bank, run by a friendly couple (and their two cats). There are just three rooms, two of which have self-catering facilities; breakfast is taken in your room. **£90**

**LONDON MARRIOTT HOTEL COUNTY HALL** > County Hall ⊖ Waterloo ☎ 020/7928 5200, ⓦ www.marriott .com. MAP P.115, POCKET MAP J19. The Marriott has taken over some of the finest rooms in historic County Hall, former home to London's government, with over three-quarters offering river views, many with small balconies. It's all suitably pompous inside, and there's a full-sized indoor pool and well-equipped gym. **£210**

**MAD HATTER** > 3–7 Stamford St ⊖ Southwark or Blackfriars ☎ 020/7401 9222, ⓦ www.fullershotels .co.uk. MAP P.115, POCKET MAP L7. Plush pseudo-Victorian Fuller's hotel above a modern pub on Blackfriars Road. Breakfast is extra on weekdays, and is served in the pub, but this is a great location, a short walk from Tate Modern and the South Bank. Rates depend on availability – weekends are usually cheapest. **£95–135**

# Bankside and Southwark

**LONDON BRIDGE HOTEL** > 8–18 London Bridge St ⊖ London Bridge ☎ 020/7855 2200, ⓦ www .londonbridgehotel.com. MAP PP.122–123, POCKET MAP N7. Perfectly placed for Southwark and Bankside or the City, with very good transport connections, this is a comfortable, contemporary hotel right by the station with flat-screen TVs, wi-fi and air-conditioning in all the rooms. **£100–170**

**ST CHRISTOPHER'S VILLAGE** > 161–165 Borough High St ⊖ Borough ☎ 020/7407 1856, ⓦ www .st-christophers.co.uk. MAP PP.122–123, POCKET MAP M8. St Christopher's run seven hostels across London, with no fewer than three near London Bridge The decor is upbeat and cheerful, the hostels are efficiently run and there's a party-animal ambience, fuelled by the hostel bars. The *Inn* has a pub attached, the *Oasis* is women only, while the *Village* has a nightclub and cinema, plus a rooftop hot tub and sauna. **Dorms from £18; doubles £50**

**SOUTHWARK ROSE HOTEL** > 43–47 Southwark Bridge Rd ⊖ London Bridge ☎ 020/7015 1480, ⓦ www .southwarkrosehotel.co.uk. MAP PP.122–123, POCKET MAP M7. The *Southwark Rose* has nice contemporary design touches that raise the rooms several notches above the bland chain hotels in the area. Giant aluminium lamps hover over the lobby, which is lined with funky photographs, while the penthouse restaurant offers breakfast with a rooftop view and free wi-fi. Rates depend on availability. **£125–190**

# Kensington and Chelsea

**ASTER HOUSE** > 3 Sumner Place ⊖ South Kensington ☎ 020/7581 5888, ⓦ www.asterhouse.com. MAP PP.130–131, POCKET MAP D10. Pleasant, award-winning B&B in a luxurious South Ken white-stuccoed street with a lovely garden at the back and a large conservatory where breakfast is served. **£180**

**B+B BELGRAVIA** > 64–66 Ebury St ⊖ Victoria ☎ 020/7823 4928, ⓦ www .bb-belgravia.com. MAP PP.130–131, POCKET MAP F9. Very close to the train and coach station, this is a real rarity in this neck of the woods – a B&B with flair. The rooms are boutique-hotel quality, with original features as well as stylish modern touches. Communal spaces are light and well designed, and staff welcoming and enthusiastic. Free in-room internet access. **£115**

**CARING HOTEL** > 24 Craven Hill Gardens ⊖ Bayswater, Queensway or Lancaster Gate ☏ 020/7262 8708, Ⓦ www.caringhotel.com. MAP PP.130–131, POCKET MAP C6. The decor isn't to all tastes, but the rooms are clean; the cheaper ones have shared facilities. **£55**

**CARTREF HOUSE** > 129 Ebury St ⊖ Victoria ☏ 020/7730 6176, Ⓦ www .cartrefhouse.co.uk. MAP PP.130–131, POCKET MAP F9. Clean Georgian B&B situated in a white-stuccoed street round the back of Victoria station. The couple who run it are very friendly and all rooms are en suite. **£102**

**COLUMBIA HOTEL** > 95–99 Lancaster Gate ⊖ Lancaster Gate ☏ 020/7402 0021, Ⓦ www.columbiahotel.co.uk. MAP PP.130–131, POCKET MAP C7. This large hotel, once five Victorian houses, offers simply decorated rooms, some with views over Hyde Park, a spacious public lounge with a vaguely Art Deco feel, and a cocktail bar. Said to be a rock-star favourite, but surprisingly good value for all that. En-suite triples and quads also available. **£90**

**GARDEN COURT HOTEL** > 30–31 Kensington Gardens Square ⊖ Bayswater or Queensway ☏ 020/7229 2553, Ⓦ www.garden courthotel.co.uk. MAP PP.130–131, POCKET MAP B6. Nicely refurbished family-run B&B close to Portobello Market; rooms are small, and the cheaper ones have shared facilities. English breakfast. **£75**

**THE HALKIN** > 5 Halkin St ⊖ Hyde Park Corner ☏ 020/7333 1000, Ⓦ www .halkin.como.bz. MAP PP.130–131, POCKET MAP B19. A luxury hotel that spurns the chintzy country-house theme: elegant, East-meets-West minimalism prevails in each of the 41 rooms. The contemporary theme is continued in the Michelin-starred Thai restaurant, which overlooks a private garden. **£250–450**

**HOLLAND HOUSE YHA** > Holland Walk ⊖ Holland Park or High Street Kensington ☏ 0845/371 9122, Ⓦ www.yha.org.uk. MAP PP.130–131, POCKET MAP A8. Idyllically situated in Holland Park and fairly convenient for the centre. Kitchen available and café. Popular with groups. Dorms (4–10 beds) only. **Dorms £25**

**THE MAIN HOUSE** > 6 Colville Rd ⊖ Ladbroke Grove or Notting Hill Gate ☏ 020/7221 9691, Ⓦ www .themainhouse.co.uk. MAP PP.130–131, POCKET MAP A6. Bright and cheerful place that manages to be both homely – thanks to some lovely period furniture – and chic. Perfectly placed for Portobello Road. Breakfast not included. **£110**

**MEININGER** > Baden Powell House, 65–67 Queen's Gate ⊖ Gloucester Road or South Kensington ☏ 020/3051 8173, Ⓦ www.meininger-hostels.com. MAP PP.130–131, POCKET MAP C9. Bright and cheerful modern hostel, part of a German chain, run with Teutonic efficiency and located near the South Ken museums. Free wi-fi. Kitchen, but no laundry; breakfast not included. Dorms (4–6 beds) available. **Dorms from £19; doubles £45**

**MILLER'S RESIDENCE** > 111a Westbourne Grove ⊖ Bayswater ☏ 020/7243 1024, Ⓦ www.millersuk .com. MAP PP.130–131, POCKET MAP B6. Every inch of this grandiose and eccentric B&B is littered with nineteenth-century antiques, from the sumptuous baronial drawing room (much in demand for fashion shoots) to the bedrooms. Some rooms are a little small and dark for the price, but the welcome is warm and the ambience unique. Access from Hereford Road. **£180**

**PAVILION HOTEL** > 34–36 Sussex Gardens ⊖ Edgware Road ☏ 020/7262 0905, Ⓦ www.pavilionhoteluk.com. MAP PP.130–131, POCKET MAP D5. A decadent rock star's home from home, with outrageously over-the-top decor and every room individually themed, from "honky-tonk Afro" to "Highland Fling". Service can be erratic but it's perfect for those who like their hotels a bit quirky. **£100**

**PORTOBELLO GOLD** > 95–97 Portobello Rd ⊖ Notting Hill Gate or Ladbroke Grove ☏ 020/7460 4910, Ⓦ www.portobellogold.com. MAP PP.130–131, POCKET MAP A6.

A fun and friendly option above a cheery modern pub/seafood restaurant. The seven rooms are plain and some are tiny, with miniature en-suite bathrooms, but the hotel also has a great apartment (sleeps 6 – at a bit of a pinch), with a dinky Caribbean-themed bathroom and fantastic roof terrace (and putting green). Breakfast not included. **£70**

**ST DAVID'S HOTELS** > 14–20 Norfolk Square ⊖ Paddington ☎ 020/7723 3856 or 4963, Ⓦ www.stdavidshotels .com. MAP PP.130–131, POCKET MAP D6. Inexpensive, family-run B&B, famed for its substantial English breakfast. Most rooms are en suite, and the large family rooms make it a good option for families on a budget. **£60**

**VICARAGE HOTEL** > 10 Vicarage Gate ⊖ High Street Kensington or Notting Hill Gate ☎ 020/7229 4030, Ⓦ www .londonvicaragehotel.com. MAP PP.130–131, POCKET MAP B8. Ideally located B&B on a quiet street a step away from Kensington Gardens. Clean and smart floral rooms with shared facilities; full English breakfast included. **£93**

# Regent's Park and Camden

**NEW INN** > 2 Allitsen Rd ⊖ St John's Wood ☎ 020/7722 0726, Ⓦ www .newinnlondon.co.uk. MAP P.145, POCKET MAP D3. Landlady Jan runs an excellent B&B with just five rooms above a nice pub (with good Thai food), in a quiet street a few minutes' walk from the north edge of Regent's Park. Breakfast is £5–8 extra. **£75**

# Hampstead and Highgate

**HAMPSTEAD VILLAGE GUESTHOUSE** > 2 Kemplay Rd ⊖ Hampstead or Hampstead Heath Overground ☎ 020/7435 8679, Ⓦ www.hampsteadguesthouse.com. MAP PP.152–153. Lovely B&B in a freestanding Victorian house on a quiet backstreet between Hampstead village and the Heath. Rooms (most en-suite) are tiny but characterful, crammed with books, pictures and handmade and antique furniture. **£75**

**LANGORF HOTEL** > 20 Frognal ⊖ Finchley Road or Finchley Road & Frognal Overground ☎ 020/7794 4483, Ⓦ www.langorfhotel.com. MAP PP.152–153. Pristinely maintained if rather old-fashioned hotel in a trio of red-brick Victorian mansions, with a walled garden. Apartments (sleeping 3–4) also available. **£90–100**

# Greenwich

**DEVONPORT HOUSE** > King William Walk ⊖ Greenwich DLR or train station from Charing Cross ☎ 020/8283 3121, Ⓦ www.deverevenues.co.uk. MAP P.158. Right in the centre of Greenwich, these conference-centre rooms are functional, but worth it if you can find an online bargain. **£80–170**

# Kew and Richmond

**THE OLD STABLES** > 1 Bridle Lane, Twickenham. St Margarets train station from Waterloo ☎ 020/8892 4507, Ⓦ www.oldestables.com. MAP P.163. Three bedrooms and one studio apartment in a lovely house in a quiet street right by the train station; walking distance to Richmond and the Thames. No onsite staff, but the manager is a phone call away. **£75**

# Hampton Court

**PADDOCK LODGE** > The Green, Hampton Court Road. Hampton Court train station from Waterloo ☎ 020/8979 5254, ✉ paddocklodge @compuserve.com. MAP P.169. A secluded Palladian villa set down a leafy lane amidst wonderful gardens, with just two luxurious rooms. Excellent breakfast; four-course dinner available by arrangement. **£90**

ESSENTIALS

# Arrival

The majority of visitors arrive in London at one of its five airports, all but one of which can involve an expensive trip to the centre. Those arriving by train or bus are dropped right in the middle of the city, with easy access to public transport.

## By plane

Flying into London, you'll arrive at Heathrow, Gatwick, Stansted, Luton or City **airport**, each of which is less than an hour from the city centre.

### HEATHROW

Heathrow Airport (☏ 0870/000 0123, Ⓦ www.heathrowairport.com) lies around fifteen miles west of central London, and is the city's busiest airport, with five terminals and three train/tube stations: one for terminals 1, 2 and 3, and separate ones for terminals 4 and 5. The fastest **train** service into London is the high-speed, non-stop Heathrow Express to Paddington station (daily 5am–11.30pm; journey 15–21min); tickets cost £16.50 one way or £32 return. Heathrow Connect trains stop at intermediate stations (Mon–Sat 5.30am–midnight, Sun 6am–midnight; every 30min; journey 25min) but tickets cost just £7 single and £14 return. A cheaper alternative is to take the Piccadilly **Underground** line, which connects the airport to numerous tube stations across central London (Mon–Sat 5am–11.30pm, Sun 6am–11.30pm; every 5min; journey 50min); tickets cost just £4.50 single, or £7.50 for an Off-Peak One-Day Travelcard (Zones 1–6) (see "City transport", p.000). A **taxi** from Heathrow will cost in the region of £50–70, depending on traffic and the time of day.

### GATWICK

Gatwick Airport (☏ 0870/000 2468, Ⓦ www.gatwickairport.com) is around thirty miles south of London, and has a train station at its South Terminal. Non-stop Gatwick Express **trains** run between the airport and London Victoria (daily 4.30am–12.30am; every 15min; journey 30min); tickets cost around £17 single, £29 return. It's cheaper, however, to take a Southern train to Victoria (every 15min; journey 35min), or a First Capital Connect train to one of various stations within London (every 15–30min; journey 30–40min), including London Bridge and King's Cross; tickets for either cost around £10 single. easyBus (Ⓦ www .easybus.co.uk) runs **buses** to Fulham Broadway tube (6.40am–11pm; every 15–20min; 1hr 10min), with online tickets going for as little as £2 single (£10 if you buy on board). National Express buses run from Gatwick direct to central London (5am–9.30pm; hourly; 1hr 30min): tickets cost around £7 single, £15 return. A **taxi** will set you back a ludicrous £90 or more, and take an hour or more.

### STANSTED

Stansted Airport (☏ 0870/000 0303, Ⓦ www.stanstedairport.com) is roughly 35 miles northeast of the capital. Stansted Express **trains** run non-stop to Liverpool Street (5.30am–12.30am; every 15–30min; journey 45min), and cost £18 single, £30 return. easyBus (Ⓦ www .easybus.co.uk) runs buses to Baker Street tube (daily 7am–1am; every 20min; 1hr 30min), with online tickets going for as little as £2 single (£10 if you buy on board). National Express runs buses 24 hours a day calling at various places in London en route to Victoria Coach Station (every

10–30min; journey 1hr–1hr 40min), with tickets for around £10 single. Terravision (☎ 01279/680028, ⓦ www .terravision.eu) also runs coaches to Liverpool Street (daily 7am–1am; every 30min; journey time 1hr–1hr 15min), with tickets £9 single, £13 return. A **taxi** will set you back £80 or more, and take at least an hour.

## LUTON

London Luton Airport (☎ 01582/405100, ⓦ www.london -luton.com) is roughly thirty miles north of London and mainly handles low-cost flights. A free shuttle bus takes five minutes to reach Luton Airport Parkway station, which is connected by **train** to King's Cross St Pancras (every 15–30min; journey 35–40min) and other stations in central London; single tickets cost around £11. All year round, 24 hours a day, Green Line (ⓦ www.greenline .co.uk) and easyBus (ⓦ www .easybus.co.uk) run up to three buses an hour from Luton to Victoria Station (every 15–30min; journey 1hr 20min), stopping at several locations en route, including Baker Street; tickets cost as little as £2 if you book in advance online (or £12 single, £15 return if you don't). A **taxi** will cost in the region of £60 and take at least an hour to central London.

## CITY

London City Airport (☎ 020/7646 0000, ⓦ www.londoncityairport .com), the capital's smallest and used primarily by business folk, is situated in the Royal Albert Docks, ten miles east of central London, and handles almost exclusively Euro-pean flights. The **Docklands Light Railway** (DLR) takes you straight to Bank in the City (Mon–Sat 5.30am– 12.30am, Sun 7am–11.30pm; every

8–15min; journey 20min), where you can change to the tube; single tickets cost around £4. A **taxi** from the airport to the City's financial sector will cost around £20, and take half an hour or so.

## By train and coach

**Eurostar** (☎ 0870/160 6600, ⓦ www.eurostar.com) trains arrive at the beautifully refurbished St Pancras International train station, next door to King's Cross, which is served by several Underground lines. Arriving by **train** from elsewhere in Britain (☎ 0845/748 4950, ⓦ www.nationalrail.co.uk), you'll come into one of London's numerous mainline stations, all of which have nearby Underground stations linking into the city centre's tube network. Trains from the Channel ports arrive at Charing Cross or Victoria, while boat trains from Harwich, on the North Sea coast, arrive at Liverpool Street. Coming into London by **coach** (☎ 0870/580 8080, ⓦ www. nationalexpress.com), you're most likely to arrive at Victoria Coach Station, a couple of hundred yards south down Buckingham Palace Road from Victoria train station and tube.

### Fly Less – Stay Longer!

Rough Guides believes in the good that travel does, but we are deeply aware of the impact of fuel emissions on climate change. We recommend taking fewer trips and staying for longer. If you can avoid travelling by air, please use an alternative, especially for journeys of under 1000km/600 miles. And always offset your travel at ⓦ www .roughguides.com/climatechange.

# Getting around

London's transport system has definitely improved over the past decade. The congestion charge reduced traffic by thirty percent within central London, and much of the money was ploughed into improving the buses. That said, London still has one of the most expensive transport systems in the world.

**Transport for London** (TfL) provides excellent free maps and information on bus and tube services from its six **Travel Information Centres**: the most central one is at Piccadilly Circus tube station (daily 9.15am–7pm), with other desks at Heathrow arrivals (terminals 1, 2 and 3), Victoria, Euston and Liverpool Street train stations, and Camden Town Hall, opposite King's Cross St Pancras. There's also a **24-hour helpline** and an excellent website (☏ 020/7222 1234, ⊛ www.tfl.gov.uk).

For transport purposes, London is divided into six concentric **zones** (plus a few extra in the northwest), with fares calculated depending on which zones you travel through: the majority of the city's accommodation and sights lie in zones 1 and 2. If you cannot produce a valid ticket for your journey, or travel further than your ticket allows, you will be liable to a **Penalty Fare** of £50, reduced to £25 if you pay within 21 days. Try and avoid travelling during the **rush hour** (Mon–Fri 8–9.30am and 5–7pm) if possible, when tubes can become unbearably crowded and hot, and some buses get so full they literally won't let you on.

## Oyster cards and tickets

The cheapest, easiest way to get about London is to use an **Oyster card**, London's transport smartcard, available from all tube stations and TfL Travel Information Centres, and valid on the bus, tube, Docklands Light Railway (DLR), Tramlink, Overground and almost all suburban rail services. The simplest way to use an Oyster card is as a pay-as-you-go card – you can top-up your card with credit at all tube stations and most newsagents. As you enter the tube or bus, simply touch in your card at the card reader and the fare will be taken off. If you're using the tube or train, you need to touch out again or up to £6.50 will be deducted. Oyster operates daily price-capping so that when you've paid the equivalent of a daily Travelcard (see below), it will stop taking money off your card, though you still need to touch in (and out). To obtain an Oyster card you must hand over a £3 refundable deposit; visitors can buy one for just £2 online.

If you don't have an Oyster card, you can still buy a paper **Travelcard** from machines and booths at all tube and train stations (and at many newsagents too – look for the sign). Anytime Day Travelcards start from £7.20 (zones 1 and 2); Off-Peak Travelcards are valid after 9.30am on weekdays and all day at the weekend, and cost £5.60 (zones 1 and 2), rising to £7.50 for zones 1–6. If you need to travel before 9.30am, it's worth considering an Anytime 3-Day Travelcard, which costs from £18.40 (zones 1 and 2), .

**Children** under 11 travel for free; children aged 11–15 travel free on all buses and trams and at child-rate on the tube; children aged 16 or 17 can travel at child-rate on all forms of transport. However, all children over 10 must have an Oyster photocard to be eligible for free travel – these should be applied for in advance online. Without a photocard, you can buy an Off-Peak Day Travelcard (zones 1–9) for children aged 11–15 for just £1, providing they're travelling with an adult.

## The tube

Except for very short journeys, the **Underground** – or tube, as it's known to Londoners – is by far the quickest way to get about. Eleven different lines cross the metropolis, each with its own colour and name – all you need to know is which direction you're travelling in: northbound, eastbound, southbound or westbound (this gets tricky when taking the Circle Line). As a precaution, it's also worth checking the final destination displayed on the front of the train, as some lines, such as the District and Northern lines, have several different branches.

Services are frequent (Mon–Sat 5.30am–12.30am, Sun 7.30am–11.30pm), and you rarely have to wait more than five minutes for a train between central stations. **Tickets** must be bought in advance from automatic machines or from a ticket booth in the station entrance hall. Single fares are outrageously expensive – a journey in the central zone costs an unbelievable £4 – so if you're intending to make more than one journey, an Oyster card or a Travelcard is by far your best option.

## Buses

London's famous red double-decker **buses** are fun to ride on, but struggle to run to a regular timetable due to the volume of traffic. In the Pay Before You Board zone in central London, and on all the extra-long "bendy buses", you must have a valid ticket before boarding, whether an Oyster card, Travelcard, or a single ticket (£2) from the bus-stop ticket machines (which don't give out change); elsewhere, you can buy it from the driver.

A lot of bus stops are **request stops** (easily recognizable by their red sign) – stick your arm out to hail the bus or it will pass you by, and when on board ring the bell to request it to stop. Some buses run a 24-hour service, but most run between 5am and midnight. **Night-buses** (prefixed with the letter "N"), operating outside this period, depart at twenty- to thirty-minute intervals, more frequently on some routes and on Friday and Saturday nights.

## Suburban train lines

To reach some of London's far-flung sights, you may need to use the suburban **train** network, sections of which are now known as the London Overground. For enquiries, call ☎ 0845/748 4950 or visit ⓦ www .nationalrail.co.uk. In East London, the **Docklands Light Railway** (DLR) runs driverless trains to Docklands, Greenwich and beyond. Oyster and Travelcards are valid on all suburban, Overground and DLR trains.

## Cycling

Cycling is increasingly popular in London because – in the centre at least – it's the fastest way to get around. Only folding bikes can be taken on public transport, although conventional bikes can go on certain tube and railway lines at off-peak times – check ⓦ www.tfl.gov.uk for details. **Cycle Hire** is London's public bicycle sharing scheme, perfect for short journeys, with over 400 docking stations. It's £3 for a key, and £1 for access, after which the first 30 minutes are free, the first hour's £1, increasing rapidly after that to £15 for three hours. Bikes can be **rented** from the London Bicycle Tour Company, 1a Gabriel Wharf on the South Bank (☎ 020/7923 6838, ⓦ www.londonbicycle.com), costing around £20 a day or £50 a week.

## The London Pass

If you're thinking of visiting a lot of fee-paying attractions in a short space of time, it's worth considering buying a **London Pass** (ⓦwww .londonpass.com), which gives you free entry to a whole host of attractions including Hampton Court Palace, Kensington Palace, Kew Gardens, London Zoo, St Paul's Cathedral and the Tower of London. The pass costs around £39 for one day (£26 for kids), rising to £89 for six days (£62 for kids). The London Pass can be bought online or in person from tourist offices and from London's mainline train and principal underground stations.

## Taxis

Compared to most capital cities, London's metered **black cabs** are an expensive option unless there are three or more of you. The minimum fare is £2.20, and a ride from Euston to Victoria, for example, costs around £12–15 (Mon–Fri 6am–8pm). After 8pm on weekdays and all day during the weekend, a higher tariff applies, and after 10pm, it's higher still. Tipping is customary. An illuminated yellow light tells you if the cab is available – just stick your arm out to hail it. London's cabbies are the best trained in Europe; every one of them knows the shortest route between any two points in the capital, and they won't rip you off by taking another route. They are, however, a blunt and forthright breed, renowned for their generally reactionary opinions. To order a black cab in advance, phone ☎0871/871 8710, and be prepared to pay an extra £2.

**Minicabs** look just like regular cars and are considerably cheaper than black cabs, but they cannot be hailed from the street. All minicabs should be able to produce a Public Carriage Office licence on demand. There are hundreds of minicab firms in the phone book, but the best way to pick is to take the advice of the place you're at, unless you want to be certain of a woman driver, in which case book a cab from Ladycabs (☎020/7272 3300), or a gay/ lesbian-friendly driver, in which case call Freedom Cars (☎020/7739 9080). Avoid illegal taxi touts, who hang around outside venues alongside licensed cabs, and always establish the fare beforehand as minicabs are not metered.

Last, and definitely least, there's currently a plague of pedicabs or **bicycle taxis** in the West End after nightfall. The oldest and biggest of the bunch are Bugbugs (☎020/7353 4028, ⓦwww.bugbugs.com). The rickshaws take up to three passengers and fares are negotiable, so you should always agree a price beforehand, based on a fare of around £3–5 per person.

## Boats

Unfortunately, **boat services** on the Thames are not fully integrated into the public transport system. Timetables and services are complex – for a full list pick up a booklet from a TfL information office (see p.000) or visit ⓦwww.tfl.gov.uk /river. You can pay for your fare using your Oyster card (and get 10 percent off single fares), but price-capping doesn't apply. One of the largest companies is Thames Clippers (ⓦwww.thamesclippers.com), who run a regular **commuter service** (Mon–Fri 7am–11.30pm, Sat and Sun 9am–11.30pm; every 20–30min) between Waterloo and Greenwich (including the Dome), with some boats going as far as Woolwich. Typical fares are £5 single, with an unlimited hop-on, hop-off River Roamer day ticket costing £12.

Other companies run boats upstream to Kew, Richmond and Hampton Court (see box, p.164). Look out, too, for the MV *Balmoral* and paddle-steamer *Waverley*, which make regular visits to Tower Pier in the summer and autumn (☎ 0845/130 4647, ⊛ www.waverleyexcursions .co.uk).

## Sightseeing tours and guided walks

Standard **sightseeing tours** are run by several rival bus companies, their open-top double-deckers setting off every thirty minutes from Victoria station, Trafalgar Square, Piccadilly and other conspicuous tourist spots. You can hop on and off several different routes as often as you like with The Original Tour (☎ 020/8877 1722, ⊛ www.theoriginaltour.com; daily 8.30am–6pm; every 15–20min; £24). Alternatively, you can climb aboard one of the bright-yellow World War II D-Day amphibious vehicles used by London Duck Tours (☎ 020/7928 3132, ⊛ www.londonducktours .co.uk), which offers a combined bus and boat tour (daily 9.30am–6pm or dusk; £20). After departing from behind County Hall, near the London Eye, you spend 45 minutes driving round the usual sights, before plunging into the river for a half-hour cruise; advance booking is essential.

A much cheaper option is to hop on a real **London double-decker** – the #11 bus from Victoria station, for example, will take you past Westminster Abbey, the Houses of Parliament, up Whitehall, round Trafalgar Square, along the Strand and on to St Paul's Cathedral. Alternatively, you can take an old double-decker **Routemaster**, with open rear platform and roving conductor, on two "heritage" routes (daily every 15min 9.30am–6.30pm): #9 from the Royal Albert Hall to Aldwych and #15 from Trafalgar Square to Tower Hill.

**Walking tours** are infinitely more appealing and informative, mixing solid historical facts with juicy anecdotes in the company of a local specialist. Walks on offer range from a literary pub crawl round Bloomsbury to a roam around the East End. You'll find most of them detailed in *Time Out* magazine (see p.193); as you'd imagine, there's more variety on offer in the summer months. Tours cost around £5 and take around two hours; normally you can simply show up at the starting point and join. If you want to plan – or book – walks in advance, contact the most reliable and well-established company, Original London Walks (☎ 020/7624 3978, ⊛ www.walks.com).

---

## Congestion charge

All vehicles entering central London on weekdays between 7am and 6.30pm are liable to a congestion charge of £8 per vehicle. Drivers can pay the charge online, over the phone and at garages and shops, and must do so before midnight the same day or incur a £2 surcharge – 24 hours later, you'll be liable for a £120 **fine**. Local residents, the disabled, motorcycles, minibuses and some alternative-fuel vehicles are exempt from the charge, but must register in order to qualify. For more details, visit ⊛ www.tfl.gov.uk.

# Directory A–Z

## Addresses

London addresses come with postcodes at the end. Each street name is followed by a letter or letters giving the geographical location of the street in relation to the City (E for "east", WC for "west central" and so on) and a number that specifies its location more precisely. Unfortunately, this number doesn't correspond to the district's distance from the centre. Full postal addresses end with a digit and two letters, which specify the individual block, but these are only used in correspondence.

## Cricket

Most years three Test matches are played in London each summer: two at **Lord's** (☎ 020/7432 1000, ⓦ www.lords.org; ➜ St John's Wood), the home of English cricket; the other at **The Oval** (☎ 0871/2461 100, ⓦ www.britoval.com; ➜ Oval). There are also numerous one-day internationals and Twenty20 matches, some of which are usually held in London.

## Crime

Should you have anything stolen or be involved in an incident that requires reporting, go to the local **police station** (ⓦ www.met.police.uk) or phone ☎ 0300/123 1212; the ☎ 999 number should only be used in emergencies. Central 24hr police stations include: Charing Cross, Agar St ➜ Charing Cross; Holborn, 10 Lambs Conduit St ➜ Holborn; Marylebone, 1–9 Seymour St ➜ Marble Arch; and West End Central, 27 Savile Row ➜ Piccadilly Circus. The City of London Police (☎ 020/7601 2222, ⓦ www.cityoflondon.police.uk) are separate from the Metropolitan Police, and have their headquarters at 182 Bishopsgate ➜ Liverpool

Street. If there's an incident on public transport, call the British Transport Police on ☎ 0800/405040. For **Rape Crisis**, contact ☎ 020/8683 3300, ⓦ www.rapecrisis.org.uk.

## Electricity

Electricity supply in London conforms to the EU standard of approximately 230V. Sockets are designed for British **three-pin plugs**, which are totally different from those in the mainland EU and North America.

## Embassies and consulates

**Australian High Commission** Australia House, Strand ☎ 020/7379 4334, ⓦ www.australia.org.uk; ➜ Temple tube. **Canadian High Commission** 1 Grosvenor Square ☎ 020/7528 6600, ⓦ www.dfait-maeci.gc.ca; ➜ Bond Street. **Irish Embassy** 17 Grosvenor Place ☎ 020/7235 2171, ⓦ www.embassyofireland.co.uk; ➜ Hyde Park Corner. **New Zealand High Commission** New Zealand House, 80 Haymarket ☎ 020/7930 8422, ⓦ www.nzembassy.com; ➜ Charing Cross. **South African High Commission** South Africa House, Trafalgar Square ☎ 020/7451 7299, ⓦ www.southafricahouse.com; ➜ Charing Cross. **US Embassy** 24 Grosvenor Square ☎ 020/7499 9000, ⓦ www.usembassy.org.uk; ➜ Bond Street.

## Football

Over the decades, London's most successful club by far has been **Arsenal** (☎ 020/7704 4040, ⓦ www.arsenal.com). However, since the arrival of Russian oil tycoon Roman Abramovich, fellow London club **Chelsea** (☎ 020/7386 9373, ⓦ www.chelseafc.com) have had a resurgence, winning the league for the first time in fifty years in 2005. Chelsea's closest rivals (geographically) are **Fulham** (☎ 0870/442 1234,

## Emergencies

For **police**, fire and ambulance services, call ☎ 999.

ⓦ www.fulhamfc.com), while Arsenal's are **Tottenham Hotspur** (☎ 0870/420 5000, ⓦ www .tottenhamhotspur.com). East London's premier club is **West Ham** (☎ 0871/222 2700, ⓦ www.whufc .com). Tickets for most Premier League games start at £30–40 and are virtually impossible to get hold of on a casual basis, though you may be able to see one of the Cup fixtures. A better bet is to head to one of London's numerous, less illustrious clubs such as **Crystal Palace** (ⓦ www.cpfc.co.uk), **Millwall** (ⓦ www.millwallfc.co.uk) or **Queens Park Rangers** (ⓦ www.qpr.co.uk).

### Gay and lesbian travellers

London Lesbian and Gay Switchboard (☎ 020/7837 7324, ⓦ www.llgs.org .uk) has a huge database of everything you might ever want to know, plus legal advice and counselling. Lines are open 24hr: keep trying if you can't get through.

### Health

For minor complaints, pharmacists, known as **chemists** in England, can dispense a limited range of drugs without a doctor's prescription. Most pharmacies are open standard shop hours, though some stay open later: Zafash, 233–235 Old Brompton Rd, SW5 (☎ 020/7373 2798; ⊖ Earl's Court), is open 24 hours; while Bliss, at 5–6 Marble Arch, W1 ☎ 020/3302 8345 (⊖ Marble Arch), is open daily 9am till midnight. Every police station keeps a list of late-opening pharmacies.

If there's an emergency, you can turn up at the **Accident and Emergency** (A&E) department of your local hospital, or phone for an ambulance (☎ 999). A&E services are free to all. You can also go to a **Minor Injuries Clinic** such as the one at St Bartholomew's Hospital, West Smithfield (☎ 020/7601 7407; ⊖ Farringdon), or get free medical advice from NHS Direct, the health service's 24-hour helpline (☎ 0845/4647, ⓦ www.nhsdirect.nhs. uk). For emergency **dental treatment**, make for Guy's Hospital, St Thomas St SE1 (Mon–Fri 9am–5pm; ☎ 020/7188 7188; ⊖ London Bridge).

### Internet

Many hotels and hostels in London have internet access. After that, your best bet is a café with **wi-fi**; try the one in Foyles bookshop at 113–119 Charing Cross Rd (⊖ Tottenham Court Road). Alternatively, to find an **internet café** (£2–5 per hour) log on to ⓦ www.easyinternetcafe.com. In addition, most **public libraries** offer free access.

### Left luggage

**Airports** Gatwick: North Terminal ☎ 01293/502013 (daily 5am–9pm); South Terminal ☎ 01293/502014 (24hr). Heathrow ☎ 020/8759 3344: Terminal 1 (daily 6am–11pm); Terminal 2 (daily 5.30am–11pm); Terminal 3 (daily 6am–10pm); Terminal 4 and 5 (daily 5.30am–11pm). London City ☎ 020/7646 0000 (daily 6am–10pm). Luton ☎ 01582/405100 (24hr). Stansted ☎ 01279/663213 (4am–midnight). **Train stations** All are open daily 7am–11pm except where noted: Charing Cross ☎ 020/7930 5444; Euston ☎ 020/7387 1499; King's Cross ☎ 020/7837 4334; Liverpool Street ☎ 020/7247 4297; Paddington ☎ 020/7262 0344; St Pancras ☎ 020/7833 1596 (Mon–Sat 6am–10pm, Sun 7am–10pm); Victoria ☎ 020/7963 0957 (daily 7am–midnight); Waterloo ☎ 020/7401 8444.

## Lost property

**Airports** Gatwick ☎ 01293/503162 (Mon–Sat 8am–7pm, Sun 8am–4pm); Heathrow ☎ 020/8745 7727 (Mon–Sat 8am–7pm, Sun 8am–4pm); London City ☎ 020/7646 0000 (daily 6am–10pm); Luton ☎ 01582/395219; Stansted ☎ 01279/663293 (daily 9.30am–4.30pm). **Buses** ☎ 020/7222 1234, ⊛ www.tfl.gov.uk (24hr). **Eurostar** ☎ 0870/160 0052. **Train stations** ☎ 0870/000 5151, ⊛ www.networkrail.co.uk: Euston ☎ 020/7387 8699 (Mon–Fri 9am–5.30pm); King's Cross ☎ 020/7278 3310 (Mon–Sat 9am–5pm); Liverpool St ☎ 020/7247 4297 (Mon–Fri 9am–5.30pm); Paddington ☎ 020/7313 1514 (Mon–Fri 9am–5.30pm); St Pancras ☎ 020/7833 1596 (Mon–Sat 6am–10pm, Sun 7am–10pm); Victoria ☎ 020/7963 0957 (Mon–Fri 9am–5.15pm); Waterloo ☎ 020/7401 7861 (Mon–Fri 7.30am–7pm). **Tubes and black cabs** Transport for London Lost Property Office, 200 Baker St NW1 ☎ 020/7918 2000, ⊛ www .tfl.gov.uk (Mon–Fri 8.30am–4pm).

## Money

The basic unit of **currency** is the pound sterling (£), divided into 100 pence (p). Coins come in denominations of 1p, 2p, 5p, 10p; 20p, 50p, £1 and £2; notes come in denominations of £5, £10, £20 and £50. Many shopkeepers may not accept £50 notes – the best advice is to avoid having to use them. The exchange rate can fluctuate considerably, but at the time of writing, £1 was worth $1.50, €1.10, C$1.55, A$1.65, NZ$2.20 and ZAR11.30. For the most up-to-date exchange rates, see the useful currency converter websites ⊛ www.oanda.com or www.xe.com.

**Credit/debit cards** are by far the most convenient way to carry your money, and most hotels, shops and restaurants in London accept the major brand cards. There are ATMs all over the city and every area has a branch of at least one of the big-four high-street **banks** (NatWest, Barclays, Lloyds TSB and HSBC); opening hours are generally Mon–Fri 9.30am–4.30pm. Outside banking hours go to a **bureau de change**; these can be found at train stations and airports and in most areas of the city centre.

The high **cost** of accommodation, food and drink make London a very expensive place to visit. Staying in a budget hotel and eating takeaways, you'll still need in the region of £50 per person per day. Add in a restaurant meal and tourist attraction or two, and you are looking at £75–100.

## Opening hours

Generally speaking, opening hours are Monday to Saturday 9am or 10am to around 6pm and Sundays noon to 6pm. Some places in central London stay open until 7pm, and later on Thursdays and Fridays (around 9pm).

## Phones

Public **payphones** are ubiquitous on the streets of London. Most take all coins from 10p upwards (40p minimum), some take only phonecards and credit cards, and some take all three. Discount call cards with a PIN number are the cheapest way to make international calls. If you're taking your **mobile/cell phone** with you, check with your service provider whether your phone will work abroad and what the call charges will be. Unless you have a tri-or quad-band phone, it's unlikely that a mobile bought for use in the US will work in London. Mobiles in Australia and New Zealand generally use the same system as the UK so should work fine.

## Post

The only (vaguely) late-opening post office is at 24–28 William IV St, near Trafalgar Square (☎ 020/7930 9580; Mon–Fri 8.30am–6.30pm, Tues opens 9.15am, Sat 9am–5.30pm); it's also the city's poste restante collection point. For general postal enquiries phone ☎ 0845/774 0740 (Mon–Fri 8am–6pm, Sat 8am–1pm), or visit ⓦ www.royalmail.com.

## Smoking

Smoking is banned in all indoor public spaces including all cafés, pubs, restaurants, clubs and public transport.

## Time

**Greenwich Mean Time** (GMT) is used from the end of October to the end of March; for the rest of the year the country switches to **British Summer Time** (BST), one hour ahead of GMT. GMT is two hours behind South Africa, five hours ahead of the US East Coast; eight ahead of the US West Coast; and nine behind Australia's East Coast.

## Tipping

There are no fixed rules for tipping. However, there's a certain expectation in restaurants or cafés that you should leave a tip of ten percent of the total bill – check first, though, that service has not already been included. Taxi drivers also expect tips – add about ten percent of the fare – as do traditional barbers. The other occasion when you'll be expected to tip is in upmarket hotels where porters and table waiters rely on being tipped to bump up their often dismal wages.

## Toilets

There are surprisingly few public toilets in London. All mainline train and major tube stations have toilets. Department stores and free

museums and galleries are another good option.

## Tourist information

The chief tourist office in London is the **Britain & London Visitor Centre**, 1 Regent St (April–Sept Mon 9.30am–6.30pm, Tues–Fri 9am–6.30pm, Sat 9am–5pm, Sun 10am–4pm; times vary slightly in winter and June–Sept; ⓦ www .visitbritain.co.uk; ⊖ Piccadilly Circus). Also useful is the **London Information Centre**, a tiny window in the tkts kiosk on Leicester Square (daily 10am–6pm; ☎ 020/7292 2333, ⓦ www.londontown.com; ⊖ Leicester Square).

The most useful listings magazine for visitors is **Time Out** (ⓦ www .timeout.com), which comes out every Tuesday and has a virtual monopoly on listings. It carries critical appraisals of much of the week's theatre, film, music, exhibitions, children's events and much more besides.

## Travellers with disabilities

London is an old city, not well equipped for travellers with disabilities, though all public venues are obliged to make some effort towards accessibility. Public transport is slowly improving, with most buses now wheelchair-accessible, and up to a quarter of all tube stations – they're marked with a blue symbol on the tube map.

## Travelling with children

London is a great place for children and needn't overly strain the parental pocket. The city boasts lots of excellent parks and gardens, public transport is free for under 11s and many of the major museums can be visited free of charge. For the most part kids are tolerated in most cafés and restaurants, less so in pubs.

# Festivals and events

## LONDON PARADE

**January 1** W www.londonparade.co.uk.
At noon, a procession of floats, marching bands, cheerleaders and clowns wends its way from Parliament Square to Green Park. Admission charge for grandstand seats in Piccadilly, otherwise free.

## CHINESE NEW YEAR

**late January/early to mid February**
W www.londonchinatown.org.
Soho's Chinatown, Leicester Square and even Trafalgar Square all erupt in a riot of dancing dragons and firecrackers – expect serious human congestion. Free.

## OXFORD AND CAMBRIDGE BOAT RACE

**late March/early April**
W www.theboatrace.org.
Since 1845 rowers from Oxford and Cambridge universities have battled it out over four miles from Putney to Mortlake. The pubs at prime vantage points pack out early. Free.

## LONDON MARATHON

**Third Sunday in April**
W www.london-marathon.co.uk.
The world's most popular marathon, with around 40,000 masochists sweating the 26.2-mile route. Most of the competitors are running for charity, often in some ludicrous costume. Free.

## IWA CANALWAY CAVALCADE

**May Bank Holiday weekend**
W www.waterways.org.uk.
Lively three-day celebration of the city's inland waterways, held at Little Venice, with scores of decorated narrow boats, Morris dancers and lots of children's activities. Free.

## BEATING RETREAT

**early June** W www.army.mod.uk.
Annual military display on Horse Guards' Parade over two consecutive evenings, marking the old custom of drumming and piping the troops back to base at dusk. Tickets must be booked in advance.

## TROOPING THE COLOUR

**second Saturday in June**
W www.army.mod.uk.
Ticket-only celebration of the Queen's official birthday featuring massed bands, gun salutes and fly-pasts. The royal procession along the Mall allows you a glimpse for free, and there are rehearsals (minus Her Majesty) on the two preceding Saturdays.

## WIMBLEDON LAWN TENNIS CHAMPIONSHIPS

**last week of June and first week of July**
W www.wimbledon.org.
This Grand Slam tournament (played on grass) is one of the highlights of the sporting and social calendar.

## PRIDE LONDON

**late June or early July**
W www.pridelondon.org.
Colourful, whistle-blowing lesbian and gay march through the city streets followed by a rally in Trafalgar Square.

## HENRY WOOD PROMENADE CONCERTS

**mid-July to mid-September.**
W www.bbc.co.uk/proms.
Commonly known as the Proms, this

series of nightly classical concerts at the Royal Albert Hall (and elsewhere) is a well-loved British institution.

## NOTTING HILL CARNIVAL

**last bank holiday weekend in August**

Ⓦ www.thenottinghillcarnival.com.

World famous two-day street festival established nearly fifty years ago, Carnival is a tumult of imaginatively decorated floats, eye-catching costumes, thumping sound systems, live bands, irresistible food and huge crowds. Free.

## OPEN HOUSE

**third weekend in September**

Ⓦ www.londonopenhouse.org.

A once-a-year opportunity to peek inside over 650 buildings around London, many of which don't normally open their doors to the public. You'll need to book in advance for some of the more popular places. Free.

## STATE OPENING OF PARLIAMENT

**late October/early November**

Ⓦ www.parliament.uk.

The Queen arrives by coach at the Houses of Parliament at 11am accompanied by the Household Cavalry and gun salutes. The ceremony itself takes place inside the House of Lords and is televised; it also takes place whenever a new government is sworn in. Free.

## LONDON FILM FESTIVAL

**November** Ⓦ www.bfi.org.uk/lff.

A two-week cinematic season with scores of new international films screened at the BFI Southbank and some West End venues.

## BONFIRE NIGHT

**November 5**

In memory of Guy Fawkes – who tried to blow up King James I and the Houses of Parliament in 1605 – effigies are burned on bonfires all over London, and numerous council-run fires and fireworks displays are staged. Free.

## LORD MAYOR'S SHOW

**second Saturday in November**

Ⓦ www.lordmayorsshow.org.

Big ceremonial procession from the Law Courts on the Strand to the Guildhall of some 140 floats, military bands and even the odd piece of military hardware, followed by the new Mayor in his gilded coach and a whole train of liverymen in carriages. After dark, there's a fireworks display on the Thames. Free.

## NEW YEAR

**New Year's Eve** Ⓦ www.london.gov.uk.

New Year is welcomed by thousands of revellers who get to enjoy a spectacular firework display centred on the London Eye. TfL runs free public transport all night, sponsored by various public-spirited breweries. Free.

## Public holidays

You'll find all banks and offices closed on the following days, while everything else pretty much runs to a Sunday schedule (except on Christmas Day when everything shuts down): New Year's Day (January 1); Good Friday (late March/April); Easter Monday (late March/April); Spring Bank Holiday (first Monday in May); May Bank Holiday (last Monday in May); August Bank Holiday (last Monday in August); Christmas Day (December 25); Boxing Day (December 26). Note that if January 1, December 25 or December 26 falls on a Saturday or Sunday, the holiday falls on the following weekday.

# Chronology

**43 AD** > Romans invade and establish a permanent military camp by the Thames called Londinium.

**c.61** > Queen Boudica, leader of the Iceni tribe, burns Londinium to the ground.

**c.100** > Londinium becomes the capital of the Roman province of Britannia, eventually boasting a vast basilica, a forum, an amphitheatre and several baths.

**410** > The Romans abandon Londinium and leave the place at the mercy of marauding Saxon pirates.

**871–1066** > The Danes and Norwegians fight it out with the kings of Wessex over who should control London.

**1066** > Following the defeat of the English King Harold at the Battle of Hastings, William the Conqueror, Duke of Normandy, is crowned king in Westminster Abbey.

**1290** > King Edward I expels London's Jewish population.

**1348** > The Black Death wipes out a third of London's population of 75,000.

**1381** > During the Peasants' Revolt, London is overrun by the rebels who lynch the archbishop, plus countless rich merchants and clerics.

**1532–39** > The Reformation: King Henry VIII breaks with the Roman Catholic church, establishes the Church of England, dissolves the monasteries and executes religious dissenters.

**1553–58** > The religious pendulum swings the other way as Elizabeth's fervently Catholic sister, forever known as "Bloody Mary", takes to the throne and it's the Protestants' turn to be martyred.

**1558–1603** > During the reign of Elizabeth I, London enjoys an economic boom and witnesses the English Renaissance, epitomized by the theatre of William Shakespeare.

**1603** > James VI of Scotland becomes James I of England, thereby uniting the two crowns and marking the beginning of the Stuart dynasty in England.

**1605** > The Gunpowder Plot to blow up the Houses of Parliament (and King James I along with it) is foiled and Guy Fawkes and his Catholic conspirators executed.

**1642–49** > English Civil War between the Parliamentarians and Royalists ends with the victory of the former under the leadership of Oliver Cromwell. King Charles I (1625–49) is tried and beheaded in Westminster.

**1660** > The Restoration: Charles I's son, Charles II (1660–1685), returns from exile to restore the monarchy and as the "Merry Monarch" actively encourages the development of the arts and sciences.

**1665** > The Great Plague kills some 100,000 Londoners, around a fifth of the population.

**1666** > The Great Fire rages for four days, kills just seven people but destroys four-fifths of the City.

**1714–1830** > The Georgian period: from the reign of George I to George IV, London's population doubles to one million, making it Europe's largest city. The period is one of boom and bust, gin drinking, rioting and hanging.

**1750** > Westminster Bridge opens, the first rival river crossing to London Bridge in over seven centuries.

**1836** > London gets its first railway line from London Bridge to Greenwich.

**1837–1901** > During the reign of Queen Victoria, London becomes the capital of an empire that stretches across the globe. Its population increases to nearly seven million, making it the largest city in the world. Industrialization brings pollution, overcrowding and extreme poverty.

**1851** > The Great Exhibition is held in a giant glasshouse known as the "Crystal Palace", erected in Hyde Park.

**1855** > The Metropolitan Board of Works is established to organize the rapidly expanding city's infrastructure.

**1914–18** > During World War I, London experiences its first aerial attacks, with Zeppelin raids leaving some 650 dead – a minor skirmish in the context of a war that takes the lives of millions.

**1939–45** > During the course of World War II, London suffers a lot of bomb damage, with 60,000 killed and many thousands more made homeless.

**1948** > The SS *Windrush* brings the first postwar immigrants to London from the West Indies; over the next two decades, thousands more follow suit from former colonies all over the world.

**1951** > The Festival of Britain is held on the south bank of the Thames in an attempt to dispel the postwar gloom. The Royal Festival Hall is its one lasting legacy.

**1960s** > Pop music and fashion helps turn London into the epicentre of the "Swinging Sixties", with King's Road and Carnaby Street the hippest places to shop and be seen.

**1980s** > Under the Conservative Thatcher government, the gap between rich and poor grows. Homelessness returns to London in a big way and London's governing body, the GLC, is abolished, leaving London as the only European city without a directly elected body to represent it.

**2000** > London gets to vote for its own Mayor (Ken Livingstone) and its own elected assembly. London's national museums introduce free entry, the London Eye enhances the city's skyline and the Millennium Dome opens for one year, and proves a critical and financial flop.

**2005** > London wins the right to hold the 2012 Olympic Games. A day later on July 7, the city is hit by four suicide bombers who kill themselves and over fifty commuters in four separate explosions.

**2008** > Conservative candidate Boris Johnson defeats Ken Livingstone and becomes Mayor of London.

## PUBLISHING INFORMATION

This first edition published January 2011 by **Rough Guides Ltd**

80 Strand, London WC2R 0RL

11, Community Centre, Panchsheel Park, New Delhi 110017, India

**Distributed by the Penguin Group**

Penguin Books Ltd, 80 Strand, London WC2R 0RL

Penguin Group (USA) 375 Hudson Street, NY 10014, USA

Penguin Group (Australia) 250 Camberwell Road, Camberwell, Victoria 3124, Australia

Penguin Group (NZ) 67 Apollo Drive, Mairangi Bay, Auckland 1310, New Zealand

This paperback edition published in Canada in 2010. Rough Guides is represented in Canada by Tourmaline Editions Inc., 662 King Street West, Suite 304, Toronto, Ontario, M5V 1M7

Typeset in Minion and Din to an original design by Henry Iles and Dan May.

Printed and bound in China

© Rob Humphreys 2011

Maps © Rough Guides

Contains Ordnance Survey data © Crown copyright and database rights 2011

No part of this book may be reproduced in any form without permission from the publisher except for the quotation of brief passages in reviews.

208pp includes index

A catalogue record for this book is available from the British Library

ISBN 978-1-84836-274-1

The publishers and authors have done their best to ensure the accuracy and currency of all the information in **Pocket Rough Guide London**, however, they can accept no responsibility for any loss, injury, or inconvenience sustained by any traveller as a result of information or advice contained in the guide.

1 3 5 7 9 8 6 4 2

MIX
Paper from
responsible sources
FSC
www.fsc.org
FSC™ C018179

## ROUGH GUIDES CREDITS

**Text editor:** Edward Aves

**Layout:** Pradeep Thapliyal

**Photography**: Roger Norum, Natascha Sturny, Mark Thomas

**Cartography:** Ed Wright

**Picture editor**: Mark Thomas

**Proofreader**: Stewart Wild

**Production:** Rebecca Short

**Cover design:** Nicole Newman and Dan May

## THE AUTHOR

**Rob Humphreys** has lived in London since 1988, although he grew up in rural Yorkshire. He has recently qualified as a City of London Tour Guide and in his spare time can be found steering a Norfolk reed cutter up and down the Thames.

## HELP US UPDATE

We've gone to a lot of effort to ensure that the first edition of **The Pocket Rough Guide to London** is accurate and up-to-date. However, things change – places get "discovered", opening hours are notoriously fickle, restaurants and rooms raise prices or lower standards. If you feel we've got it wrong or left something out, we'd like to know, and if you can remember the address, the price, the hours, the phone number, so much the better.

Please send your comments with the subject line "**Pocket Rough Guide London Update**" to € mail@roughguides.com. We'll credit all contributions and send a copy of the next edition (or any other Rough Guide if you prefer) for the very best emails.

Find more travel information, connect with fellow travellers and book your trip on ⓦ www .roughguides.com

## PHOTO CREDITS

All images © Rough Guides except the following:

# Index

Maps are marked in **bold**.

SO NOW WE'VE TOLD YOU
ABOUT THE THINGS NOT TO
MISS, THE BEST PLACES TO
STAY, THE TOP RESTAURANTS,
THE LIVELIEST BARS AND THE
MOST SPECTACULAR SIGHTS,
IT ONLY SEEMS FAIR TO
TELL YOU ABOUT THE BEST
TRAVEL INSURANCE AROUND

 **WorldNomads.com**
*keep travelling safely*

RECOMMENDED BY ROUGH GUIDES

# DISCOVER IT

Disney PRESENTS

# THE LION KING

## LONDON'S LANDMARK MUSICAL

www.thelionking.co.uk

## LYCEUM THEATRE, LONDON

Photo by Lois Greenfield. Kissy Simmons as 'Nala'. © Disney.